iPhone® & iPad® for Musicians

FOR DUMMIES®

A Wiley Brand

D1306631

iPhone® & iPad® for Musicians

FOR DUMMIES®

A Wiley Brand

by Ryan Williams and Mike Levine

FOR DUMMIES®

A Wiley Brand

Contents at a Glance

Table of Contents

Introduction

A professor in one of my first music technology classes imagined a world where the recording studio wouldn't even use physical controls — instead, it would have just a series of computer panels projecting the necessary controls on the screens that interacted with human touch. Just a few (all right, slightly more than a few) years later, those virtual controls became reality. But those panels didn't remain in the confines of a recording studio. Instead, you can carry them around in your pocket or bag, laying down tracks in between social media posts and a quick game.

This book doesn't try to introduce you to the future. Instead, *iPad & iPhone for Musicians For Dummies* introduces you to the wonderful present where your iOS device can act as a virtual instrument, a guitar and pedal simulator, or even the portable recording rig you always wanted to carry around with you so you'd never forget another hit song. You can do all this and more with your device and a few apps — no need to wait for the future!

About This Book

This book includes several different parts that take a look at different aspects of making music on your iPhone or iPad. Depending on what you want to accomplish or learn about, you can skip around the book and just read what you want, or you can read the book from cover to cover. It's up to you!

Let's take a look at the parts of the book so you can make an informed decision.

Part I: Getting Started with iOS Music

This section takes you back in time, all the way back to when the first iPhone arrived to a desperate public (lo, those many years ago). When you're up to speed on your history lesson, you'll find out what makes the iOS device such a valuable musical tool, how to choose the best device for your needs, and the apps you'll need to make everything function.

Part II: Playing Music on Your iOS Device

This part contains some fun information about playing your iOS device as if it were an actual musical instrument — because it is! Whether you connect your device to an external controller or use the touchscreen to control new and different instruments, this part gets you up and running. You'll also learn how to connect other instruments (like a guitar or bass) to the device for optimum performance.

Part III: Setting Up Your iOS Studio

Want to record your songs, anytime, and anywhere? This part helps you set up your recording rig, so you can pull together all the parts you need. You'll also learn about the apps you need to make your recordings happen, along with the headphones and monitors you'll use to hear your genius once you finish (and help make it better).

Part IV: Your Recording Workflow

Whether you record in the field or at home, this part helps you plot out your recording projects. You'll gain the knowledge you need to get all of the audio you need on your iOS device and create the tracks you want.

Part V: Using Multiple Apps Together

iOS apps don't have to live separately from each other — the best music comes from using the tools you want in harmony (puns fully intended) with each other. Learn how to make Inter-App Audio, Audiobus, Virtual MIDI, and more options to get your apps interacting.

Part VI: Editing, Mixing, and Sharing Your Projects

After you record all of your audio, you must bring it all together to make the files your listeners can download or stream. This part shows you the tools and techniques you'll need to get your music together and ready to ship, from making large edits to the little tweaks that symbolize perfection. Or at least as close as you can possibly get. No judgment here.

Part VII: The Part of Tens

This part adds a little something extra to the book, giving you some insights into some other apps you can use to make music beyond what you look at in the book itself (both paid and free). You'll also get some insight to the other musical uses you have for your iOS device, from sheet music to tuning your guitar or bass.

Foolish Assumptions

This book tries to address the widest possible audience without regards to how advanced of a musician you are, but I do have to assume a couple of things to make the information in this book useful:

✔ **You must have an interest in music of some fashion:** If you're not interested in making or recording music, you probably have better things to do than read this book. Note that I'm not assuming you're a virtuoso on your chosen instrument — just that you actually want to make some righteous noise with your iOS device.

✔ **You must use an iOS device (either an iPhone, iPod touch, or iPad) running iOS 7 or 8:** No other device will work — sorry. And while you may be able to scrape by using some apps on iOS 6, the overall experience probably won't function well. The newer iOS versions just offer too much good stuff to overlook.

And that's it! Fulfill these two basic requirements, and you're good to go!

Icons Used in This Book

Throughout the book, you'll see some icons in the margins that offer some additional information. Some icons just augment your already stellar reading experience, while others contain some knowledge that definitely requires your attention. Let's take a look at those icons so you know how you wish to interact with them.

This icon gives you a little extra information beyond the current topic. You can live without it, but a little time spent on the knowledge could be helpful.

Definitely pay some attention to this icon — failure to do so could put you in danger of losing music or data. Anytime you see the lit fuse, stop and read!

I tend to get a little nerdy and drop some information in the book that appeals to those who really want to dig deep (and probably not anybody else). You can skip it and come back to it later, but I promise the information will be useful at some point.

Everybody needs a friendly reminder sometimes. This icon calls out information you should keep in mind as you go on.

Beyond the Book

A lot of extra content that you won't find in this book is available at www. dummies.com. Go online to find the following:

- **Online articles covering additional topics at**

  www.dummies.com/extras/ipadandiphoneformusicians

  Here you'll find out the four types of devices you can connect to your iPad, the four tools all recording studios need, how to record audio in a DAW, and much more.

- **The Cheat Sheet for this book is at**

  www.dummies.com/cheatsheet/ipadandiphoneformusicians

  Here you'll find a recording checklist, downloading options, and more.

- **Updates to this book, if we have any, are also available at**

  www.dummies.com/extras/ipadandiphoneformusicians

Where to Go from Here

As I stated before, you should feel free to read from cover to cover or just skip to the sections that interest you the most. Whatever gets your task accomplished! Most of all, have fun and make wonderful music!

Part I

Getting Started with iOS Music

In this part . . .

✔ Get the basics of creating music with iOS.

✔ Choose the right device for your music.

✔ Explore the iTunes App Store.

✔ Select the right apps to create your masterpieces.

Chapter 1

Digging into iOS

. . . .

In This Chapter

▶ Understanding the iOS operating system

▶ Learning how iOS and apps evolved

▶ Making iOS work as a music production tool

. . . .

*B*efore you can make music using your iPhone or iPad, you should understand the basics of the software that makes it tick (or, more appropriately, *sing*). This chapter introduces you to iOS and explores the ways you can interact with the device you're probably holding in your hand right now. (Consider putting it down somewhere nearby — it might be hard to hold both your phone and this book at the same time.) Here you learn the basic functionality of iOS, how your apps work with iOS, and why iOS can be a practical and inexpensive music production tool.

What Is iOS?

iOS is the operating system that powers all the iPhones, iPads, and iPod touches ever produced. iOS does the same job OS X does for Macs and Windows or Linux does for other computers, but Apple designers specifically programmed iOS to handle mobile devices. The operating system handles the basic functionality of every aspect of your device. It determines everything from the apps you see when you first log in to your device to the notifications you receive when you're overwhelmed with texts, phone calls, or messages. Anything your device does, it does because iOS told your device to do it. (See Figure 1-1.)

iOS is an Apple creation that's available only on Apple devices. Although this limits the available choices for iOS fans, and maybe costs a bit more, it also allows Apple to fine-tune the operating system. By restricting iOS to a specific stable of devices, Apple can tailor iOS to work better. As Apple likes to say,

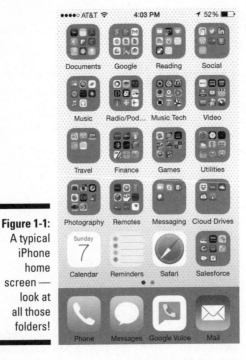

Figure 1-1:
A typical
iPhone
home
screen —
look at
all those
folders!

"It just works." You may not experience this level of satisfaction all the time (*Why does this app keep crashing?!*), but, generally speaking, iOS provides a smooth and quick performance, at least for Apple's latest generation of devices.

Understanding the History of iOS

To understand how iOS progressed since its birth, we must part the mists of time and go back all the way to 2007, when the world first learned of the Apple's new device — the iPhone. When Apple first introduced the device that would revolutionize the mobile phone world, it also introduced the world to iOS, the software that would run it. Compared to the latest iteration of iOS (8, as of this writing), the first generation seems a little . . . limited. Back then, Apple didn't even call it *iOS* — they just referred to it as a version of the OS X software Apple uses to run larger devices like the MacBook Pro or iMac. Although the fledgling iPhone's operating system basically existed only to power the device and make it functional, it also introduced a formidable touchscreen-based interface that would soon take over the mobile device world. No more keyboards, just a few buttons — everything else took place on the screen.

From that auspicious beginning, Apple began creating more versions of iOS, ones that included additional features and access to improved iPhone hardware. These features included:

✔ Access to the iTunes and Apps Stores

✔ Messaging improvements

✔ Newer and better cameras

✔ Accelerometers and gyroscopic capabilities (basically, iOS could track your phone's movements and how fast those movements occurred)

✔ Better audio and MIDI (Musical Instrument Digital Interface) capabilities

. . . and so much more, really. You can't always differentiate the evolution of software and hardware, because iOS and the iPhone/iPad/iPod touch are so tied together, but the key takeaway from the history of iOS is that a simple phone operating system evolved from a small device you hold in your hand into a full-fledged platform that allows you to imagine, create, and distribute music.

When the iPhone first came to the market, it was tied to a computer. You plugged it in to sync your information, to update apps and the operating system, and to transfer any songs or other files. As iOS and the hardware progressed, the iPhone and iPad became more autonomous. They became their own platform, and not just peripheral devices to a home computer. Nowadays you can perform any action, including syncing your information to a cloud server for instantaneous access as needed, on the iPhone or iPad itself.

These devices left the nest and flew on their own. That's pretty amazing.

Exploring the Possibilities

There are so many possibilities to explore! The iOS operating system may not cover the entire mobile world, but it does provide the most robust option for musicians wishing to create music on a mobile device. Because Apple made iOS specifically for a limited set of devices, the company can better handle issues like touch response and interactions with external hardware (such as keyboards or other MIDI controllers, as described in Chapter 5). The App Store provides the largest marketplace for mobile-device music apps, a great many of which are available for free. Although buying an iPhone or iPad may be expensive, the cost of making that device a music workstation is relatively low. Let's take a look at a broad overview of everything you can accomplish with your iPhone or iPad.

Playing music anywhere

Obviously, Apple designed the iPhone and iPad to go along with you wherever you go. With powerful onboard memory and Wi-Fi/wireless data connections, your devices travel easily and provide near-instantaneous access to your data, allowing you to carry the following devices in your pocket:

- Piano
- Modular synthesizer
- Sampler
- Drum machine/sequencer
- Guitar/bass amp
- Effects pedals
- DJ equipment
- Strange and wonderful sound generation devices
- Your entire sheet music collection

This list is only a sample. Your only limitation is the size of your device's storage, your screen size (especially if you're older and need a screen larger than an iPhone's for reading music), and your data connection. It's all so convenient: Carrying these items on your phone certainly beats carting them around in a generously sized motor vehicle!

 Apps that use a lot of small controls (such as knobs or switches) will benefit from the larger screen size of a full-sized iPad versus an iPad Mini. For example, large virtual mixers or synthesizers with a lot of controls may need a larger screen size so you can better access these controls (especially if you're performing live and don't get a shot at fixing any mistakes).

 For practical reasons, we recommend you buy a sturdy case to go along with your iPhone or iPad. Make sure the case will protect the device in case of an accidental fall, a fractured screen, an accidental spill of liquid, or other traumatic events that can occur while you're lost in playing or composing music. Musicians don't often work in sterile or clean environments, so protect your investment! Be sure that any case you buy also allows you to connect the hardware you need to make your music. We discuss that hardware more in Chapters 6 and 7.

Be careful when connecting external devices to your iOS device if you put that device in a large or bulky case. And definitely take your iPhone or iPad out of any case you normally put on it before you try to insert it in a dock. Not only will some cases block usage of external connections, but you could also damage the data connector by trying to force that connection.

Storing your sounds

There's no shortage of opinions among musicians and audiophiles, but keep in mind that opinions are always subjective. The iPhone and iPad may not have the "mojo" factor of vintage tube amps or studio-quality recording consoles, but you can still get great audio sounds out of them.

For music playback, the iPhone and iPad can handle mp3, AAC, ALAC, WAV, and AIFF files at different levels of audio quality. Apple recommends sticking with AAC and ALAC files, probably because Apple itself created the formats, but also because you get better audio quality at the same file size over other formats. You'll fill up your phone quickly with high resolution audio files (especially in ALAC, WAV, and AIFF formats), but the choice is yours. Connect a good pair of headphones (not the earbuds that come with the phone, please — it's worth investing in a better pair after you initially buy the device) and you're set. And keep the earbuds in a safe place as a backup. Just in case.

Lossy vs. lossless

The AAC vs. ALAC file formats belong to Apple, and thus work really well on an iPhone or iPad. But the main difference between these files is *lossy* vs. *lossless* data compression. When you convert an audio file to an AAC format, you retain most of the data but lose a little here and there to keep the file size down. The iTunes Store sells music files at 256 Mbps, which most listeners agree is an acceptable resolution for everyday listening.. The standard before 256 Mbps was 128 Mbps, regarded by many experts as the minimum listenable size (although some will turn their nose up at that). Anything lower than that rate and things start to get ugly: You'll hear a distorted high end (think cymbals and other high-pitched noises), and the music just won't sound . . . *good*. ALAC files, on the other hand, use lossless compression. Although ALAC files are larger than AAC files, they don't lose data, and they're smaller than the uncompressed audio of AIFF or WAV files. Again, your only limitation is the size of your device's storage and how much music you want to carry around with you at any time.

Bit depth and sample rate

If you're an experienced musician or audiophile, you may already understand what *bit depth* and *sample rate* mean for digital audio. If you're new to this concept, welcome to a broad and bitterly debated issue that will likely not see resolution (forgive the pun) in your lifetime. The terms *bit depth* and *sample rate* refer to the quality of the digital audio file (the *technical* quality, that is — even the highest levels of fidelity can't make certain recordings of "MacArthur Park" listenable). Digital audio relies on a series of samples of an audio signal (think a series of pictures, like the frames of an old movie). The *bit depth* refers to the amount of information in every sample. A low bit depth (say, 8-bit) might be the sonic equivalent of hearing a bass guitar play a note. A higher bit depth would give you enough detail to let you know that Jaco Pastorius played that note on a fretless bass live before an audience in Japan during the early '70s. The sample rate (expressed in kHz) tells you how many times per second the file samples the audio. The more samples you use, the more audio information you get and the better the file sounds. CD-quality audio files (and most of the files you can purchase on iTunes or at similar stores) use 16-bit audio. As the capabilities of iOS and the iPhone and iPad advance, you get access to higher bit depth and sample rates for your audio files.

What about recording? The iPhone and iPad can already record audio up at 32-bit and 192 kHz, depending on the audio hardware you connect to your device. For those who started home recording on an analog cassette portable studio, this jump is mind-blowing. However, this level of fidelity requires a good deal of outboard gear and the proper recording environment. We discuss these matters more in Chapters 9 and 11. For now, it suffices to say that great sound recordings will cost you a little more money than you just paid for your newest Apple toy.

Surveying the App World

Although the iPhone and the iPad don't outsell the Android devices, for app developers, iOS is a lucrative market that cannot be ignored. Historically, the Android operating system just couldn't handle real-time audio work because the OS had too much latency. Essentially, too much time elapsed between the time a player made a musical action (like pressing a key) and the time the sound actually played. This latency is getting better, but there are still additional obstacles. Because these developers must account for a small number of devices (compared to the seemingly endless Android variants), they can write better tailored and more individualized software. And iOS presents the most stable and functional platform for musical software. You can find thousands of apps on the App Store ready for your use, each

Figure 1-2:
Bebot
takes the
stage and
sings like
a bird (or a
Theremin,
or a power
synth, or
something
else . . .).

costing way less than it would cost to purchase a new synthesizer or home recording system.

The cool thing about music on iOS is that you're not limited to traditional methods of creating music. Sure, you can anticipate the sounds that the virtual strings of a guitar or the digital skins of a drum make in GarageBand. But with Bebot, a tiny robot sings his heart out for you; by adding distortion or harmony to your taste, you've got an entirely new way to make noise. (See Figure 1-2.) Turn knobs or draw new patterns in Animoog to take the classic sounds of the Moog synthesizer into a new dimension. Or use Traktor to cut your compositions together like a professional DJ (without the fog machines and flashing lights) to make your own dance sets for distribution across the world.

Because the iPhone and iPad present a new way to interface with technology and software, developers can always imagine new and different ways to create music, and the App Store allows those developers to get their software to you wherever you are (for free or a nominal fee, of course). Check back early and often to see what's new.

Scratching your iPhone or iPad

Using the term "scratch" in connection with an iPhone or iPad makes us a little queasy, but be assured that we speak metaphorically here. Professional musicians can't always be around their primary instrument — it may be easier for violinists or trumpet players, but pianists can't strap a Steinway to their back in the event that inspiration strikes. And portability doesn't always imply convenience: Even a piccolo player will annoy his fellow airline passengers when he tries out a new line at 30,000 feet.

Apps for the iPhone and iPad allow you to record your thoughts or musical ideas whenever the mood hits. Apps like Take or Loopy HD take your sung melodies and loop them into into layered songs. GarageBand presents a series of instruments you can use to tap or pluck out your rough drafts. Notion lets you create and edit sheet music on your iPad without paper and pencil (or lots of erasers).

Once you record your ideas, you can move them from your apps to their big-sibling equivalents on your home computer. Notion app files, for instance, can make the transition to Notion on your Mac or PC, and you can open your GarageBand app files in GarageBand on your Mac. So, not only can you record your initial ideas, but you can flesh them out later and transform them into staggering works of genius (or at least write a decent song, but why not dream big?). Depending on the software, you may even be able to transfer the files wirelessly!

With the available apps and the portability of your Apple device, you don't have to worry about losing inspiration ever again. On the night he came up with the riff to "(I Can't Get No) Satisfaction," Keith Richards was famously so drunk and bleary-eyed he had to sing it into a tape recorder so he wouldn't forget it. You can think of your iPhone as the modern-day equivalent. (Except, of course, you'll have a better chance than Keith did of remembering the event later.)

Using iOS as a full-fledged recording system

No matter what software you download onto your iPhone or iPad, you won't approach the sound quality of *Abbey Road* or *Electric Ladyland* any time soon. Still, even if your iPhone or iPad can't rival hundreds of thousands of dollars' worth of professional recording equipment (most of which, to be fair, you'd probably never use anyway), it can provide you with an inclusive recording system you can use to record, produce, and distribute finished tracks to the masses.

A lot of what you can do with your iPhone or iPad depends on the hardware you hook up to it (a subject we discuss in Part III, "Setting Up Your iOS Studio"). But these devices are more than capable of recording multiple audio tracks at the same time, mixing and mastering the resulting tracks into an audio file, and placing that audio file into the online distribution channel of your choice.

Software like Auria, Capture, or MultiTrack DAW (*DAW* stands for digital audio workstation, a common term used to describe software for recording, mixing, and mastering audio) make it possible to create songs from beginning to end. And you can do it for a lot less than booking time at a high-end recording studio. (Save that for your next recording contract.)

Investing in your iOS studio

Apple's hardware carries a reputation for hefty price tags, but the good news is that after that initial investment, you're not going to have to spend that much more money. And really, for all that you get for your iPhone or iPad, the cost isn't *really* that much.

The relative costs of software and hardware are as follows:

- ✔ **Software:** The apps themselves all come from the App Store, and you won't flinch when you see their price tags. Most apps cost between 99 cents and $5 apiece, so you probably have what you need to get a brand new synthesizer in your wallet right now. (I know, you'll have to use a credit card or gift card instead of cash, but the metaphor stands.) Even the more pricey recording apps come in around $25, which is still far less expensive than recording apps like Logic or Pro Tools (which also require a home computer and higher-priced hardware). And you never know when an app will go on sale (usually when developers first release their apps or around holidays or other special events).

  This low cost also means you can avoid the dreaded gear acquisition syndrome (GAS) common to musicians. No longer do you have to collect thousands of dollars to try out a new instrument or put together a portable music library you'll need a cart to transport. Try out as many apps as you want and keep only the ones you really want to use. You may not be able to return an app for a refund, but at such a low cost, you won't really miss it. And plenty of apps provide a free trial version you can take for a test-drive. This amounts to less stress on your wallet (and on your relationship with a significant other when you try to bring home *yet another musical instrument*).

  After you buy an app, you can delete and redownload it as needed. Even if that synth you bought today doesn't offer what you need now, it may come in useful down the road. However, you can't share or sell apps beyond the original purchaser and anybody involved in a family sharing circle. You won't find a secondhand app market out there like you can for vintage or used audio gear.

✔ **Hardware:** Although adding additional recording hardware might add to your cost, remember something as you go through your wish list — you've already purchased the most expensive and necessary piece of equipment: your iPhone or iPad. When it comes to creating, playing, or distributing your own music, that device will do most of the heavy lifting. Even if you decide to buy a MIDI keyboard, for example, you're not going to need to buy an entire synthesizer workstation to go with it. You only need the keys or pads themselves and the circuits necessary to tell your iOS device what to play and when. The brains of the keyboard already reside in your iPhone or iPad. All you need is the device that lets you better interact with your apps.

Chapter 2

Choosing Your iOS Device

● ●

In This Chapter

▶ Surveying the available iPhones and iPads

▶ Evaluating your device's ports and connectors

▶ Understanding the music-related improvements in iOS 8

● ●

*Y*ou might already own an iPhone or iPad, so your choice in purchasing a device might already be made. Or maybe you're considering buying a new iPhone or iPad on which to begin your music-making career. Either way, it helps to take a look at the available Apple devices (either new or used) and to better understand their capabilities.

This chapter analyzes the advantages and disadvantages of each device to see how they fit your music-making needs. We also take a look at the different iOS versions to help you find out which one you need to use (hint: it's probably the latest one).

Comparing the Advantages of iPad and iPhone

The obvious difference between the iPhone and the iPad is size — the iPhone fits into your pocket, and the iPad fits in a case or a bag or a purse or . . . anything larger than your pocket, really. But bigger isn't always better. Because your iPhone is always with you, you're more than likely to have it around whenever inspiration strikes — on an airplane, next to your bed, the next boring meeting, or wherever you happen to be, you can create or edit your musical creations.

Every iPhone comes with a persistent data connection as well. Since you must buy a data plan when you get an iPhone, your device always remains connected to the Internet either via Wi-Fi or your cellular data connections (depending on your location, of course — you may not be able to depend on your signal in the mountains of Wyoming or while attending a major sporting event). That data connection means you can always upload, download, and backup any apps or files you need to. This persistent connection also means you'll need to ensure against intrusive phone calls or text messages while recording or performing.

During extended recording or performing, put your iPhone in *airplane mode.* The airplane mode setting disables the wireless features of the iPhone in order to be compliant with airline restrictions, but it's also useful in preventing interruptions from unwanted text messages or phone calls. You can enable this setting by swiping up from the bottom of the screen and tapping the airplane icon. And you can always purchase an iPod touch to use music apps without worrying about a pesky data connection.

The larger screen of the iPad, though, doesn't just offer you more room on which to display your musical apps. Many app developers build apps specifically for iPad's larger screen, and optimize their apps for the iPad. This means that some of the app's features — or even the app itself — won't be available on any other device. The iPhone version of the App Store won't even display iPad-only apps, so you need to be aware of what's available and where you can get it.

Not all iPads come with a wireless data connection, either. You can hook up your iPad to any Wi-Fi connection (with the correct password, of course), but a wireless access point may not always be within reach. In some circumstances, then, this lack of access may make uploading and download information difficult, but at least it prevents the iPhone's phone-call and text-message interruptions.

You can make music with either an iPhone or an iPad, so that can't be a factor in your decision. Thankfully, a few other factors can help make your choice easier (and either keep cash in your wallet or blow out your bank account). Let's take a look at what might cause you to go in one direction or another in your search for the perfect device:

✔ **Apps:** As we mentioned earlier in this chapter, certain apps are available only for iPad. Other apps offer *universal* versions, which look and operate the same on either an iPhone or an iPad. And some apps developed for the iPhone may work on an iPad, but they'll appear grainy or in low resolution because the developers never intended for the app to appear on the iPad's larger screen. Do some research before buying and make sure your device runs all the apps you want to use before you make your final purchase.

If you're attached to a specific manufacturer or type of software, check out the App Store (discussed more in Chapter 3) to make sure the software runs on your device. For example, Ryan loves the Propellerhead Figure and Take apps, and luckily enough they make versions that run on both his iPhone and my iPad. But anyone who loves the LiveFX effects made by Elephantcandy will need an iPad to use that app at all. And even if you buy a version of an app on one type of device, some developers make separate versions for iPhone and iPad that require separate purchase. Caveat app-tour!

✔ **Screen size:** Yes, in this case, the size of the screen does make a huge difference. Simply speaking, it's probably easier to interact with an app's small virtual dials, knobs, or other controls on an iPad than it is on an iPhone. And you'll be able to read the text on the larger screen more easily, and you'll probably have access to more information.

That is, of course, if you plan on using only the device itself as a controller. If you plan on plugging in additional devices, like a keyboard or other type of interface, the screen size might make a little less difference. In that case, you'll be interacting with actual physical controls instead of the pixel-based versions appearing on your device's screen. Still, the increased real estate can make a huge difference, especially in performance-based situations. Ryan says he would feel quite comfortable reading sheet music off of his iPad at a gig. Off of his iPhone — not so much.

✔ **Performance:** In this case, I'm not talking about the brilliant stage show you'll no doubt put on with your new device. *Performance* refers to the processor speed and the amount of memory (otherwise known as *RAM*) on your device. Without getting too technical, newer devices boast faster processors and memory than older versions, so musicians wanting to push the limit in performance should look to the newest possible devices. If you just want to use your iPad as a sheet music reader, though, you can get away with an older device.

Note here that, unlike some computers, you can't upgrade the processor or the RAM in an iPhone or iPad — they come with what they have. Don't plan on souping anything up later. By the way, this applies to just about everything Apple makes these days, with the possible exception of the Mac Pro.

✔ **Storage:** Audio files can eat up huge amounts of space, and larger apps can take up just about as much space as a higher-resolution music album. The storage requirements of games can easily top 1GB, but you'll probably want to store a few of those on your device as well (can't be creative all the time, can you?). Right now, the local storage on an iPhone or an iPad (that is, the kind of storage physically located on your iPhone, as opposed to cloud or server storage) tops out at 128GB of storage. If you plan on making one of these your primary recording and performing device, you should get as much storage as you can afford.

Exploring Device Generation and OS Versions

The land is littered with older models of the iPhone and iPad, and Apple continues to produce newer versions of these iconic devices. So which model should you choose? Good question. For a little guidance (and a little warning), take a look at the factors below.

iOS 8 versus iOS 7

iOS 8 represents the latest and best functionality offered by Apple (including the music-specific features we discuss later in this chapter in the section called "Checking Out the Music-Related Improvements in iOS 8"). Developers will no doubt concentrate their efforts on making products for this new operating system, and anybody interested in using the most up-to-date apps will want to use iOS 8. Such is the inevitable movement of progress.

That said, Ryan still uses his original iPad (the very first version) to read sheet music and notes on gigs. It works wonderfully for that, and it hasn't caused him any problems during the entire lifetime of that device. It even occasionally gets app updates (and bless the companies that still think of older devices like this — it must be like visiting a relative in the nursing home).

If you use an iOS 7 device, developers aren't going to leave you totally out in the cold — most will maintain some sort of *backwards compatibility* (technical jargon for keeping the old devices going) as long as they can and as long as the new functionality isn't totally dependent on iOS 8 or the latest device model and features. So buy as new a device as you can, but don't throw out your older devices just yet — they can still be valuable years later.

iPhone

As of this writing, Apple offers the iPhone 6 and 6 Plus as its flagship device, backed by the older iPhone 5s. All of these devices use the Lightning connector, so the 30-pin connection has been moved to the side in favor of the inexorable march of technology.

Although you can buy any of these iPhones new, you may find a better deal on older devices like the iPhone 5 and 4s (both of which will support iOS 8, albeit at a likely slower and clunkier pace and without the necessary storage space). If you discover that the apps you want to run will perform correctly on these legacy devices, go ahead and make a deal. Just know that time is not often kind to technology, and you'll probably soon notice toys that just won't play well with your device.

iPad

Apple currently offers three different iPad models:

- ✔ iPad Air 2
- ✔ iPad Air
- ✔ iPad Mini 3
- ✔ iPad Mini 2
- ✔ iPad Mini

The iPad Air offers the highest-end capabilities of all of the models, and the Retina Display designation offers higher resolution than its counterparts. Note also that the iPad Mini offers only 16GB of local storage, so you might run out of room pretty quickly if you don't watch out.

Again, you can probably score a deal on older models (such as the third- and fourth-generation iPads, which will support iOS 8). Check out the possibilities and see what you can get by with.

Looking at Ports and Connectors

Depending on when you bought your iPhone or iPad, your headphone jack and the single port used to connect your device to other hardware, like a home computer or a recording interface, appear in different locations. And yes, these make a big difference, so pay attention.

30-pin or Lightning?

In the first iPhones, Apple included a proprietary 30-pin jack that attached to a cable in order to sync the device with a home computer. (See Figure 2-1.) Over time, Apple and other manufacturers built plenty of hardware for that 30-pin connector, and these products sold reasonable well. Ryan still has a clock radio that uses a 30-pin connector, for example.

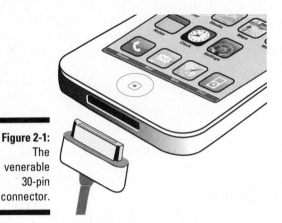

Figure 2-1:
The venerable 30-pin connector.

And then, Lightning struck. More specifically, the Lightning connector struck. (See Figure 2-2.) With the release of the iPhone 5, Apple replaced the 30-pin connector with a smaller connector that allows for additional powering capabilities and a lack of directionality. The additional powering means that your iPhone or iPad can now provide power for attached devices and can accept a higher level of power for charging purposes. But what does "a lack of directionality" mean? Basically, it means that unlike USB jacks or other types of connectors (including 30-pin), there's no wrong way to insert the connector into the iPhone or iPad jack. No matter which side you plug in on top, your connection works. Try that with a USB cable. How many years of frustration could we have eliminated with that particular advance?

But we digress.

You'll still find that Apple and other manufacturers sell 30-pin connector equipment, and Apple even sold the iPhone 4S with the older 30-pin connection until very recently. And for the foreseeable future, you can still use equipment with 30-pin connectors by purchasing Lightning adapters (available for a nominal fee, of course).

Figure 2-2:
The Lightning connector makes the scene.

These adapters support charging and audio transmission only with the analog and USB connections favored by later Apple devices. So if you've been holding on to those old Firewire-based adapters since the mid-2000s, no adapter can save you now.

Try and test everything before making a final buying decision. You don't want to be caught out in the cold with a product that won't fit your needs.

All this information basically boils down to this: You can be confident that you'll be able to connect your iPhone or iPad to just about any device you need to make music, even if you need a bunch of wires and adapters to do so. Just be aware of your device's limitations, and any cables you may need to connect all the pieces.

You can never predict what Apple might do with any degree of certainty, but the company has never walked back its decision to remove a piece of technology from its devices. The 30-pin connector will be obsolete very soon, so anyone purchasing a new Apple device should definitely choose one with the Lightning connector. Consider it future-proofing (for the foreseeable future, at least). You can also plan to use Bluetooth LE or NFC pairing in the future.

Headphone Jack

The type of headphone jack you have doesn't really matter, because jacks adhere to a standard format that's been used on all kinds of devices for many, many years. You can take pretty much any pair of headphones or earbuds and plug it into your iPhone or iPad without issue. That being said, the jack can handle special brands of headphones that include mics and volume controls in the cords, and these mics might give you slightly better recording quality than your device's internal phone mic (not by that much, though — headphone mics certainly aren't pro-level). Also, certain audio interfaces connect to the iPhone and iPad through the headphone jack, and we discuss those later, in Chapter 6. But, for the most part, it's really just a plain old jack.

The *placement* of that jack, however, can make a big difference. Beginning with the iPhone 5, the headphone jack appears at the bottom of the device, not at the top. No big deal, right? You can just turn your device and lock your screen in whichever direction you need. This is true, but make sure you pay attention to *cable strain* (the amount of pressure you put on your cable and the jack). Too much stress can cause breakage in the cable or, worse yet, in the headphone jack itself. Just make sure that you release any tension in the cable and the jack, and you should be okay. Plenty of devices include built-in cable relief parts to ensure the safety and security of your device.

Checking Out the Music-Related Improvements in iOS 8

iOS 8 brings a lot of new features to the table, but a few music-related changes stand out. These changes might not attract the attention of the general public, but they make the lives of musicians much, much easier.

Inter-App Audio

iOS 8 introduced the new version of Inter-App Audio, but this feature existed before iOS 8 entered the public view. Basically, Inter-App Audio lets you send sound from one source or *node* (such as the Animoog synth app) to a *host* app (such as GarageBand). Think of it as running a cable from one app to another (without having to use an actual cable — which is nice because we constantly lose cables).

The new version of Inter-App Audio allows quicker switching between these connected apps so you can move from one app to another quickly. We discuss these changes more fully in Chapter 16.

Native Bluetooth MIDI Support

Before iOS 8, you had to use a series of interfaces and cables to communicate MIDI data from one source to another (and remember how we feel about cables). Now, with iOS 8, you can establish a Bluetooth connection between your iPhone or iPad and a controller like a MIDI keyboard or other device. You can use this feature both in the studio (imagine using your iPhone and iPad as a separate control surface for synths) and in performance (to connect your foot controller to change effects in guitar apps, for instance).

Not all of this functionality will appear instantaneously in your favorite apps. Developers may need to add additional code to their apps to get these features to work, so don't expect miracles in the early days of any iOS update. Check in with developers via social media for more information.

Upgrading the operating system of your device can cause problems for existing apps. Make sure you know exactly how your existing apps (if any) will respond to using the new iOS before upgrading or updating your apps and devices. Check with manufacturers and users before causing yourself any heartbreak.

Chapter 3

Downloading Apps from the iTunes Store

*O*ne of the many great features of your iOS device is that you choose which apps run on it, which gives you a virtually open-ended ability to customize. Your only real limitations are the storage space on your device — apps can use up a lot — and the amount you want to spend. With over 1,000,000 apps available on the iTunes App Store, there's a lot to choose from. Naturally, only a percentage of these are music apps, but there are still plenty of them, with more becoming available all the time.

In this chapter, we start with the basics. For those who have yet to dip their toes into the iOS world, we explain the nuts and bolts of setting up your iTunes account. If you already have an iOS device, and you're up to speed on that, feel free to skip ahead to the next section of this chapter, where we show you how to find good music apps in the App Store. We also discuss the "in-app purchase" process, which makes it easy to expand an app's capabilities or sound collection.

Setting Up Your Account

Before you buy an app from the App Store — either from iTunes on your computer or from the App Store app on your iOS device —you first must establish an Apple ID and set up an iTunes Store account. If you already download music from the iTunes Store, you can use your existing Apple ID and account.

After you've set up an active App Store account, you can download apps either directly from your iOS device or from a computer that you sync it to.

To get the process started, open the Settings app on your iOS device and scroll down until you see iTunes & App Store. Tap this choice, and you'll find an option for creating an Apple ID (see Figure 3-1), which requires that you first agree to the terms and fill in some additional information, including your password and security questions. You're also asked to provide an email address, which will be used as your Apple ID.

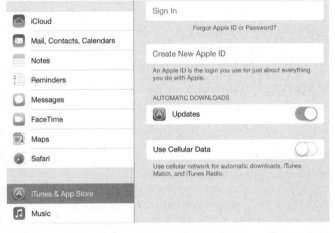

Figure 3-1:
Tap "Create New Apple ID" from the iTunes & App Store tab in the Settings App.

When creating your ID, you have the option to set up what's called a "rescue email address," which Apple recommends. A rescue address is a secondary email address, different from the one you're using as your Apple ID, at which Apple can reach you. If you forget your password or the answers to your security questions, Apple can send a reset request to your rescue address. Since your primary email address *is* your Apple ID, it's not as safe to have your security-related correspondence with Apple go to it. Having a rescue address prevents someone logged in to your email address from being able to easily procure your Apple ID password.

When your ID has been set up, you're given the option to set up your iTunes Store account. Fill in your credit card number and all other required info, and hit the Next button. After that, you're asked to verify your info: Apple will send you an email containing a Verify Now link. Pressing it will take you to a screen requesting your Apple ID and password, which, when correctly entered, verifies your account. Now you're ready to start downloading apps.

For additional safety and security, consider adding two-factor authentication to your Apple ID. This process requires you to log in and enter a security code sent to your mobile device, helping to ensure your information and credit card information remains safe.

Understanding iPhone, iPad, and Universal Apps

Apple offers three types of iOS apps:

- **iPhone apps:** These run on any iOS device, but they're optimized for the smaller screen of the iPhone and the iPod touch. If you install and run these apps on an iPad or iPad mini, you get the choice to view them at two settings: By default, they open at the 1X setting, which is their actual size, but by tapping the 2X button, you can view them at double size. The 1X size is small for the iPad or iPad mini screen, but it has sharper graphics than 2X. Because 2X simply expands the 1X image without adding any pixels, the image can look blown out, depending on the app.

- **iPad apps:** iPad apps run on the iPad or iPad mini, but not on the iPhone or iPod touch. If you access the App Store from your iPhone or iPod touch, you won't even see these apps listed.

- **Universal apps:** These are designed to run on both the iPhone/iPod touch and iPad/iPad mini, so they'll open with the correct graphics for the device on which they've been installed. The functionality is usually the same across all devices, but sometimes features aren't included when a universal app opens on the iPhone or iPod touch.

Searching for Apps

With the incredibly high number of apps available in the App Store, finding good apps can be a bit of a challenge. Whether you're searching on your iOS device's App Store app or on your computer in the iTunes Store, the experience of searching is pretty similar. We look at both here.

If you sync your iOS device to a computer, you may find it easier to search for apps on its bigger screen, using iTunes, rather than on your iOS device, especially if you have an iPhone or iPod touch. Be sure to leave enough room on your hard drive to store backups of your apps if you do this, though.

Searching the iTunes App Store on your computer

On the App Store main page is a search window in which you can type in a word or phrase to search for apps. Inputting *music,* for example, returns search results not just for apps, but also for other iTunes Store categories as well — such as albums, books, and podcasts. (See Figure 3-2.) You can return only the app results by clicking the iPad Apps or iPhone Apps links in the menu on the right, but even these results are too broad: You may find a couple of instrument or recording apps here, but *music* is too general a search term, and you'll end up with more apps for listening to music than for making it.

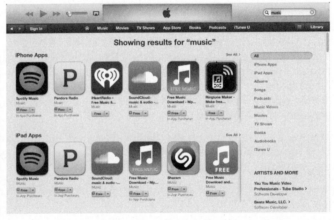

Figure 3-2: Search results for the general term *music* include few instrument or production apps.

So, clearly you have to use more specific terms. If you're interested in synths, for example, searching under *synth* or *synthesizer* will give you much better results (see Figure 3-3).

To refine the results even more, you can also add a second search term, separated by a comma. For example, trying *synth, free* (see Figure 3-4) presents you with a list of free synths without a lot of unrelated apps cluttering up the results.

Another way to find instrument and recording apps is to go to the App Store home page and, at the top, choose either iPad or iPhone, then open the category pull-down menu on the far right and select Music. This takes you to the main iPad or iPhone Music home page, which offers a very broad selection, but has some interesting subcategories.

Figure 3-3:
Using
a more
specific
term, like
synth,
works
better.

Figure 3-4:
Adding a
second
search term
can help
refine your
results.

If you scroll down on the Music home page, you'll find the Band in Your Hand section, which includes separate icons for GarageBand, Guitars and Strings, Audible Oddities, Vocals, Pianos and Synths, Producers and DJs, and Drums and Beats. Clicking any of these icons — except for the GarageBand icon, which is for Apple's recording and production app — reveals collections of apps from within those categories. Unfortunately, the collections aren't comprehensive, but they do contain a lot of good choices (see Figure 3-5).

You can find even more apps in the Related tab on any individual app's page. Just click on any individual app in the search field to bring up that app's page, and then click the Related tab near the top of the page. On this tab you can find a selection of apps deemed similar by Apple's search engine.

Figure 3-5:
The Pianos
and Synths
tab in the
Band in
Your Hand
section
has a good
selection of
instruments.

Apple updates iTunes pretty regularly, so it's possible by the time you read this the App Store may look a little different and have some changes in some of its features. Nevertheless, you'll certainly still have access to the search field and the category pull-downs, so the process of finding apps shouldn't change a whole lot.

Searching for apps on your iOS device

Although you'll be working with a smaller screen, searching for apps directly from your iOS device is similar to searching iTunes on your computer: Just type in specific search terms and survey the results, or tap categories in the App Store to see collections of apps.

By virtue of its screen size, the App Store app for iPhone/iPod touch can show only a little data about the app at a time. You have to scroll through the results (see Figure 3-6).

At the top of the iPad App Store page are several menus with choices that let you refine your searches:

✔ **The Any Price menu** lets you choose between paid and free apps.

✔ **The All Categories menu** makes it possible to search within a category, so set it to Music.

✔ **The By Relevance menu** (see Figure 3-7) gives you choices to present the results by Relevance, Popularity, Rating, and Release Date.

✔ **The All Ages menu** lets you narrow results to apps aimed at kids of various ages. Unless you're looking for a music app specifically for children, you probably won't need this menu.

Figure 3-6:
It's slower
to search
for apps on
an iPhone
because
you have
to scroll
through the
results
individually.

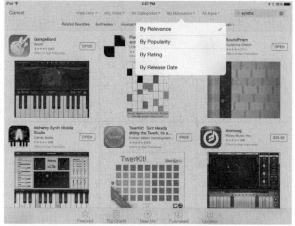

Figure 3-7:
The search
results
screen on
the iPad lets
you choose
ways to
organize
the results,
such as "By
Relevance."

As in the iTunes App Store, the App Store app also offers a Related tab for finding similar apps. When you search from the iPad App Store app, you get a list of Related Searches near the top of the page, which can offer good leads for finding more good apps.

You can run iPhone apps on the iPad, but you might not see these apps immediately when you conduct a search. Tap the iPad Only drop-down and switch it to iPhone Only to see those apps.

Researching Apps before Buying

Okay, you've found an app you're interested in. What next? If it's a free app, you may as well give it a try, but if you have to pay for it, you may want to do some research about it first, and the App Store gives you some good ways to dig deeper for information about the apps it sells.

When you select an app in the store by tapping on its icon, you're taken to its dedicated App Store page. Here you'll find screenshots and a short description of the app, as well as a What's New list that offers the latest version of the app. Tapping the little blue More link at the bottom-right (see Figure 3-8) expands the description to its full length, where you can find a lot more information about the app, including a detailed list of features.

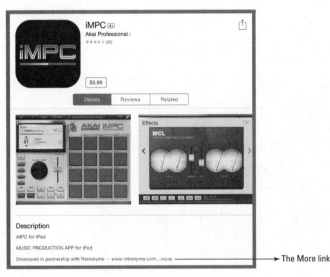

Figure 3-8: By tapping More, you get a much fuller description, usually including a feature list.

The More link

When reviewing these features, pay attention to hardware details. If it's an instrument app, for instance, look to see if it supports MIDI (for more details on MIDI, see Chapter 5), which would allow you to play it from external keyboards, and in some cases from other apps that are active at the same time in your device (for more about Virtual MIDI, see Chapter 18). Also see if it supports Audiobus or Inter-App Audio, both of which facilitate the use of multiple apps together (see Chapters 17 and 18).

The description should also tell you what the expansion options are for the app via in-app purchases, which can give you an idea of some of the additional features or sounds you can add. (We cover in-app purchases later in this chapter in the "Expanding Your Apps via In-App Purchases" section.)

For related apps, it's also helpful to look at the Customers Also Bought section, often found at the bottom of an app's dedicated page.

If you go to the top of an app's page and tap on Reviews, you can check out the Customer Ratings section. Even if you only read a few reviews, check out the Average Rating box and the list (near the top and middle of the page) that shows the distribution of the app's star ratings. When an app has predominantly 4- and 5-star reviews, you can be pretty confident you won't be wasting your money. Tap Reviews and select All Versions to go beyond the reviews for the most recent version and see all available reviews for the app.

Finally, try entering the app's name in Google or another search engine. These results should bring you some additional information that might be useful in your decision.

Installing and Managing Your Apps

To buy an app directly from your device, open the app's dedicated page and tap the price button, which then changes to a Buy button. Tap again, and you're asked to enter your Apple ID (see Figure 3-9). This is a security measure to make sure that only authorized users purchase apps. If you buy additional apps during the same App Store session, you most likely won't need to enter your password again.

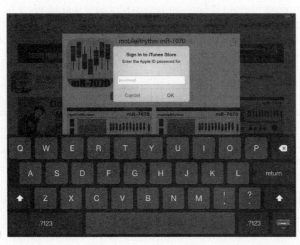

Figure 3-9:
Make
sure you
remember
your
password,
as you'll
need it to
purchase
and
download
apps.

After you correctly enter your password, the credit card you set up in your App Store account is charged (unless, of course, it's a free app) and the app begins downloading onto your device. When the download completes, tap Open to open the app. Where can you find the app on your iOS device? Well, that depends on the location and number of other apps already installed. You can review how you organize apps in the "Arranging Apps on Your iOS Device" section later in this chapter.

Buying apps from the iTunes App Store on your computer works a little differently. When you go to purchase an app there, you first get the password sign-in screen, which looks a little different than the sign-in screen at the iOS App Store. (See Figure 3-10.) When you've successfully entered your password and tapped Buy, the button under the app will say "Downloading," and the app will be downloaded onto your computer and stored only in iTunes until you sync your device.

Figure 3-10:
The iTunes App Store sign-in has a different look from the app version.

The next time you plug in your device to your computer with the sync cable, the syncing process should begin automatically and install your newly purchased apps to your iPhone, iPod touch, or iPad. An icon for your device should appear on the left side of the iTunes screen. Once the sync ends, click this icon, and make sure Apps is selected in the top horizontal row of categories. A list of apps appears on the left, which should include the ones you purchased (refer to Figure 3-10). Next to each app is one of three buttons:

- **Remove:** The app is installed. Clicking Remove and then syncing removes the app from your device, although it will remain stored in your iTunes application on your computer.

- **Install:** The app is currently in iTunes but not installed on your device. Clicking Install changes the button to Will Install.

- **Will Install:** Will Install indicates iTunes will attempt to install the app next time you sync.

Arranging Apps on Your iOS Device

When you have only a few apps on your device, finding a specific one isn't a problem, but as your app collection grows — presumably you'll have a lot of non-music apps on your device, as well — the need to organize your apps grows along with it. Often an app will install on a different home screen on your device than you'd like it to. As with purchasing, you can move and arrange apps on your device either directly from your device or via the iTunes application on your computer, where the changes you make won't take effect until you sync your device.

Using either method you can:

- ✔ Move apps between home screens
- ✔ Rearrange apps within a home screen
- ✔ Create folders for organizing multiple apps
- ✔ Rename the folders as you see fit
- ✔ Rearrange the folders

Arranging apps on your iOS device

If you want to move an app from one home screen to another — your device can provide multiple screens (up to the hardware and OS limitations of your device — older devices can't handle as many screens as newer devices) — first press and hold the app's icon until a little X appears there in the left corner and the app icons begin to wiggle (see Figure 3-11). This indicates that you can now slide the app icons around to change their positions, both within and outside of the screen they're on.

When the apps are in their wiggling state, they're not always so cooperative, and at times seem to have minds of their own. Sometimes it seems like every time you try moving an app to an adjacent screen, it slips off your finger just at the screen's edge.

If you want to move an app to an adjacent screen, slide it to the edge of the screen so part of it is under the black border. Keep your finger on it and hold it, and it will slide into the next screen on its own. Release your finger when you get to the screen you want it in.

Changing an app's position within a screen full of apps can be tricky. If you try to move an app from, say, the bottom of the screen to the top, other apps will scatter in its wake like scared animals, and will move to seemingly

Figure 3-11:
When the apps are wiggling, they can be moved by dragging them with your finger.

random locations. The best approach is to go slowly, sliding the app over the rows until you reach a position just beneath the row you want to place it in. If there's no open space in that row, moving the new app in between any two apps forces the rightmost app to accommodate it by moving one space to the right. This is a lot easier to accomplish on an iPad or iPad mini, because the space between the apps is a lot larger than on an iPhone or iPod touch. It may take you a little while to get things arranged the way you'd like.

To stop the icons from doing their little dance, press the Home button (the round, tactile button situated below the screen) and they'll return to their normal state.

If you want to put your apps into categories, you can also create folders. Simply dragging one app over another and holding for a second creates a new folder that opens with the two apps inside. iOS guesses what to name the folder based on the apps inside. Usually, it's a pretty generic name, like "Music," but it's easy to change: Tap the name field and the iPad or iPhone's keypad opens. Then erase the name — either with the Delete key or by tapping the little X to the right of the name — and enter the name you want. If you want to add additional apps to the folder, just drag them over the folder and hold. To close a folder, just tap outside of it; to open it, tap the folder itself.

Even if you carefully organize all your apps, you may not always be able to find an app that you know is on your device. A reliable way to find it is to type a few letters of the app's name into your device's search field. When the app you're looking for appears in the search results, tap it to open it. In versions of iOS before iOS 7, you could bring up the search field by swiping to the right from the main home screen, but more recent devices use a different approach. In iOS 7 or iOS 8, place your finger on any of your home screens and drag it slowly downward while maintaining pressure. The search box appears at the top of the screen as you drag your finger down. Just don't drag from the top of the screen down, as that brings up the Control Center. Stick closer to the middle of the home screen.

Arranging apps via iTunes on your computer

With your device connected to your computer, select it on the left side of iTunes and click Apps at the top of the screen. Then, on the right side a graphic depiction of your device appears, showing your home screens and all your apps situated where they would be on the actual device. A magnification bar lets you zoom in on the screens (see Figure 3-12).

Figure 3-12: Arranging your apps is easy when you do it in iTunes.

From this window you can drag apps from one home screen to another, drag one on top of another to create folders, and rename the folders. When you've arranged your apps to your satisfaction, hit the Apply button in the lower right, and the changes sync to your device, arranging the apps on your device as you specified in iTunes.

Although you have to sync to actually apply these changes to your device, organizing your apps in this manner is a lot easier.

Updating Your Apps

Changes and improvements made to the apps you've installed come in the form of *updates.* You can tell how many of your apps have updates available when a little red number appears on the upper-right corner of your device's App Store app icon (see Figure 3-13). When you open the App Store app and go to the Updates section, you'll see a list of all your apps with updates available.

Figure 3-13:
The red number on the App Store app icon indicates the presence and number of updates available.

You can find out what's included in the update by going to the correct page. On the iPad, you'll see info about what's new in the app in the Updates page. On the iPhone and iPod touch, you have to tap on the What's New link, which opens a window with the update information. After you've read the info about the update, simply press the Update button and the new version will load onto your device automatically. Updates are free. You can update all apps simultaneously by pressing Update All.

Don't use the Update All feature if you want to be able to run one of the apps being updated right away. The apps being updated will be out of commission until they've received their updates. The entire process can take anywhere from a few minutes to half an hour or so, depending on the number of apps being updated and the speed of your Internet connection. So if you want to upgrade and then use the app right away, just update it individually, and update your other apps later.

Apps get updated for several reasons, and a new version may have changes in more than one of the following categories.

Make sure you use a WiFi connection when updating apps, if possible. You'll speed up the process and keep your data usage rates under control.

- ✔ **Bug fixes:** Minor or major software bugs are fixed to increase the app's performance.

- ✔ **Minor feature introductions:** New capabilities that add functionality but aren't major overhauls.

- ✔ **Major feature introductions:** Major updates include revised user interfaces and significant new features.

As long as you're not having any performance issues with an app, you don't have to upgrade it as soon as a new version becomes available. That said, upgrading is always a good idea unless you have an older device on which the upgrade runs badly. That info should be stated in the App Store upgrade notes, so keep an eye out for that if you're using an older iPhone, iPod touch, or iPad.

Music apps can take a little while to update after a major iOS release. If you depend on a specific app (especially if that app uses Inter-App Audio, Audiobus, or CoreAudio functionality — and most do), wait until the developer of that app gives the all clear.

App version numbering is usually either in a two-digit format (such as, for example, 1.0, 1.1, 1.2, and so on) or a three-digit format (like 1.0.0, 1.0.1, 1.0.2, and so on). In the case of the former, any update that increments the number on the right by one is usually a small-to-medium-sized update, and could include either bug fixes, new features, or both. Increments to the number on the left, say to 2.0 from 1.9, indicate major updates, which contain significant changes, revisions and capabilities.

The three-digit system is supposed to correspond to major, minor, and bug fix updates, respectively. So update 1.1.2 from 1.1.1 indicates a bug fix; 1.2.0 from 1.1.1 indicates a minor feature introduction; and 2.1.0 from 1.1.1 indicates a major overhaul. Although Apple recommends that apps use the three-digit system, they don't require it, so variations are common. Don't get too hung up on the meaning of these version numbers, however, because iTunes always gives you a description of the update that you can read before you install it.

Expanding Your Apps via In-App Purchases

Many apps offer the option of unlocking additional functionality or more sounds via the in-app purchase capabilities in iOS. In-app purchases affect the same Apple account that you use in the App Store or iTunes App Store, but you make them from inside the app itself (see Figure 3-14). In some apps, a

Figure 3-14: In-app purchases on offer in the JamUp simulator.

window pops up to ask if you'd like to make a purchase. In others, you access a Store section within the app to find all the in-app purchases available.

Like in the App Store, when you've said yes to a purchase, you're asked for your Apple ID to confirm your identity before the purchase goes through. For most in-app purchases, you don't have to download anything — the additional features, music, or MIDI files you buy are simply "unlocked" from within the app, so accessing them is instantaneous. Some in-app purchases, such as the downloadable sound collections for IK Multimedia's SampleTank app, are so large that you have to download them from a server rather than unlock them from within the app, but these are exceptions.

If you purchase an app and later upgrade to a different device, not only will your app collection be available for your new device (assuming the apps are compatible with it), but your in-app purchases will be as well. A feature called *Restore Purchases* makes this possible. When you open an app in the new device, you'll likely get a pop-up window saying, "Restore In-App Purchases?" If you say yes, and enter your Apple ID, then your purchases will be unlocked.

For some reason, sometimes your purchases won't appear on your device — even when you haven't switched devices. When this happens, using the Restore In-App Purchases option lets you retrieve your purchases.

Part II
Playing Music on Your iOS Device

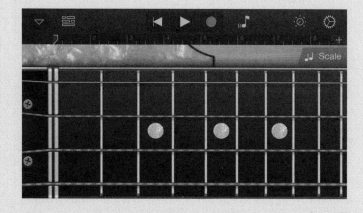

In this part . . .

- ✔ Explore the types of musical instruments you can find in the App Store.

- ✔ Connect MIDI and other controllers to your mobile device.

- ✔ Connect your electric guitar or bass to your mobile device and play through a mountain of virtual amps and effects.

- ✔ Link your microphone to your mobile device and get your voice or instrument the best sound possible.

Chapter 4

Exploring iOS Instruments

. . . .

In This Chapter

▶ Evaluating the available instruments for your iPhone or iPad

▶ Playing familiar instruments on your iOS device

▶ Discovering new touchscreen-based instruments

. . . .

*O*ne of the best parts about playing music on an iPhone or iPad is the amazing diversity of instrument options available to you. For a few bucks (or sometimes even for no bucks at all) you can install a synthesizer on your iOS device whose real-life counterpart might have cost you hundreds of dollars. All that sound for a fraction of the cost — and it's available for a few taps in the App Store.

This chapter takes an extensive look at all the types of sounds you can load on your iPhone or iPad. We can't tackle all of the possible apps, because new and different apps come along every day, but we can take a look at the types of apps you'll run into and the sorts of things those apps can do. Whether you decide to stick to more familiar synths and drum machines or dive into instruments specifically designed for touchscreen use, you'll have plenty of options to work with. And apps are far easier to carry with you than four or five trailer's worth of keyboards and other equipment.

Emulating Conventional Instruments

The App Store contains a staggering number of apps that seek to capture and translate the sound of familiar instruments to a new platform. Maybe you always wanted to be a bassist (don't we all), but you never found the time to pick up the instrument. Still, you find you need to add some bass parts to a song you're working on, and you're unable to locate a real live bassist (undoubtedly because of all those gigs we're playing at the moment). The App Store can solve your problem. You can find an app that will allow you to approximate that all-important bass sound so you can record the song you need at that precise moment, or at least until that bassist you know comes back from the gig.

The important concept to remember here is that app emulators can create the sounds of a familiar instrument that you might not otherwise have access to. The makers of these apps sometimes try to reproduce the real-life version of the instrument in the app's *user interface* (the buttons and functions you see, touch, and interact with onscreen). Take a look at the version of the bass guitar contained in the GarageBand app in Figure 4-1.

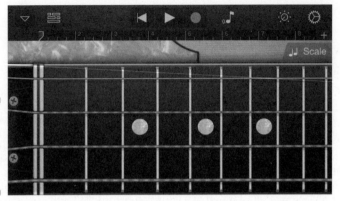

Figure 4-1:
Plucking
the virtual
GarageBand
bass guitar.

All of the screens in this chapter came from the iPhone version of GarageBand. iPad users may see some slight differences in controls or screens because of the extra available space.

Touch the fretboard, and you'll hear the sound of the chosen bass guitar model. You can even bend the strings or slide up and hear realistic effects from the app. Depending on how the developers designed the app, you may be able to access all kinds of sounds and effects modeled from the original source (maybe even by using samples of an actual instrument).

In this section, we take a look at the common types of emulations you'll encounter and what you can expect when you download one of these apps.

Even though you're using a virtual approximation of the instrument on your iPhone or iPad, a little knowledge of the actual instrument goes a long way. If you understand what the instrument is capable of, you can make the emulation sound more realistic. And most app designers restrict their emulations to "realistic" limits. If you try to make a bass clarinet play in the piccolo range, you may find that listeners are troubled by the odd sound. With this knowledge, you can avoid that odd sound and make your performance more realistic — unless, of course, you're *trying* to make that odd sound, and more power to you if you are.

Synths

Compared to many of the instruments you see emulated in the App Store, synthesizers are relatively modern and easy to replicate. After all, digital synthesizer technology entered the consumer and technology all the way back in the late '70s, and improvements in modern technology only helped these synthesizers become more available and accessible. Their transition to the iOS platform was both inevitable and a relatively short jump.

The iOS makes several different kinds of synthesis available to you, and most of these probably won't make much difference to you unless you're really into electronic music. But a little knowledge about the types of synthesis available may give you a better idea of the sounds you're buying:

- **Additive synthesis:** The synthesizer starts with a relatively basic sound and then adds sounds and filters to make the sound more rich and unique. Kawai produced the more popular additive synthesizers.

- **Subtractive synthesis:** The synthesizer starts with a rich and complex sound and then subtracts frequencies to make the sound more unique. If you're looking for that classic analog synth sound (coming from your purely digital device), this is the process to look for.

- **Granular synthesis:** The synthesizer starts with several smaller samples (called *grains*) and then adds processing to those sounds to achieve the final sonic products. You'll find most granular synthesizers as part of software packages like Native Instruments Reaktor or Propellerheads Reasons.

- **FM synthesis:** The synthesizer takes a basic signal and uses oscillators to modify that signal. (FM stands for "frequency modulation.") This type of synthesizer became extremely popular in the '80s when Yamaha introduced the legendary DX7.

- **Wavetable synthesis:** The synthesizer uses a series of digital audio samples to play back the initial sound smoothly transition to another sound for the release after you take the pressure of the key or other triggering action. The PPG synthesizer became one of the more famous examples of wavetable synthesis.

- **Physical modeling:** The synthesizer stores a ton of complex formulas that describe how the sound should react and plays that sound back (depending on how the controls are set).

Again, these types of synthesis might not mean much to you now, but what if we tell you that additive and subtractive synthesis probably powered the synth sounds from the '60s and '70s? Or that you probably heard a ton of FM synthesizers in '80s music? Or that physical modeling became more prevalent in the last few years as computers grew more powerful and gained the ability to reproduce these sounds? This should give you a clearer idea of the nature of these sounds, along with the app descriptions you see in the App Store. You'll also recognize some familiar synth names in the App Store (like Korg, Moog, and Yamaha) and other companies that seek to approximate the sound of these classic instruments (without necessarily using the proper trademark).

Knowing a little about what actually makes these synthesizers function can help you craft your own sounds, but you don't necessarily need that knowledge to play tunes. The app developers nearly always include a ton of presets designed to get you up and running in a short amount of time anyway. So let's get away from the theory — time to start playing with the toys! Take a look at some of the more common features you'll find in synthesizer applications — we'll start from the bottom up.

Keys

The obvious first step in playing a synthesizer is figuring out exactly what you press to make the sound. Take a look at the example of the Animoog synthesizer in Figure 4-2, and notice how the app presents a keyboard.

Synth emulations usually give you a familiar keyboard you can use to trigger all of the sounds you'll need. Some use the standard black-and-white keyboard pattern familiar from all of those piano lessons you took as a child, whereas others pick a common scale (in Figure 4-2, you see a C Major scale) that you

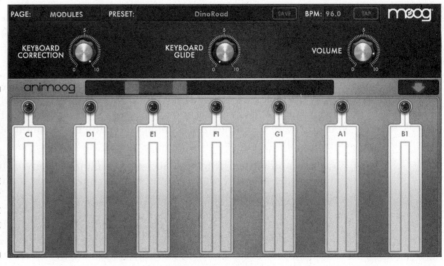

Figure 4-2: The simplified Animoog keyboard makes it easier for you to hit the right note.

can play without fear of accidentally hitting the wrong note (although even if you do hit it, you'll never blow up like a character in a Warner Brothers cartoon — we promise). The slider just above the keys in Figure 4-2 lets you select which octave you play the scale in. Without getting into too much music theory (because experts can and have written multiple volumes on the subject), you can get a sense of the octaves just by taking a look at the number after the note names on the keys. As those numbers get higher, the pitch of the notes gets higher as well.

The keys aren't just on/off switches for the notes, though. In this synthesizer, the *modulation* of the notes changes as you slide your finger up and down the key. In this case, modulation refers to the cutoff frequency of the filter on the sound. Now, again, what we just wrote might not make that much sense if you're not versed in synthesizers, but try to see it like an old tone knob on a radio or amp. As you raise the tone knob, you get more high frequencies in the sound. Turn it down, and you hear lower frequencies more. The great part about playing with touchscreens is that you can do more than just simply play notes. You can modify the sound by moving and sliding your fingers across the screen. Moving your finger up and down the key in Animoog roughly equals moving the modulation wheel in a physical synthesizer.

You hear the word *modulation* in reference to music a lot, and the term doesn't always mean the same thing. Frequency modulation synthesis isn't the same thing as cutoff frequency modulation, and neither of these has much to do with a key modulation (more music theory!). Just know that modulation refers to a control or concept that changes or affects the music.

You can modulate by moving and sliding your fingers across the touchscreen, but no matter how hard you hit the screen, you won't change the sound. If you're used to using *aftertouch* when playing a synthesizer on a real keyboard —aftertouch is adding pressure to a key to change the sound — you'll need an actual MIDI keyboard with aftertouch capabilities to simulate this effect on your device. You just connect that MIDI keyboard to your iPhone or iPad. We talk more about how to make this connection in Chapter 5.

Knobs and switches

Synthesizers wouldn't be *nearly* as fun without all of the knobs and switches you can play with while you're designing your sounds. Presets are great places to start, but tweaking your own sounds until they're just right really adds another dimension to your sound. Figure 4-3 shows you some common configurations for these controls.

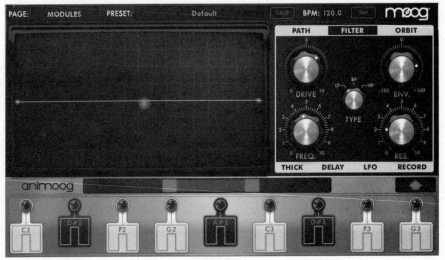

Figure 4-3:
Common
controls
from the
Animoog
app.

Figure 4-3 shows the controls you can use to alter the filter affecting the sound you play:

- ✔ **Drive** adds a bit of gritty overdrive for a little more aggressive sound.

- ✔ **Freq** selects the cutoff frequency of the filter.

- ✔ **Type** select the general band that the filter affects, as follows:

  - *LP* stands for low pass, where the filter primarily affects low frequencies.

  - *BP* stands for band pass, where the filter primarily affects midrange frequencies.

  - *HP* stands for high pass, where the filter primarily affects high frequencies.

- ✔ **Env** selects the level of the envelope modulation on the sound.

- ✔ **Res** selects the amount of oscillation the filter puts on the cutoff frequency.

Manufacturers adhere to no set standards when it comes to labeling these controls. Look for edgy misspellings (such as, say, REZ instead of Res) or labels that suggest the names of more famous synths that the developers couldn't secure the rights for. The ultimate judge of functionality comes from your ears.

You can see in the words around the knobs and switches other screens you can flip to. Not all synthesizers use all of these kinds of controls, but you'll find certain common controls on most of them, such as:

✔ **Delay** includes controls on the amount of time, the amount of feedback, and the ratio of delayed (or *wet*) signal heard to non-delayed (or *dry*) signal heard. Think of this as the amount of echo you hear when you play the sound.

✔ **LFO** (not the '90s boy band) includes the rate (or speed) and shape (such as sine, triangle, or square waves) of the low frequency oscillator that affects the sound. You don't actually hear the low frequency oscillator, but you can hear the effect the LFO has on the audible sound. It sounds more like a wobble in the sound, from a smooth and slow motion to a fast, jittery effect.

✔ **Think** actually refers to common effects like chorus or bitcrushing. You can add multiple union voices to make a sound thicker and louder, detune a second signal slightly for a shimmering chorus effect, add more drive (some synth designers really like drive), or add *bitcrushing* (reducing the amount of details in the sound information to make it sound more harsh and gritty).

Views

Sometimes synth apps possess so many controls and information that you can't physically view them all on one screen at the same time. In these cases, the synth will offer different views. In Figure 4-3, the Page setting in the top-left corner of the screen is an example — you can select from the different available views using this control. In this case, you can select to alter more sounds, perform configuration options on the synth, or change the scales available on the keyboard.

Familiarize yourself quickly with the views of your chosen synth apps so you can navigate between these views as part of your natural playing activities. All synths will require some view changes, so being able to move effortlessly between these views will help your overall playing and performance.

Presets

Ah, presets. Every synth you purchase or download likely comes with a long, long list of sounds created either by the developers or by celebrity musicians or sound designers (and which you'll probably end up paying a little extra for). In the Animoog app, tapping the Preset setting shown in Figure 4-3 takes you to the screen shown in Figure 4-4.

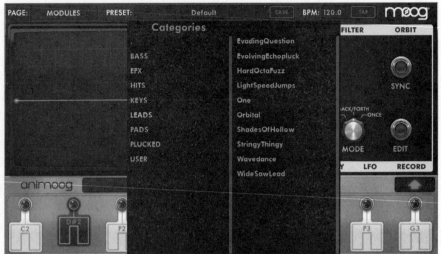

Figure 4-4:
Just a
sampling of
the presets
available
within the
Animoog
app.

Just tap a preset (also known as a *patch*) and load the configuration for that sound automatically. Most apps use these presets to capture commonly expected sounds or show off the most radical or impressive features of the synth. Think of presets as shortcuts to the sound you want.

Everybody uses presets, but you don't have to use that preset just for that sound. Suppose you want to jazz up a lead sound with a little bit more drive or echo. Dial up a preset that's close to what you want, and then tweak it from there. Most synthesizers let save your modifications as separate presets that you can call back later. Just be careful not to save over the original preset!

MIDI configuration options

If you want to play your synthesizers using external controls, such as a MIDI keyboard or a foot control, you'll need to make sure your controller can speak effectively with your app. To do this, you need to set the MIDI configuration for the app.

These controls vary from app to app, again because each synthesizer comes with its own functionality. However, take a look at the controls of the Animoog synth in Figure 4-5 to see the basic features.

Among the features here, you'll probably be most concerned with the MIDI Inputs function, since this determines where the incoming MIDI commands

Figure 4-5:
MIDI con-
figuration
options for
the Animoog
synth.

come from. Follow the steps below to connect a MIDI controller to the Moog
synth app:

1. **Connect your MIDI interface and controller to your iPhone or iPad.**

2. **Open the Animoog app.**

3. **Click Page and select Setup.**

4. **Select MIDI.**

5. **Click the controller you wish to use in the MIDI Inputs section.**

   If you don't see your controller, make sure everything is connected and
   powered up and click Refresh.

This process takes care of the note values, but many controllers contain
additional controllers, such as knobs or switches, that you can map to other
controls. Fortunately, touchscreen apps make this mapping process easy —
just tap the control you want to modify on the screen, move the knob on the
controller you wish to use, and everything is linked up. In the Animoog app,
follow the steps below to map a control:

1. **Tap the MIDI CC Mapping button.**

2. **Navigate to the control (surrounded by a red square) you wish to map
   to the controller.**

   The red square indicates you can map a MIDI command to that controller.

3. **Tap the control.**

   The square turns green.

4. Move the corresponding control on your MIDI controller.

The control on the screen will move as you turn the controller.

Don't forget to save your MIDI CC mappings when you finish the process. This might be easier said than done, though — the iPad version of the Animoog app permits saving CC mappings, but the iPhone app does not. Just check ahead before you get started, and you'll know how much work (or repetition) you'll need to perform for each synth app you buy.

Apps don't all map MIDI controls in the same way (unless they come from the same developer, or if both the controller and the app comes from the same company). Make sure you check out all directions from the developers and follow their instructions correctly to make sure the controller and the app match up.

MIDI CC refers to *control channel* information — basically this refers to any MIDI information that doesn't trigger an actual note. Think of pitch bend or modulation (there's that word again!) controls. These controls allow you a little more control over your sound than just what note you play.

Each synth behaves differently to different MIDI commands and controls, so you must spend a little time with the documentation for each app. Documentation for an app?! Yes, some of these programs require a little more information than Flappy Angry Birds With Friends. Just do a little reading, and you'll save yourself a lot of time and heartbreak in the future.

Background audio

No, this switch doesn't turn on soothing light jazz to relax (or irritate) you while you try to figure out your latest musical masterpiece. Most synths include a control that allows the app to continue to play sound while you switch to another app. (It moves that app into the foreground while the synth continues playing in the background.) This setting is important because it allows you to quickly check something (such as an email or a text) while you're in the middle of laying down tracks. It also prevents the synth from stopping if you accidentally switch to another app or get an interruption you didn't expect (such as an email or text).

In Animoog, you set the background audio option by following these steps:

1. Open the Animoog app.

2. Tap Page and select Setup.

3. Tap Audio.

4. Tap Background Audio.

After you enable this option, the synth and any recordings remain available while you do other things on your iPhone or iPad.

Inter-App Audio and Audiobus (discussed in Chapters 16 and 17, respectively) only use synths and other apps that implement background audio.

Panic!

Okay, don't let this button alarm you. Even though it comes with big letters an exclamation point, you should not really panic. This button doesn't even really make the iPhone or iPad panic, either. Although the label isn't really accurate, Panic buttons persisted since the beginning of MIDI, so you should familiarize yourself with them now.

If you hit the Panic (shown in Figure 4-5) button when everything is fine, nothing happens. But if you notice that a note keeps playing after you let off the key (when this isn't supposed to happen) or that controls refuse to respond, *that's* when you hit the Panic button. This control basically sends a message to every component of your MIDI setup that says, "Stop. Calm down. Let's try this again."

After you hit the Panic button, go ahead and keep playing. Unless you're doing something really wrong, you probably won't have to hit the button again anytime soon.

If you keep encountering Panic issues, check your connections with hardware and reboot the iOS device.

Samplers

Samplers came to popularity with the rise of hip-hop music (and, as drummer and musical historian extraordinaire Ahmir "Questlove" Thompson pointed out, after a fateful appearance by Stevie Wonder on an episode of "The Cosby Show" in which he demonstrated sampling technology via one of his keyboards). We take this trip back through time to demonstrate that what used to take a huge keyboard or sampler and a mic now resides in an app that comes free with your iOS device of choice, as shown in Figure 4-6.

Samplers record audio (anything that your microphone can pick up) or import loops from audio stored in your phone. Within GarageBand, you can choose from Apple Loops (audio that changes tempo to match the master setting of your song, a concept we talk more about in Chapter 10) or music from your music library. You can edit these samples in several ways, including reversing the audio or trimming the beginning or end of the sample to change what you hear. From there, you can use the keys within the sampler to play back the sample at different assigned pitches.

Figure 4-6:
The sampler
inside
Garage-
Band.

You can use several different samplers on your iPhone or iPad, depending on your personal preference (and budget), but for this example, stick with GarageBand. It performs the basic actions easily and gives you a little flexibility with your sounds.

If you bought a new iOS device recently, GarageBand probably came with the sampler. If you use an older device, you might have to purchase the sampler as part of an in-app purchase.

Choosing your sample

As we mentioned earlier, you can either record your own sample or import your sample from somewhere else. Let's start with recording your own sample for playback (see Figure 4-7):

1. **Open your GarageBand app.**

2. **Navigate to the sampler and tap the icon.**

3. **Tap New Sample.**

4. **Hold your mic (either an internal mic or an external mic, as explained in Chapter 7) close to the source of the sound you intend to sample.**

5. **Tap Start.**

6. **When the sound ends, tap Stop.**

That was simple! Press the keys at the bottom of the screen to play back the sample at whatever pitch you choose. Have some fun with that for a bit — we can wait.

Figure 4-7:
Recording
your
sample.

If you want to load a sample, tap the Import button shown in Figure 4-7. You'll see a choice of Apple Loops or Music. Take a look at Figure 4-8 to see the Apple Loops choice.

You can tap the loop to hear a preview of what it sounds like, and you can filter the list using the controls at the top of the screen:

 ✔ Tap Instrument to sort the loops by a specific instrument.

 ✔ Tap Genre to select loops from a specific type of music (no progressive bossa nova death metal?!).

 ✔ Tap Descriptions to sort the apps by a predefined set of adjectives (such as Acoustic, Relaxed, Cheerful, and others).

When you find the loop you want, tap the download icon at the right side of the loop to download and insert it into your sampler.

Reset		Apple Loops	Music		Cancel
Instrument		Genre		Descriptors	
None		None		None	

〰 60s Shuffle Drumset 01	2 bars	⬇
〰 60s Shuffle Drumset 03	2 bars	⬇
〰 60s Shuffle Drumset 06	2 bars	⬇
〰 60s Shuffle Fill 07	2 bars	⬇
〰 70s Electric Piano 06	2 bars	⬇

Figure 4-8:
Loading an
Apple Loop
into your
sampler.

If you want to sample some music you stored on your phone, select the Music tab to see the screen shown in Figure 4-9.

You can navigate through many options (including Songs, Artists, Genres, and Playlists) to find the song you want. Then, just tap the download icon at the right side of the loop to put it right into your sampler.

	Apple Loops	Music		Cancel
🎵	Albums			>
👤	Artists			>
🎸	Genres			>
📄	Playlists			>
🎵	Songs			>

Figure 4-9: Loading music into your sampler.

The GarageBand sampler also comes with a few presets (such as Kids Cheering and Party Horn, to name a couple of extremely valuable options!). If you want to explore those, click My Samples and select one of the options on the right of the screen. Tremendously easy, if not really worth all that much.

If you have some music files left over from the iTunes Music Store back when those songs were saddled with unfortunate *digital rights management* (DRM) software, be aware that those songs will not work in the sampler unless you purchase the unlocked version from the iTunes Music Store. Sorry.

Sampling music from iTunes or other commercial sources and releasing it as part of your own music without permission is a good way to get sued by the original artist. Messing around with these samples for fun or education is a great way to learn, but be sure to get permission from the original artist if you decide to post it for public consumption.

Editing your sample

After you load your sample into the sampler, you can play around with it a little bit. From the main sampler screen, click the arrow to see the screen shown in Figure 4-10.

Figure 4-10:
Editing your
sample.

Figure 4-10:
Editing your
sample.

Let's start with the options under the sample, from left to right:

✔ **Shape:** You're not playing with blocks here — *shape* refers to the way the loop sounds during playback. If you want to get fancy, the technical term for this concept is the *envelope* of the sound, and each of the dots shown in Figure 4-11 refers to specific elements of that envelope, as follows:

• The first point represents the *attack* of the sample, or how quickly you hear the sound from the sample.

• The second point represents the *decay* of the sample, or when the sample volume changes from the attack of the sample to the main sound of the sample.

Figure 4-11:
The
envelope
for your
sample,
even though
you're not
mailing it
anywhere,
really.

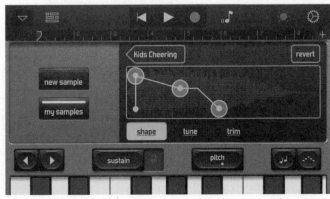

- • The third point represents the *sustain* of the sample, or how long the main part of the sound.

- • The fourth point represents the *release* of the sample, or when the sound finally stops . . . sounding.

Imagine a snare drum hit — loud attack, short decay and sustain, and a quick release. A piano note might also have a loud or soft attack, depending on how hard you hit it, and the decay and sustain depend on how long you hold the key down and which pedals you use to dampen or enhance the strings vibrating. A cello has a soft attack (you may not even hear the bow start the note), but the decay and sustain can actually get louder and go longer depending on how hard you press on the bow while playing. This control is your virtual chance to manipulate these elements of the sound envelope each time you play the sample.

Just drag the points wherever you want and experiment with the sound. If you get to a place you like, keep it. If you want to start over again, tap Revert to move the envelope back to the original settings.

✔ **Tune:** Tune lets you alter the pitch of the sample before you even touch a key on the keyboard, as seen in Figure 4-12.

The Course Tune control lets you move the pitch of the sample up or down by three octaves either way (which may be a little arbitrary if your sample isn't of an instrument and doesn't have a standard pitch) in *half-steps.* If you don't know your scales or music theory (no judgment here), just think of a half-step as a key on a piano. The Fine Tune control moves the sound up or down by 50 *cents* either way. These cents have nothing to do with finances or a certain hip-hop artist, though. Each half-step includes 100 cents, so this control allows you to move a half of a half-step, either up or down.

Figure 4-12:
Tuning
up your
sample.

Tweak to your heart's content. Remember, this setting sets the initial pitch of the sample before you even hit a key. And, as always, tap Revert to get back to where you began.

✔ **Trim:** Jump back to Figure 4-10 for a minute and notice that big blob or squiggle on the screen. That blob or squiggle is kind of a picture of your sample. The left is the beginning of the sound, the right is the end of the sound, and the blob gets bigger or smaller as it gets louder or softer. So what if you want to just use a little bit of the sample? Just like a haircut, you just trim the sample!

Trimming is a fairly easy prospect in theory, but you're going to be doing it for a bit and using a lot of trial and error. The easy part is actually modifying the sound — just tap the controls (the double bars that indicate a draggable point) and move them to the beginning and end of the section of sound you wish to use.

That simple, eh?

Well, if you're on an iPhone and you have big fingers like me, you might not possess the level of precision necessary to get exactly what you want. So move slowly and carefully, and remember that a little bit of the sample goes a long way. You probably want to move the control until the loop begins and ends seamlessly exactly where you want it, but feel free to play around and stop when it sounds right — and "right" can mean anything you find useful, really.

Remember that you can also tap the Rev control to reverse the sample and play it back backwards (like a Jimi Hendrix guitar solo or dialogue from Twin Peaks) or tap Loop to play the sound over and over as long as you hold down a key. Fun, huh? (The Loop function really needs a sample with a seamless beginning and ending to function well.)

Playing your sample

It's not that hard. Just press the key. And another key. Then a third, and so on.

Okay, so there's a little more to it than that. Jump all the way back to Figure 4-6 and notice all the controls just above the keyboard. Most of these controls refer to standard piano and keyboard functions, so we tackle them in more detail later in this chapter in the section called (appropriately enough) "Pianos." But for now let's take a quick look at these controls and see how they apply to samplers:

✔ **The arrow keys:** The two arrows that point left and right move the location of the virtual keyboard up or down. Traditional pianos have 88 keys, and most synthesizers have anywhere from 25 to 61. It's difficult to fit even the smallest of these on a small iPhone or iPad screen. These arrows let you move up and down the length of the keyboard to play higher and lower notes.

✓ **The Sustain switch:** The Sustain switch adds more of the previously mentioned sustain to your sound. Slide the Sustain switch to the left and hold it down, then press a key. When you let off the key, the sound continues to play until you let off of the Sustain switch. No matter what the sound, it will keep going.

Now move the switch to the right and press a key. The sound will continue to play until you tap the Sustain switch again. Now that you know the choices, you can put the switch where you want and go from there.

✓ **The Glissando/Scroll/Pitch switch:** This switch determines how the keyboard reacts when you move from one key to the next. The switch starts on Glissando and cycles through three different options:

- *Glissando:* A fancy Italian music term (or a perfectly normal term if you hail from Italy) meaning that you glide from one key to the next. In fact, some apps ditch the fancy Italian and just call it Glide. The pitch of each key sounds as you move, and the keyboard stays where it's supposed to.

- *Scroll:* Your fingers stay on the keys you play, and the keyboard moves left or right depending on how you drag across the screen.

- *Pitch:* The initial key you press selects the overall pitch, and then you just drag your fingers across the screen to bend the pitch up or down. Crazy wacky fun!

The last two buttons choose scales and run a function called the *arpeggiator* that plays any notes you hold down individually in a specific order, as opposed to all at once. We reviewed altering keys for scales earlier this chapter, in a section called "Synths." The arpeggiator really applies more to pianos, however, so we discuss this functionality later in this chapter in the section, "Pianos."

Drum machines

Joke if you wish about the drum machine (just don't do it around a drummer — he or she might get angry). However you feel about the technology, you can't deny that drum machines play an amazingly large role in modern music (and have been for many years, really). At the most basic level, drum machines play prerecorded or synthesized drum samples that you can arrange into loops and songs. Again, the App Store contains a great deal of drum machines, and each of them presents drum sounds and options differently. But we focus on GarageBand's drumset for now, as shown in Figure 4-13.

Figure 4-13:
Garage-
Band's
drumset.

Open GarageBand and tap Drums (not Smart Drums — we get there later in this section). You'll see the drumset shown in Figure 4-13. This is pretty much what it looks like being behind a real drumset (aside from being in somebody's parents' basement — sorry, I couldn't resist). Now, just tap the drums. Each one you tap gives a different sound and moves accordingly.

You can change drumsets by clicking the triangle in the upper-left corner of your screen. Click the Classic Studio Kit entry in the window that pops up to see your choices. GarageBand contains six different kits — three "acoustic" drumsets, and three "drum machines." Click the Classic Drum Machine entry to see the screen shown in Figure 4-14.

Figure 4-14:
The classic
drum
machine à
la Garage-
Band.

iPad users get a little more room to see the kits, so you can just tap the kit name in the center of the screen if you're on your larger mobile device.

Each pad displayed in Figure 4-14 shows a picture of the sound it plays. Tap along to hear the different sounds. Switch between all the kits to see what's available to you. GarageBand contains a fairly limited number of kits — other programs contain many, many more.

In GarageBand's drum machine kits, notice the small dial icon in the upper-right of the screen. Tap that icon to see four controls that alter the sound of the drum machine:

✔ **Resolution:** This knob affects the quality of the sound. Turn it to the drum sound more "normal," and turn it to the left to decrease the quality of the sound. You can use this control to simulate sounds associated with classic bit-depths — time from some 8-bit video-game-like goodness with a quick left turn!

✔ **Lo-Fi:** Turn this knob to the right to add more noise and grit to the drum machine sounds.

✔ **Low Cut:** Turn this knob to the right to add more low frequencies to the sounds, and turn it to the left to take away those low frequencies.

✔ **Hi Cut:** Turn this knob to the right to add more high frequencies to the sounds, and turn it to the left to take away those high frequencies.

These sound controls are pretty basic compared to more advanced drum machines, where you can alter more sound parameters and generally tweak to your heart's content.

As an alternative to tapping your own drum sounds, Smart Drums give you the option to let GarageBand do the drumming for you. Tap the triangle in the upper-left corner of your screen again and select Instruments. Now choose Smart Drums to see the screen shown in Figure 4-15.

Figure 4-15: Drums get smarter with Smart Drums!

The Smart Drums interface lets you tell GarageBand how you want each drum sound to play. You can select from the same drum kit, but instead of tapping the sound, you drag that sound onto the grid in the middle of the screen.

Drag a sound from the right of the screen onto the grid, and that sound automatically starts playing. If you drag that sound to the left, it plays a more simple rhythm. Move it to the right, and GarageBand adds a little complexity to the beat. Drag the sound up or down to affect the volume level. As you drag each sound onto the grid, that sound falls into place with the beat, and eventually you've got a full-fledged beat ready to go. You can tap the power icon to start and stop the beat, or tap the dice icon to randomize a beat, just for the fun of it. Finally, tap Reset to move everything off the grid and start over.

Tapping and arranging all of these drum sounds is fun, but the real strength of the drum machine involves recording and playing back drum parts that keep strong, consistent time for the entire song. These controls usually (such as the tempo of the song and the length of the loops) differ from app to app, but they usually all work within the context of a *digital audio workstation,* and we tackle that information more in Chapter 10.

Pianos

When you see the word *piano,* the instrument you envision could be anything from your parents' old upright piano (which rarely receives a tuning) to a concert grand piano ready for a professional's loving touch. Or maybe you envision a smaller baby grand in a smoky jazz club, a church organ, or even a Fender Rhodes electric piano like the one on many classic soul albums. The digital equivalent of a piano usually includes all of these, giving musicians many options to fit their sound to the musical context. And because piano sounds have been digitized for many years, apps like GarageBand offer an easy transition from hardware keyboards to a touchscreen or maybe even a MIDI controller.

Open the GarageBand app and tap Piano to see the screen shown in Figure 4-16.

Figure 4-16:
Garage-
Band's
piano.

The keys and controls look like the controls shown in the Sampler section, and for the most part they have the same effect. The arrows move up and down the keyboard, the Sustain button functions the same way, and you can chose Glissando and Scroll to determine the way the keyboard moves as you play.

You can even choose the type of piano by tapping the triangle icon in the upper-left corner, selecting the current instrument, and then choosing the type of piano you wish to play. Pretty simple, eh?

It really is pretty simple. However, if you're not much of a piano player and if the sight of all those keys makes you feel a little woozy, the two buttons above the keys on the right will help you out.

Tap the note icon and GarageBand presents you with scales. As with the synths mentioned earlier in this chapter, you can choose a preset number of keys that map to specific scales (such as major, minor, and pentatonic scales). Take away the keys you don't want to play, and it's easy to play all the right notes! Just tap the scale you wish to use and play away. You can always choose a different scale later, or return to the full piano keyboard.

Feel like changing the key of the song later in your writing process? Tap the wrench icon and change it whenever you wish!

The second button looks a little like a small pyramid, but those little lines in a triangle pattern actually indicate the arpeggiator mentioned briefly in the Sampler section. Activate the arpeggiator using the following steps:

1. **Move the Run switch to On.**

2. **Select how you want the notes to play.**

   Choices here are:

   - *Up* indicates the notes you hold down will always play from lowest to highest.

   - *Down* indicates the notes you hold down will always play from highest to lowest.

   - *Up and Down* indicates the notes you hold down will play from low to high and then back to low, over and over.

   - *Random* indicates the notes play in a random, unpredictable order.

   - *As Played* indicates the notes play in the order that you hold them down.

3. **Tap Note Rate and select how quickly you want the notes to play.**

   Choices here are:

   - Normal quarter, eighth, sixteenth, or thirty-second notes.

   - Dotted quarter, eighth, sixteenth, or thirty-second notes (dotted notes play for 1.5 the amount of time as their normal counterparts).

   - Triplet quarter, eighth, sixteenth, or thirty-second notes (triplets play in groups of three as opposed to the default of four used others).

4. **Choose the number of octaves you want the arpeggiator to cover in the Octave Range menu.**

   This setting determines how high and low the notes will play.

Sounds like a lot of work, right? Maybe it does now, but after following the steps you can just hold down the notes and let the arpeggiator do all the work. Go ahead and hold down a few keys now — notice how the piano plays all the notes in the order you specified using the controls. These functions may help you sound a little more professional than you would ordinarily.

You could even select the Smart Keys app elsewhere in GarageBand that presents chords and auto-play options. The app presents all the chords in the correct key and lets you choose how those chords play. It's that simple!

These piano controls may seem a little basic, but the magic of the piano unlocks when you hook up an external MIDI keyboard (as described in Chapter 5). When you play GarageBand or a more advanced piano app using the external keyboard and other controls (such as a sustain pedal), these apps allow you to play the sounds you wish wherever and whenever you wish, either recording or performing live.

Orchestral instruments

Recording a full orchestra is a logistical nightmare. The wrong recording location, improper microphone placement, or the random human element can wreak havoc on a recording session. This situation might be necessary for professional recordings or performances, but you're just trying to sketch out some quick string parts for your song. Luckily, GarageBand and other apps let you gather together virtual violins, violas, and the rest for your inspiration.

Open the GarageBand app and select Smart Strings to see the screen in Figure 4-17.

As with the other apps, select the type of strings you wish to play by tapping the triangle icon in the upper-left corner of the screen and selecting the type of orchestra you wish to hire. Although you won't have to pick up a bow, you have a couple of options to play the strings.

Tap the chords displayed onscreen to make the orchestra sound off pizzi-cato-style. (That means the orchestra plucks the strings to make a bright but quick sound.) To make the players pick up their bows and give you a lush, sustained sound, drag your finger up and down the displayed chords.

Figure 4-17:
Plucking
and bowing
strings in
Garage-
Band.

Most music uses strings for background music (sometimes called *pads*) to fill out a song, and the plucking sound can be used for effect in music as well. No matter what style you choose, these strings can find a place in your song.

You can find more advanced string apps or samplers with string sounds in the App Store, but you should always look for at least the minimum of these controls when choosing an app.

Guitar and bass

Guitarists and bassist will tell you — you can never have too many guitars or basses. Each one has a unique sonic characteristic that warrants a place in your collection. And these players will spend hours upon hours learning their craft. But what if you just need a few notes from a guitar or a simple bass line for a demo song you're putting together?

iOS apps usually approach guitar and bass simulations either by loading sounds into a sampler and letting you play them via the keyboard or by actually visually simulating the guitar and bass on the touchscreen and letting you interact with the simulation directly. GarageBand falls into the latter category, which makes it so much fun to play. Open the GarageBand app and choose Smart Guitar to see the screen shown in Figure 4-18.

You need a little familiarity with the fretboard of a guitar to play this view with any confidence, but it's really easy to get started. Just touch the screen over a string and hear the note. Touch multiple strings at the same time to hear more notes. Slide your finger up and down the string to move the pitch up or down, and pull or push the string to the side to bend the note and alter the pitch a little. You've heard this sound before — it's the one where the guitarist makes a weird face and shakes the neck of the guitar a little. You may find yourself making the same face as you do this. It's only natural. Go ahead.

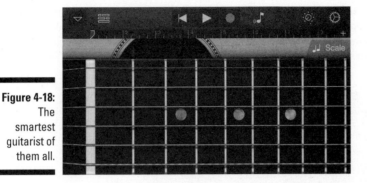

Figure 4-18:
The smartest guitarist of them all.

If you want to move away from the fretboard to play chords (that sound good immediately), tap the dial icon in the upper-left corner to see the screen in Figure 4-19.

Move the switch on the right from Notes to Chords to bring up a screen similar to the string screen in Figure 4-17. In this case, though, you can touch the name of the chords to play the full chord at the same time. If you move your finger up and down the chord, the notes sound as if you were strumming a chord on a real guitar. You can even touch the strings in a different order to simulate fingerpicking on a real guitar. The iPhone may lack the romantic sentiment of a guitar played around a campfire, but at least the sound is there.

The Autoplay function helps you choose a pre-determined strumming pattern, in case you want to spare yourself a little more work. The dial defaults to Off, but you can experiment by moving the dial to one of the four pre-sets and testing it out. Choose the one that feels first to you, then move back to the strumming screen and tap the chord name.

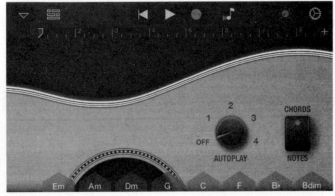

Figure 4-19:
Tying your chords together.

Finally, you can move from the acoustic guitar to the electric guitar by tapping the triangle icon in the upper-left corner and selecting the current instrument. GarageBand includes four guitar models, and three of those models imitate electric guitars. Tap the Roots Rock instrument to see the screen in Figure 4-20.

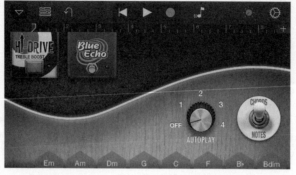

Figure 4-20: Plugging in your virtual guitar.

Notice a couple of extra toys at the left of the screen (guitarists and bassist *love* toys). These icons represent effects pedals. Tap the High Drive button to give your guitar a little more high frequency boost, and tap the Blue Echo button to hear your delayed signal repeated back as you play. Each electric guitar has two effects of its own, and they're all insanely jealous of the other choices. Just like real guitarists!

The Bass app in GarageBand behaves in much the same manner (it's shown back in Figure 4-1, because the bass should *always* come first), although you don't get the same chording options. Lower frequencies tend to sound a little muddy and jumbled in chords, so instead the bass app gives you the notes in the chords and lets you play them one by one.

With GarageBand or other apps, you get a decent simulation of these instruments for use in your songwriting or recording pursuits. And you'll never break a string!

Exploring Dedicated iOS Instruments

So far, this chapter outlined the ways the iPhone and iPad can simulate existing real-word instruments in their apps. Because these sounds are so familiar to listeners, you can understand why so many people want to simulate these sounds in their songs. But some developers and designers see the new touchscreen interface as a place to create new and different sounds. Their apps take advantage of the different things you can do with your iOS device.

New and different user interfaces

The apps in this chapter use visual representations of the instruments they sound like because it's easy to transfer previous knowledge to those apps. If you know your way around a keyboard or guitar, you can easily apply that knowledge to these simulations. Easy enough, right?

Some of the apps we looked at previously already show hints of new touch-screen functionality. Take a look at Figure 4-3, and notice the line drawn across the grid on the Animoog screen. That lines gives you a visual repre-sentation of the sound, and moving that line around (or redrawing it entirely) makes the sound change in new and different ways. As with the grid from the Smart Drums app (shown in Figure 4-15), the volume and tone of the synth change as you move that line across the screen. Touch the screen, and the sound changes as you move along.

But if you want to make new sounds — sounds people don't hear every day — you need to look at new methods of interacting with the devices that make that sound. Techie types call these *user interfaces,* but this concept basically refers to the way you make the device create the sounds you want to hear. The touchscreen presents a whole new way of interacting with sound-making devices, and gestures such as touches and swipes can count for all kinds of actions. In the next section, we look at three different apps that change the way iOS makes music.

An all-new world of sounds

The three apps in this section throw away the standard ways you approach music and make sound. These apps help you create new music and think about sound in a much different way. Or they let you make a whole bunch of racket if you forget to plug in your headphones. Either way, the whole pro-cess becomes pretty fun in short order.

Figure

Propellerheads (the company that makes Figure) kept the standard electronic music components of drums, bass, and melody in its Figure app. But it defi-nitely changed the way you produce the music, as shown in Figure 4-21.

Switch between the three parts by tapping the tabs at the top of the screen, and change the rhythm and range of the parts using the dials in the middle of the screen. You can quickly tap out notes on the bars on the screen, or you can hold down and move your fingers around the bars to produce a rhythmic track based on the Rhythm setting you chose.

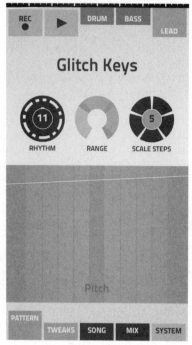

Figure 4-21:
Tapping
along with
Figure.

After you record your parts, you can mess with the tempo and keys to produce an entire song. You might not get a ton of choices (although Figure does offer a bunch of sound options for the parts), but you can get a song down quickly, easily, and mess with music in a new and different way.

Bebot

Okay, so first off — Bebot is cute. This app looks more like a cartoon robot dressed up for a night on the town, as shown in Figure 4-22.

Figure 4-22:
Bebot hits
the stage.

But once you put your finger down, Bebot starts to sing. Move your finger from left to right to raise the pitch of the sound, and move your finger up and down to add higher frequencies. Technically, this kind of app uses an *x-y axis* (made popular by the physical Korg Kaoss pad and the Kaossilator app), but that sounds too much like math and not like music. If you double-tap the small arrow icon in the corner, you can change several different preset sounds, add some sound effects, or even save your own patches. What looks like a simple app turns into a fun music machine that's inspired some additional apps (including efforts by Dream Theatre keyboard player Jordan Ruddess, who has performed with this app before — go look up some YouTube videos for a sample of what's possible).

Bloom

This app actually debuted a few years ago, but it presents a revolutionary way of approaching music, in that you are a participant in the music without retaining total control of the music. Bloom (and its sister app Scape) make *generative* music — you select some presets (shown in Figure 4-23) and let the app go to work.

You can let Bloom do all the work if you wish, but that's not really being a musician, is it? When you get to the main Bloom screen, you can tap over the screen to create a series of chiming sounds, as shown in Figure 4-24.

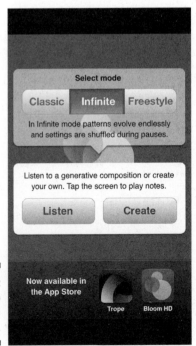

Figure 4-23: Options to make music Bloom.

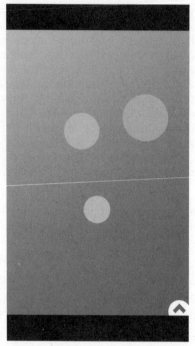

Figure 4-24:
Ringing the
chimes in
Bloom.

These chimes play in a loop that stretches time as the app plays on, so it creates more of a meditative sound than a cohesive music piece. But Bloom gives you an idea of what's possible and how you can interpret sound on the iPhone or iPad. Or just chill out between sessions. Whatever works best for you.

Chapter 5

Playing iOS Instruments

· ·

In This Chapter

▶ Playing from the touchscreen

▶ Playing from an external keyboard

▶ Connecting a MIDI controller

▶ Features of a typical controller keyboard

▶ Using alternate controllers

· ·

Your iOS device and the apps available for it are so versatile that they've probably replaced or duplicated the functions of many individual devices and items that you used to use separately, including your phone (if you have an iPhone), your GPS, your camera, your video camera, your calendar or datebook, your address book, your music player — the list goes on and on.

For musicians, iOS apps can replace your tuner, your metronome, your multitrack recorder, and, what we're going to be talking about here, your electronic instruments.

In this chapter, you learn about the plusses and minuses of playing iOS instruments from the touchscreen. You delve into the world of MIDI, and find out how to connect external keyboards to your iPad, iPhone, or iPod touch. We also look external controllers for iOS that use non-keyboard interfaces.

Playing from the Touchscreen

One of the cool things about iOS instruments is that you can play them directly from the device's touchscreen. The great majority of iOS instrument apps — pianos, organs, synthesizers, and so forth — feature onscreen, piano-style keyboards. Although the touchscreen keyboard isn't the most efficient way to play such instruments, it gives you instant access to their sounds, without needing any additional hardware, unlike most Mac- or PC-based software instruments.

Although playing from the touchscreen is convenient and fun, a keyboard player of almost any skill level will find it pretty restrictive. The built-in, onscreen keyboards on instrument apps can fit only one or two octaves of playable-size keys at a time, which makes them virtually impossible to use for two-handed parts.

To help mitigate this problem, onscreen keyboards let you change octaves as you're playing. Sometimes you can change octaves by pressing an arrow on the keyboard, and sometimes you can just scroll from octave to octave by flicking the keyboard with your finger.

In addition, some apps — such as, for example, IK Multimedia's SampleTank (see Figure 5-1), a sample-playback groove-creation app — offer a *double manual,* which is keyboard jargon for one keyboard placed above another. This way, one can be assigned to bass notes and the other for the melody or chords of a two-handed part. You can even find apps that arrange the keys for use by two people at the same time — fun at parties!

Where the touchscreen really shines, though, is for instruments whose interfaces are designed specifically for your iPad or iPhone or iPod touch — that is, instruments that don't use the piano-keyboard paradigm, such as Wizdom Music's MorphWiz or Audanika's free SoundPrism app (see Figure 5-2). These apps have unique user interfaces that are totally unlike piano keyboards.

Figure 5-1:
A double manual keyboard, such as this one on IK Multimedia's SampleTank, makes it easier to play two-handed parts.

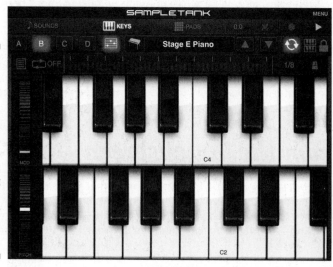

Figure 5-2:
Audanika's
SoundPrism
is an iOS-
specific
instrument
that doesn't
use the
"piano
keyboard"
paradigm.

MorphWiz, for example, works similarly to the instrument it's based on, an alternate MIDI controller called the Hakken Continuum, which you play by sliding your finger across the playing surface. Each space on SoundPrism's grid can produce either a note or a chord. Sliding your finger vertically gives you different inversions of the chord, horizontally moves pitch up or down, and your left hand plays a vertical row of bass notes.

Playing from an External MIDI Keyboard

If you want a keyboard experience closer to the real thing, you can plug an external keyboard into your iOS device — using the methods we describe a little later in this chapter — to use as a *MIDI controller* keyboard. But before we talk more about MIDI controllers, let's take a quick look at some MIDI basics.

MIDI is an acronym that stands for *musical instrument digital interface,* which is a set of standards for instrument and software designers, originally developed back in the 1980s. MIDI makes it possible for hardware-based instruments, signal processors, apps, and computer software to all "speak" a common language.

As long as they're properly connected to each other, even products from different manufacturers can communicate and exchange commands to play notes, change sounds, turn up the volume, and much more. As a result, you can control one MIDI instrument from another. In the case of iOS devices, this usually takes the form of controlling an instrument app from an external MIDI controller.

MIDI doesn't send actual audio through its connections. Instead, it sends real-time data that tells an instrument what note to play and when, how hard to strike the note, when to release it, and much more. In its totality, MIDI is quite a complex subject, but one of the beauties of it is that you only need to master the basics to be able to use it, and you can learn more on an "as-needed" basis. See the sidebar for quick definitions of some key MIDI terms.

Important MIDI terms

Here are explanations of some key MIDI concepts you should familiarize yourself with:

Aftertouch: Parameter measuring pressure on the key after it's been struck. Some controllers support it but others don't.

Continuous controller: Control change messages for any continuously variable parameter, such as volume, pan, or wah. Note the difference between these messages and the control change messages defined below: Continuous controller messages address ongoing live performance data, whereas the messages defined below change settings that you make and leave alone.

Control change: MIDI messages that control various parameters in a connected instrument or device. Turning a MIDI knob or moving a MIDI fader triggers a control change message.

iOS MIDI interface: A hardware device that connects to the dock connector on your iOS device, and adds MIDI ports for connecting external devices to use with your apps.

MIDI cable: This cable features a 5-pin male DIN jack on each end, and is used for connecting two hardware devices.

MIDI channel: Every MIDI connection has 16 channels, all of which can be used simultaneously for different messages.

MIDI in port: A physical connection on a hardware instrument or device into which MIDI data flows. This data flows through a MIDI cable that's connected to the MIDI out port of another device.

MIDI out port: A physical connection on a hardware instrument or device out of which MIDI data flows. This data flows through a MIDI cable that's connected to the MIDI in port of another device.

MIDI thru port: A physical connection on a hardware instrument or device that mirrors what's flowing into the MIDI in port, allowing for daisy-chaining of additional instruments or devices.

Modulation: A standard MIDI control change message sent from a mod wheel on a controller that modulates the pitch of the note or notes.

Note-on: A MIDI message telling an instrument to play a particular note.

Note-off: A MIDI message telling an instrument to stop playing a particular note.

Pitch bend: A standard MIDI parameter that is usually sent from a pitch wheel on a controller, and which can bend the pitch of a note up in real time.

USB MIDI (aka "MIDI over USB"): MIDI data can be sent to an app using the USB standard, assuming your iOS device has the optional Apple Camera Connection Kit (for devices with 30-pin dock connectors) or Lightning-to-USB camera adapter (for Lightning-equipped devices) attached. These Apple adapters turn the iOS device's dock connector into a USB jack.

Velocity: A MIDI message telling the instrument how hard to hit a note, which has a major impact on the note's volume.

Velocity-sensitive keys: Keys on a controller that respond to velocity, allowing you to play with dynamics. Almost all controllers support velocity-sensitive keys. If not, all notes are triggered at the same level.

An iOS app will only respond to MIDI if it's compatible with Apple's *Core MIDI* standard, which was introduced in version 4.2 of iOS. It's always good to check whether your app is Core-MIDI compatible if you're planning to use a MIDI controller with it. Check with the App Store description first, then go to the developer website and contact it directly if you don't get the answers you need.

Apple's Core MIDI for iOS lets you:

✔ Play an app from an external MIDI keyboard, pad unit, or other type of controller.

✔ Control one app from another app's onscreen keyboard or other instrument interface.

✔ Control sound parameters in a Core MIDI app from the knobs and switches on a MIDI controller.

✔ Change sound presets in an app from an external controller.

✔ Control external hardware instruments from an iOS app.

Connecting a MIDI Controller

With the exception of a few dedicated iOS-specific models, most MIDI controller keyboards require another piece of hardware to be placed in between them and your iOS device in order for your Core MIDI apps to recognize and respond to your MIDI controller. You have a few different ways you can go.

iOS MIDI interface

One way to go is to purchase a dedicated iOS MIDI interface, or an iOS audio-and-MIDI interface that gives you microphone or guitar connections (or both) in addition to a MIDI connection. Examples of audio-and-MIDI interfaces on the market include the IK Multimedia iRig PRO, the Alesis I/O Dock II (see Figure 5-3), and the Behringer iS202.

If you only need MIDI and don't plan on recording audio, a dedicated iOS MIDI interface is an economical way to go, and more are being released all the time. For instance, the new IK Multimedia iRig MIDI 2 (see Figure 5-4) gives you the option of Lightning and 30-pin connections for iOS, or USB connections for Mac and PC. It features MIDI in, out, and thru ports.

Figure 5-3:
The Alesis I/O Dock II is both an audio and a MIDI interface.

Figure 5-4:
The IK Multimedia iRig MIDI 2 is a small MIDI interface that connects to your iOS device's dock port.

If you want to have the option to set up a multi-machine setup with four MIDI ins and four MIDI outs, and the ability to pass audio from one machine to the next, you might consider iConnectivity's new iConnectMIDI4+, which, with all its capabilities, sells only for about $200.

To connect a controller keyboard with an iOS interface, first connect the interface to your iOS device's dock port. Next, plug the keyboard's MIDI out to the MIDI in on the interface using either a standard MIDI cable or a cable that comes with the unit, depending on the interface you have. The keyboard's MIDI out is where messages coming from the keyboard — including note-ons and note-offs, CC data, and more — are sent.

The interface's MIDI in port takes that data and brings it into your iOS device and makes it available for your app (see Figure 5-5).

Before MIDI came along (back in the dusty mists lost to time), synthesizers used *control voltage* (or *CV*) to pass messages like notes and performance data between different devices. CV isn't common to iOS interfaces yet, but some enterprising souls allow you to pass MIDI to digital devices and CV to analog devices for some truly impressive synth rigs. If you feel like geeking out, check out apps like Brute LFO and buy the cable you'll need (one end should be the standard headphone to plug into the phone, and the other end whatever the analog synth accepts).

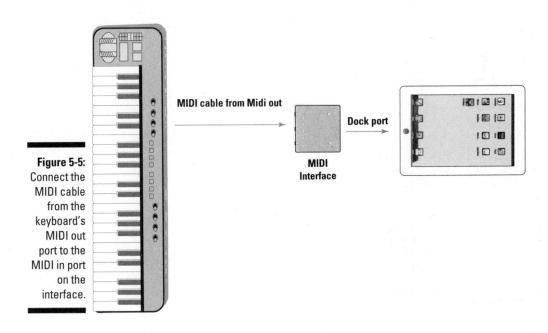

MIDI cable from Midi out

Dock port

MIDI Interface

Figure 5-5: Connect the MIDI cable from the keyboard's MIDI out port to the MIDI in port on the interface.

Connecting controllers to iOS devices using USB

Another option for plugging in an external keyboard is to use a standard USB MIDI controller. "But wait, there's no USB port on an iOS device," you say. This is technically true, but you can add one very easily with Apple's inexpensive Lightning-to-USB-camera adapter, for Lighting-equipped devices, or the Camera Connection Kit for iOS devices with 30-pin dock connectors (see Figure 5-6).

When you do this, the MIDI controller world is your oyster, as you can choose from a large selection of USB MIDI interfaces.

In order to work with Apple's Core MIDI, a USB MIDI controller must be *USB Class Compliant,* which means that it's designed to work with your iOS device (or a computer) without the need to install a software driver. If driver installation is required, it won't work on your iOS device.

A large percentage of USB controller keyboards are USB Class Compliant, and some even advertise themselves as being iOS compatible, if you use one of the Apple camera adapters described earlier.

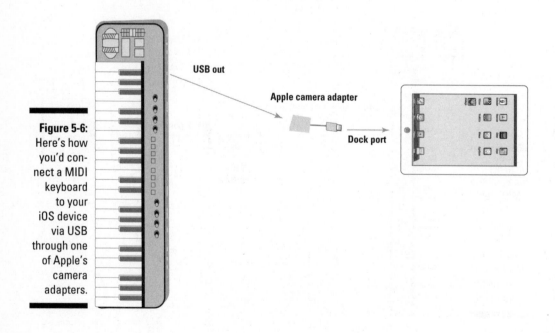

Figure 5-6:
Here's how you'd connect a MIDI keyboard to your iOS device via USB through one of Apple's camera adapters.

USB out

Apple camera adapter

Dock port

Do your research and make sure your USB MIDI controller will work with iOS devices. Manufacturers who do produce compatible equipment will usually fall over themselves advertising this fact.

One more big advantage of connecting via USB to your iOS device is that you don't need to plug a power adapter into the keyboard; it will be bus powered, which means it gets its power through the USB cable. As a result, you can connect your MIDI keyboard in places where there's no AC power available — as long as your iPad's battery is charged. However, longer chains of devices or larger devices might still need a separate power source — do your research and test first.

Features of a Typical Controller Keyboard

Obviously, all MIDI controller keyboards have piano-style keys, but the size and number of those keys vary greatly. MIDI keyboards range from 25 to 88 keys, but for a mobile studio, you'd probably want something no larger than 49 keys.

Don't expect the keys to feel like a piano, because almost all MIDI controller keyboards have "synth action" keys, which are much lighter and have less resistance when you play them. That being said, some 76- and 88-key controllers have "weighted-action" keys, which are similar in feel to those on an acoustic piano, but such units are typically a lot more expensive. You might also look at semi-weighted keys to provide a little resistance without shelling out too much money or putting too much weight in your controller to move easily.

The keys on a MIDI controller send MIDI note on, note off, velocity, and in some cases aftertouch data in real-time as you play, which instantly triggers the appropriate notes from your software instrument. (See the sidebar, "Important MIDI terms," earlier in this chapter for definitions of these terms.) Note that not all apps accept aftertouch data, though. That feature remains in the hands of the developers.

Although some controllers just have keys plus Modulation and Pitch wheels, most also have additional controls that can send MIDI Control Change data to your instrument or other Core MIDI app on your iOS device.

Here are the types of controls, besides the keys, which you might find on your MIDI controller:

- **Knobs:** Many controller keyboards feature one, two, or even eight or more MIDI assignable knobs (also known as *encoders*) on them. Turning the knobs sends control change data to your app, which can adjust all sorts of parameters, such as volume, effects, and much more. Each knob is set to send a particular type of control change message, but can be adjusted from the keyboard to send a different one (or even better, the app can be adjusted to match the physical controller using the MIDI Learn feature, as explained in the next section).

- **Sliders:** Many controllers also have sliding levers called *sliders,* which otherwise function just like knobs.

- **Buttons or switches:** If your controller has MIDI assignable buttons or switches on it, these can control MIDI parameters with on/off functions (such as, for example, switching a reverb effect on and off).

- **Pads:** Some controller keyboards offer pads, which send note on, note off, and velocity data, similar to the data a key would send. However, these are designed for triggering drum and percussion sounds by tapping on them with your fingers.

How Control Change Messages Work

Each type of MIDI control change (CC) message has its own number assigned to it, from 0 to 127. When a MIDI device or app receives a message with that number, it changes the parameter that's assigned to the same number.

Some CC numbers are standardized to specific parameters — for example, 1 controls modulation, 7 controls volume, and 10 controls pan — whereas others are unassigned in the MIDI standard but can be designated by the app developer to control specific functions in the instrument.

Apps that include advanced MIDI control usually include documentation that list all CC numbers for the app. Consult that knowledge base if you don't feel like experimenting for a good, long time.

Although it sounds complicated, most apps make using control change messages really easy by providing a feature usually called *MIDI Learn* or *MIDI Mapping.* Typically, this feature is activated by pressing and holding an onscreen control. After a few seconds, you're presented with a screen that tells you to move a knob, slider, or switch on your controller in order to assign it control of that parameter (see Figure 5-7).

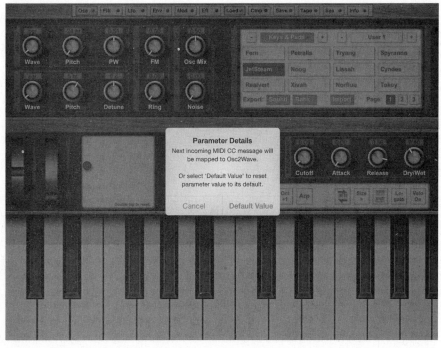

Figure 5-7:
The synth
app NLog
Synth Pro
from Tempo
Rubato in
MIDI Learn
mode.

Playing with Alternate Controllers

Keyboards are by far the most common MIDI controllers, but they are by no means the only type of MIDI controllers available.

Pad controllers typically offer 16 pads that send note on, note off, and velocity and pressure (aftertouch) messages, and often have additional programmable buttons and knobs (see Figure 5-8). Pad controllers are mainly used for playing drum and percussion apps, or triggering looped parts and creating beats. They pair exceptionally well with beat-based apps like iMaschine and iMPC. Many are based on the 16-pad arrangement of Akai's classic MPC series of hardware beat boxes, which are huge in the hip-hop production world. Most pad controllers are designed to be played with your fingers.

Although you can do the same type of triggering from a MIDI keyboard, a pad controller is better suited for the task, based on the more "drumlike" feel of the pads, and their physical arrangement, which is more convenient for tapping out drum and percussion parts than a piano-style keyboard.

Figure 5-8:
The Akai MPD32, based on the company's iconic MPC series, offers 16 pads, along with knobs, sliders and more.

With a MIDI interface connected to your iOS device, you can choose from a wide range of alternate controllers. Although most are not specifically designed for iOS, if they have a standard MIDI out, they'll connect through a physical MIDI port on a MIDI interface and then into your iOS device.

So what other types of controllers are out there? You can get MIDI guitar controllers; MIDI drum sets that can be played with sticks just like a regular kit; MIDI wind controllers that are played like a clarinet or saxophone; and MIDI theremins and alterative controllers, such as the Hakken Audio Continuum, among others.

Some alternate controllers are used just for sending out control change data, such as the IK Multimedia iRig BlueBoard, which is billed as the "The first wireless MIDI pedalboard controller for iPhone, iPad, and Mac." The BlueBoard lets you remotely send CC messages to control effects in MIDI-compatible apps and software, and is especially designed for use with amp and effects modeling apps and software.

IK also released iRing (see Figure 5-9), a gesture-based controller that wirelessly sends control change messages and note information, and can be used to make music by waving one's hands on one of the dedicated apps the company has published for them, including iRing FX Controller or iRing Music Maker.

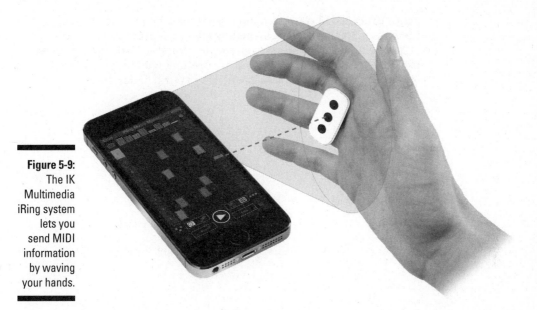

Figure 5-9:
The IK
Multimedia
iRing system
lets you
send MIDI
information
by waving
your hands.

Understanding and Minimizing Latency

Whether you're using your iOS device's touchscreen or a MIDI controller of any kind, one issue you often have to deal with is called *latency*. Latency is the split-second delay between when you touch the screen to play a note (or press a key or any other note trigger on an external MIDI controller), and when the note actually sounds. Although measured in milliseconds, latency delays can be enough to throw off the rhythm of your playing. Latency is also an issue when recording audio into your device.

So what causes latency? The delay occurs between the time it takes the app to recognize the note you've triggered from the touchscreen or a controller and when the note is heard on the speaker or headphone output of your device. Many instrument apps, especially the more consumer-oriented ones, have a distracting amount of latency when you're playing. For apps aimed at professional and semi-pro musicians, more time and effort is spent in the design stage to minimize latency, but even so, it can still sometimes be an issue.

Many music apps have a low-latency setting that you can turn on in your iOS device's Settings app. Open Settings and look for the name of the app in the main app list on the left, and when you select it, see if you are given a low-latency option. The reason this isn't switched on by default is that it takes more processor power to minimize latency, so in order to keep performance as high as possible, the low-latency feature is an option. We haven't found that turning low-latency on for the music apps causes any discernable processor issues, but theoretically it could. Also remember that any audio interfaces you connect to your iOS device can affect latency as well.

Chapter 6

Playing Your Guitar or Bass through Your iOS Device

. . . .

In This Chapter

▶ Choosing your connection options

▶ Using multi-effects modeling apps

▶ Playing through amp-and-effects modelers

▶ Finding the best amp modeling apps

▶ Using modelers onstage

. . . .

Keyboardists aren't the only musicians who have great options for playing and recording into iOS devices — guitarists and bassists do, too. Whether you're recording, performing, or just jamming, there are apps and hardware accessories that allow you to tap into the power of your iPad, iPhone, or iPod touch.

In this chapter, we show you how to set up a monster iOS rig and talk about some of the coolest apps and products out there for guitarists and bassists.

Choosing Your Connection Options

In order to take advantage of the great guitar-processing apps available, you need a way to get the signal from your guitar or bass into your iOS device. For that, you'll need a dedicated guitar interface or a more fully featured audio interface that can handle not only guitar and bass connections but also microphones and sometimes even MIDI as well. We look at those devices in depth in Chapter 7, but here we focus on dedicated guitar/bass interfaces.

Two different types of guitar/bass interfaces are available on the market:

- ✔ Digital interfaces, which connect through the dock port on your device
- ✔ Analog interfaces, which connect through the headphone jack on your device

Going digital

Initially you could only find analog guitar interfaces for iOS, but the last couple of years have brought forth plenty of digital models. These offer better sound quality than the analog ones, because they convert your instrument signal into digital audio and keep it in the digital domain as it goes into your device. Conversely, analog interfaces bring the signal in through the analog headphone jack, and it doesn't get digitized until it gets into your device.

These digital interfaces offer 24-bit audio resolution, which is the same resolution used in most professional computer recording software. The result is that your guitar or bass will sound the same going into an app as it does coming out of your guitar, and no noise will be added.

Some of the best-known interfaces of this type include:

- ✔ Apogee Jam
- ✔ Apogee Jam 96K
- ✔ Griffin Guitar Connect Pro
- ✔ IK Multimedia iRig HD
- ✔ Line 6 Mobile In
- ✔ Peavey AmpKit Link HD
- ✔ Positive Grid's JamUP Plug HD (see Figure 6-1)
- ✔ Sonoma Wireworks GuitarJack Model 2

The only disadvantage to digital interfaces is their cost, which is typically in the $90 to $120 range, depending on the product.

Connecting one of these interfaces to your device is easy: Just plug it in to the dock connector, plug your guitar or bass into its 1/4" input jack, and you're ready to rock.

Note that some interfaces feature the older-style 30-pin connectors, which means if you have one of the newer generation of Lightning-equipped iOS devices, you'll need one of Apple's Lightning-to-30-pin adapters in order to

Figure 6-1:
The JamUP Plug HD interface is Positive Grid's digital follow-up to its original, analog JamUp Plug interface.

connect it to your device. This adapter will set you back about $30, so figure that into your budget, or choose an interface such as IK Multimedia's iRig HD (see Figure 6-2), or Griffin's Guitar Connect Pro, which supports both formats out of the box.

If you plan on using both MIDI and audio in your live rig, make sure you buy an interface that supports both. You only have one data connector, after all — don't make your devices fight for space!

Figure 6-2:
IK Multimedia's iRig HD instrument interface offers detachable cables for Lightning, 30-pin, and USB (Mac) connections.

The analog alternative

Analog instrument interfaces offer an inexpensive alternative to the digital products discussed earlier. Although analog audio isn't as clean and pristine as digital audio, for a lot of applications, the difference won't be particularly noticeable. Analog guitar interfaces tend to sell in the $20 range, for the most part, so if you're willing to live with a signal that might be slightly noisy at times, you can save quite a bit.

These interfaces connect through your device's headphone jack, using a kind of connector called TRRS (see Figure 6-3), which is a special type of mini-plug that allows audio to travel both in and out of your iPad, iPhone, or iPod touch. This is important because not only do you want your guitar signal to go into your iOS device, you want to be able to hear it and any background tracks or other music you're playing with it at the same time.

Figure 6-3:
A TRRS connector, which (as you can tell from the extra ring on the jack) lets audio flow both ways.

If you're wondering where you'll be able to plug your headphones into, since the interface is connected to your headphone jack, there's a simple answer. All of these analog interfaces have their own built-in headphone output jack, so you can listen to the audio coming out of your device at the same time as your guitar's signal goes in through the iOS device's headphone jack.

Because they're 30-pin devices (a format that Apple has replaced), analog interfaces may not remain on the market all that much longer. But at the time of this writing, these three were still available, all at reduced prices (under $30):

✔ IK Multimedia iRig
✔ Positive Grid JamUp Plug
✔ Griffin Guitar Connect Pro

Using Multi-Effects Modeling Apps

When you have an interface, you'll be ready to start making some music with your guitar or bass. If you want to get authentic-sounding amp and effects pedal sounds, you'll want to use a guitar multi-effects app featuring digital amp and effects modeling, or a multitrack recording app like GarageBand, which has modeled amps and effects included with it.

You can also send your guitar signal into a multi-effects app and then into a recording app, using the Inter-App Audio feature Apple introduced in iOS 7, or the Audiobus 2 app. Both facilitate sharing audio between apps in your device. (These topics, and more about using multiple apps together, are covered in Part V of this book.)

Guitar multi-effects apps with modeling explained

Digital modeling is a process by which the circuitry and sound of a particular hardware audio device — it could be a guitar amp, speaker cabinet, effects pedal, or any unit that outputs audio — is painstakingly re-created in digital form. The basic idea is that you can duplicate the sound of the device being modeled by designing digital circuitry that mimics the behavior of the original. And it works pretty well. Is it a perfect replication? No, but it's often very tough to tell the difference.

A number of years back, a major music technology magazine conducted a blind listening test in which amp modeling software for the Mac was compared against the actual amps being modeled. A panel of engineers listened to examples, not knowing whether they were coming from actual amps or models. When asked to choose which examples were from the real amps and which were from the modeled amps, they were fooled about 40 percent of the time.

Although some guitar-tone aficionados might disagree, digitally modeled amp or effects tones generally sound authentic, and are now staple tools in the arsenals of many guitarists and bassists. You can find amp and effects modeling technology in computer software, hardware multi-effects pedalboards, and even in guitar amps that are made to sound like other amps.

In iOS, many guitar multi-effects apps feature modeling technology, and these apps typically let you choose from various amp types and pick the effects in your virtual pedalboard (see Figure 6-4). With an instrument plugged in through an interface to your iOS device, it can sound, in your headphones, as if you're playing through a massive gear rig.

All the apps give you graphic representations of the amps and effects they're modeling, and on most, you can control the amps and effects from their virtual knobs. This is very cool for duplicating the experience of using real gear, but it's hard to be precise when turning a virtual knob.

Figure 6-4:
Guitar
effects
apps, such
as Positive
Grid's
JamUP Pro
XT, give you
a virtual rig,
including
amps, cabi-
nets, and
effects.

Amp types

Let's look at some of the amp types typically modeled in iOS multi-effects modeling apps. In most cases, the manufacturers of these apps haven't licensed the names of the actual amps or pedals being modeled, so they can't refer to their models in that way. Instead, they have to come up with clever names for their models that are suggestive of what they're being modeled on, without violating trademark or copyright law. Here are some of the most commonly modeled amp types:

✓ **Fender:** Fender amps have been an integral part of the guitar gear industry since the 1940s, and the amps they made in the late '50s to mid-'60s are considered particularly desirable. As a result, virtually every product featuring amp modeling includes some Fender models. The Deluxe Reverb, Twin Reverb, and Super Reverb are combo amps (head and speakers in one unit) that are typically modeled, as is the Bassman, a separate amp head that plugs into a speaker cabinet (this configuration is referred to generically as a "stack"). IK Multimedia even has an app totally devoted to Fender amps and effects called AmpliTube Fender, which was created in conjunction with the manufacturer.

✓ **Marshall:** Emulations of these legendary British amps are also found in virtually every modeling product. Most of the classic Marshall amps are stacks. Two of the amps you find frequently in modeling software are the JCM800 and JCM900, and the speaker configuration of the cabinets usually modeled with them is 4x12, which means it has four 12" speakers in it.

✓ **Mesa/Boogie:** This American amp maker is best known for its Dual Rectifier amp, which offers a smooth, high-gain sound, and for its Mark I model that's used by Carlos Santana. Most amp-modeling products offer at least one Mesa/Boogie model, usually the Dual Rectifier.

✔ **Vox:** The Vox AC30, a British amp with a distinctive sound, has been used by many top guitarists, including Brian May of Queen and The Edge from U2. There were many different versions of the AC30 made, but the one called AC30 Top Boost is the one you'll find in most modeling apps and hardware.

Other amps you often see modeled are from Orange, HiWatt, Ampeg, Soldano, and Peavey, among others.

Bass players will be happy to know that some guitar multi-effects apps also include bass amp models. These might be modeled from Ampeg, Gallien-Krueger, Acoustic, or others. You can also find dedicated bass amp modeling apps such as PocketGK from PocketLabWorks (see Figure 6-5), a bass amp app designed to emulate the sound of Gallien-Krueger bass amps. Like with real guitar and bass amps, it generally sounds better for a bass to go through a virtual bass amp rather than a virtual guitar amp. Some bass amps, most notably the Fender Bassman, are actually used mostly by guitarists, but that is an exception.

Figure 6-5:
The PocketGK app offers dedicated Gallien-Krueger bass-amp modeling.

When you choose an amp type in a modeling app, it will typically be "matched" automatically with its corresponding speaker cabinet, which allows you to instantly get a close replication of the sound associated with that particular amp.

However, one of the cool things about modeling apps is that they make it easy for you to mix and match amp components, including amp heads, power amps, preamps, and, of course, speakers. This allows you to create hybrid setups that aren't readily available in the real world, which can be cool for creating unique amp sounds. Positive Grid's Bias, an amp-design app that works in conjunction with the company's JamUp Pro apps, even lets you change components inside the amplifier to create custom setups (see Figure 6-6).

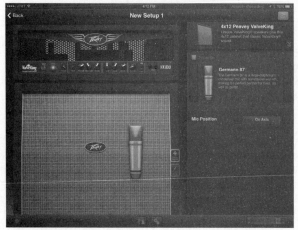

Figure 6-6:
Tweak your amp as much as you want with Bias.

Even though a combo amp is a one-piece unit with speakers integrated into it, amp modelers usually treat a combo's speaker section as a separate component, allowing you to mix and match its amp or speaker section with other models.

Mic models

Modeling apps not only simulate the sounds and architecture of an amp and speaker cabinet, but also the microphones placed in front of a speaker cabinet, like you'd have in a recording studio or stage situation. Once again, modeling comes into play in apps that give you choice of a virtual mic type — usually either a dynamic mic, which tends to offer a fatter sound, or a condenser mic, which usually has a brighter, crisper response (see Figure 6-7).

Figure 6-7:
Many guitar-effects apps, such as Sonoma WireWorks GuitarTone, offer more than one type of virtual mic.

Some apps, such as Agile Partners/Peavey Electronics AmpKit+, even let you move the mic's position on the cabinet to change the sound. AmpKit+ gives you three choices:

- ✔ **On Axis:** This setting simulates the mic pointed directly at the cabinet, and is the brightest setting.

- ✔ **Off Axis:** With this setting, the virtual mic is angled a bit as it points to the cabinet, and has less high end.

- ✔ **Distant:** This setting has more "air" (a term musical folks use to describe hearing more sound from the room as opposed to directly from the amp) in it, as it's emulating a mic placed back from the amp (see Figure 6-8).

Typically, you get a choice of a dynamic mic model and a condenser mic model (see Chapter 7 for more info on microphone types). Usually, the dynamic is modeled from a Shure SM57, perhaps the most popular mic for guitar amps of all time. The condenser is usually designed to emulate a classic studio condenser like the Neumann U87. As they do with the names of amp or effects models, the app developers usually use suggestive names rather than the actual names of the mics in order to avoid trademark and copyright violations.

Adding a Virtual Pedalboard

Effects pedals, a.k.a. *stompboxes,* are a key part of most players' setups, and modeling apps offer virtual versions aplenty of such pedals. You usually get a virtual pedalboard with slots into which you can load several effects from an available collection (see Figure 6-8).

Figure 6-8: In Garage-Band, you can access up to four stompbox effects at a time.

You can usually put the effects in whatever order you'd like, and they usually have on/off switches and virtual knobs you can use for changing parameters, just like real pedals do. The next few sections look at some basic stompbox types and some of the typical effects types you'll find in them.

Distortion and overdrive

Although you can usually get distortion and crunchy sounds from an amp model by turning up its Gain or Preamp control, if you want to add more grit or to distort a clean amp, a distortion pedal or overdrive effect is your ticket. The difference between the two is that distortion is a more intense effect, not only distorting the sound but also adding a lot of sustain. Fuzz boxes are another type of distortion effect. Heavy distortion tends to be used more in metal and other rock styles. Both guitar and bass can use distortion effects.

Overdrive is designed to break up the guitar sound as well, but in a more subtle way. It's good for crunchy sounds with less mayhem than you'd get with distortion, but it too adds some sustain and plenty of warmth.

There are several iconic distortion and overdrive pedals emulated in most modeling apps. Like with amps, unless the software manufacturer has a licensing deal with the gear company, the pedals will look reminiscent of the original but have a name that's only suggestive of it. For instance, one of those classic pedals is the ProCo RAT, which might be called something like "The Brat" or "The Rodent." Between the look and the similar-sounding name, it's should be clear which pedal each is supposed to be.

In addition to the RAT, another oft-modeled pedal is the Ibanez Tube Screamer. Often referred to by the model number of its most iconic incarnation, the TS-9, it's probably the most famous overdrive pedal of all time. It has Gain, Tone, and Level controls, and gives you a beefy overdrive sound that borders on distortion when the Gain control is turned all the way up (see Figure 6-9).

With overdrive and distortion pedals (and their modeled emulations), the Gain parameter is what controls how intense the effect will be. The higher the gain, the more distorted and "pushed" your guitar will sound. The same is true with Gain controls on an amp. When you hear of a "high-gain amp sound," it's usually the amp supplying most of the distortion right from its own circuitry (or virtual circuitry in the case of modeling apps), or possibly the sound is being achieved by a combination of an amp with a distortion or an overdrive pedal.

Other overdrive/distortion pedals often emulated in modeling apps are the Boss OD-1, a yellow overdrive pedal; the Boss DS-1 distortion; the Boss Metal Zone distortion; and the Electro-Harmonix Big Muff fuzz box.

Figure 6-9:
AmpliTube, like most modeling apps, features a model of the famous Ibanez Tube Screamer overdrive.

Modulation effects

Several different types of processes fall under the general category of modulation effects. In all of them, your signal is being modulated by something else, be it a duplicate copy or some other type of signal. Common modulation effects include the following:

- **Chorus:** This effect gives your signal a lush, wider sound by combining it with a duplicate signal that's slightly detuned and slightly delayed. If you've ever heard a 12-string guitar, which has many pairs of unison strings, the effect is somewhat similar.

- **Flanger:** Flanging was invented in the days of analog tape. It was achieved back then by playing two tapes with duplicate material in unison, with the engineer pressing on the edge (flange) of one of the reels to change speed. This effect adds a sort of rising and falling whooshy sound to your guitar or bass. Today's flangers achieve the effect digitally — no need for tape machines.

- **Phase Shifter:** A phase shifter also creates its effect by duplicating your original sound and modulating it. Its effect is similar to a flanger, but subtler.

Filter effects

Filter effects pass your guitar signal through a filter of some sort, which cuts or boosts particular frequencies (see Figure 6-10). These effects run the gamut from basic EQ to wild, synthlike effects.

Figure 6-10:
The wah
pedal from
AmpliTube
offers three
different
operating
modes: On
(manual),
Auto, and
Tilt.

Wah pedals are also filter effects. Guitar effects apps often feature wah pedals, and usually one is an auto-wah, which acts on your audio automatically based on the level of the input signal, without the need for an expression pedal. Of course, if you have a MIDI expression pedal, which sends continuous controller information (see Chapter 5), you can use it on "manual" wahs in the collection. You can also move the virtual wah pedal with your hand on your devices screen, although it's hard to do that while you play!

Auto-wahs, though convenient, don't offer the level of control of manual ones. IK Multimedia's AmpliTube has a wah that can switch between Auto, Manual, and a mode called Tilt, which lets you operate the wah by literally tilting your device.

Dynamics effects

Dynamics effects impact the amplitude (volume) of your guitar signal, and most modeling apps offer two types:

✔ **Compressor:** The first is a *compressor.* Compressors even out the dynamics of your guitar or bass signal by squashing down the louder parts. Guitar or bass stompbox compressors typically have a sustain control or compression control for increasing the intensity of the compression effect, a Level control for adjusting the output, and an Attack control. The attack governs the speed at which the compressor acts on a note that passes through its circuitry. Faster attacks tend to heighten the effect, but soften the initial transient of the note (the first part, where the pick hits the string, rather than the portion of the note that sustains).

Well-known compressors that are often included in modeling apps include the MXR DynaComp (see Figure 6-11), one of the earliest compressor pedals to hit the market, and the Boss CS-2, a blue stompbox that's found in the pedalboards of many guitarists.

Figure 6-11:
The red
compressor
pedal from
JamUp Pro
XT emulates
the clas-
sic MXR
DynaComp.

✔ **Noise gate:** The other dynamics effect you'll see in virtually every modeling app is a *noise gate* (see Figure 6-12). These are not typically modeled
from a classic pedal effect (we're not sure something as utilitarian and
mundane a noise gate would be considered classic), but they are very
important for keeping buzz from the app's virtual amp from getting into
the signal.

Here's how they work. If you have a noisy, high-gain tone selected in the
modeling app, there's a good chance it will create a constant buzz. While
you're playing, the buzzing will most likely not be too noticeable but
when you stop it will be readily audible. When properly set, a noise gate
shuts down the audio when you stop playing.

Figure 6-12:
The Noise
Gate helps
keep the
buzz from
amps and
effects from
being audi-
ble during
pauses.

Noise gates (or simply "gates") usually have a Threshold control (also called Sensitivity or Depth), which sets the level below which the gate will close. If you set the Threshold too high and there's a relatively quiet part of your song or a long held note, the gate may cut it off prematurely. So sometimes you have to experiment a little to find a good setting.

Noise gates can also help out with vocal signal chains, if you decide to get experimental and run your vocals through these kinds of apps. Have fun!

Ambient effects

Two other common effects types are *reverb* and *delay.* In a lot of guitar multi-effects apps, the reverb is an emulation of the amp's own spring reverb. In some apps, that reverb is controlled by a single knob that's a virtual version of the reverb knob on the emulated amp's face (see Figure 6-13). The spring reverb on a real amp takes the signal and runs it through a chamber with a vibrating spring inside it. The reverb control adjusts how much of it is added to the signal.

Figure 6-13:
The reverb control on a modeled amp is sometimes just a single knob that mimics the one on the amp.

Many apps offer other ways to get reverb into your signal, often in the form of virtual reverb pedals. Emulations of digital reverb pedals can give you choices of emulations of different types of spaces such as halls, rooms, chambers and plates.

Plate reverbs were artificial reverb units used in the pre-digital days, which were made from large metal plates and had a speaker and a microphone built into them. The audio to be reverberated was sent through the speaker, where it bounced around inside the plate and was picked up again by the microphone.

Chamber refers to an echo chamber, which, despite having the word *echo* in it, was designed for creating reverb effects. It was typically a dedicated room with hard surfaces for the sound to bounce around in. Like with a plate, the audio to be reverberated was piped into, played through a speaker, and miked.

TIP

Reverb and delay effects often have a wet/dry control (also called Effect Level), which determines the proportion of effected *(wet)* to non-effected *(dry)* signal sent to the output. Typically, you'd want that knob to be set much closer to the dry setting or the guitar will sound like it's being played inside a large cavern.

Another important reverb parameter is *decay time,* (sometimes called *room size*). It determines how long it a note will reverberate. The larger the size of the virtual space, the longer it will take the sound to decay. Overly long decay times will also produce a cavelike sound (see Figure 6-14).

Figure 6-14: The key reverb parameters are Decay Time (shown here as the Time knob) and Effect Level (a.k.a. Wet/Dry ratio, shown here as the E Level knob).

Delay, which is also referred to as *echo,* not only has wet/dry controls, but also the very important Delay Time knob. Delay time is typically measured in milliseconds (1/1000 of a second). With the delay time set between 50 to 120 ms, you get what's essentially a doubling effect. From 120 to 175 ms, you get a "slapback" effect, which is a staple of rockabilly and country, and was the type of delay that was used on Elvis Presley's vocals in his early career. Delays that are above about 250 ms are heard as distinct echoes.

Another important setting on a delay is called *feedback* (see Figure 6-15). It determines how many times the echo will repeat. Be careful not to set it too high, or you'll create a feedback loop.

Any effects that are time-based, such as delay, as well as most modulation effects, often have a button on them called Sync, BPM Sync, or BPM (refer to Figure 6-15). When you activate the Sync button, the effects are synced to the tempo of the metronome or the recorder (if the app has one).

When an effect is tempo-synced, instead of adjusting by time parameters like milliseconds or seconds, you it to rhythmic values such as quarter notes,

Figure 6-15:
A delay's
feedback
control
determines
how many
times
the echo
repeats.

eighth notes, sixteenth notes, and so on. This allows the effects work in time with the music. Particularly for delay, it sounds really good when the echoes repeat in sync with song's tempo.

Exploring the Features in Guitar Multi-Effects Apps

Modeling apps offer you features beyond just their sounds. Let's look at some of the more common ones:

- ✔ **Tuner:** It's hard to imagine being a guitarist or bassist without a tuner, but back before the late '70s, most guitarists had to tune only by ear. (Yikes!) The results could be hideous, and in live performances, the audience often had to sit through guitarists tuning between songs ("Give me an A!"). Luckily, tuners are now ubiquitous, and they're even built into modeling apps for iOS. Virtual tuners function just like outboard hardware tuners do, and usually feature a user interface with a faux needle or faux LED step-style display. Many tuners mute your guitar's signal while you're tuning, sparing everyone from having to listen to the process. If the tuner is having trouble giving you a steady display of the note you're playing, try tuning to a 12th-fret harmonic, which is easier for tuners to read. You will also always get a stronger signal for your tuner if you plug your instrument directly into your iOS device, as opposed to using the built-in mic.

- ✔ **Recorder:** Most modeling apps offer some sort of recording option. Usually, you have to pay extra via an in-app purchase to be able to record more than one or two tracks. These recorders typically have mixers and console effects, and give you the tools you need to record multitrack projects. IK Multimedia's AmpliTube app even offers a DAW-like editing section for its recorder as an in-app purchase.

✔ **Metronome:** A metronome is very handy for practicing. It helps you develop your rhythmic skills, and is also great for giving you a rhythmic structure when working on scales. Most modeling apps offer a metronome, which might be part of a recording section or just a standalone feature.

✔ **File Player:** Something you'll find in many apps is a file player, which lets you import audio files from your iTunes library and elsewhere to jam along with. In a number of apps, you get controls to slow down the audio for practicing purposes. This kind of functionality often requires you to plug your iOS device into your computer for syncing, though.

✔ **Low-Latency Option:** Latency (explained in Chapter 5) — the miniscule delay between when you play a note and when you hear it coming from your device — is not only a problem with MIDI instruments, but with guitars and basses, too. Some apps offer a "super-low" or "ultra-low" latency option, which reduces it further than the default setting. The trade-off is that it's more taxing on your device's processor. If you're using an old iOS device, this could be an issue for you, but with any of the Lightning-equipped devices, switching to the lowest latency option should be fine.

Choosing a Guitar Multi-Effects Modeling App

If you're shopping for a guitar or bass multi-effects app, you've got quite a few to choose from, and can spend anywhere from zero to $19.99, with many falling in between. Bearing in mind that new apps pop up fairly often, here's a look at what's currently available. We're only including apps that offer quality sounds.

We should also mention that ever since introducing iOS 7, Apple has been offering GarageBand for free (even if you do need to make an in-app purchase to take full advantage of the app), and while it's way more than a multi-effects app, it has a pretty nice amp and effects section. It doesn't have as many guitar-specific features as a dedicated guitar multi-effects app, but you get a lot of models and you can't beat the price. What's more, you get multitrack recording, virtual instruments, loops, and much more (see Figure 6-16).

Most guitar multi-effects apps offer in-app purchases to increase your sound collection or add features, but some are more — shall we say — *persistent* about it than others. Some of the apps offer free versions, and some, such as iShred Live, are free to begin with.

Figure 6-16:
Virtual
effects
pedals in
Garage-
Band, which
Apple now
includes
free in iOS.

Be aware that "free" apps often use what's called the "freemium" model (that's a marketing model, not an amp model), which means they give you a bare-bones feature set or sound set for free, and then offer all the rest of the amps, cabinets, effects, and extended features as in-app purchases.

Still, if you only want one sound, or a couple of effects, or just want to get a feel for an app before buying, free versions are useful.

Beware that some manufacturers list their entire collections of amps, cabs, and effects as "features," in descriptions on the App Store. This is pretty misleading when you open up an app and find only a few of these components included. The rest, of course, are available for in-app purchase. Be ready to get bombarded with annoying pop-up messages asking you if you want to upgrade to this or unlock that.

It varies from app to app, but individual components usually sell as in-app purchases for $2.99–$6.99, with amps tending to be more expensive than effects. Many in-app purchase "packs" are available, which let you purchase a collection of components at a better price than if you bought them individually.

The following are capsule overviews of the guitar multi-effects apps that we think are worth your consideration. They vary a lot in price and features, but all offer good sounding models of amps, cabinets, and effects. In addition to price information (subject to change) we included feature descriptions, and whether they're compatible with Audiobus and Inter-App Audio (see Part V for more info on using multiple apps together). The apps appear in alphabetical order by name.

AmpKit+ (Agile Partners/Peavey Electronics, $19.99, Audiobus and Inter-App Audio compatible, universal app): AmpKit+ (see Figure 6-17), which runs on both iPhone/iPod touch and iPad, comes with four amp models, six cabinet models, ten effects pedals and eight mics. Numerous additional amp models and effects pedals are available for in-app purchase.

Other features include a tuner and a metronome. You also get a single-track recording feature with backing tracks, so you can play along with drumbeats and fuller arrangements, and record the result. There's no multitrack recording, however. Unlike some other guitar effects apps, you can change your amp settings after you've made the recording, which is very cool. You can share your recordings via email, text or SoundCloud. Also offered is *AmpKit,* a free version with one amp, two pedals, and two mics included.

Figure 6-17: AmpKit+ with some of its optional amps showing on the right-hand side.

AmpliTube (IK Multimedia, $19.99, separate iPhone/iPod touch and iPad versions, Audiobus and Inter-App Audio compatible): IK Multimedia offers a wide selection of apps under the AmpliTube moniker, but the flagship is *AmpliTube* (see Figure 6-18). It comes with seven amp models (including a bass amp), six cabinet models, two microphone models, and eleven stompbox models. You can have up to four stompboxes active in a single patch. Additional components from IK's large collection can be added via in-app purchase.

Other features include a single-track recorder that's expandable to eight tracks on the iPad version and four on the iPhone, both with master effects. In addition, you can add Amplitube Studio, which is a DAW-style editor, as well. The Loop Drummer drum module that's included with AmpliTube sounds really good. It works in sync with the recorder, but it only comes with a few rock beats, so you'll likely have to buy some expansion packs for it via in-app purchase.

Other features include a file player with a speed control and "No Voice," which reduces or removes the vocal or anything else in the center

Figure 6-18:
One of
AmpliTube's
many
features
is Loop
Drummer, a
built-in drum
machine.

channel from the song you're listening to. *AmpliTube LE* ($2.99) and *AmpliTube FREE* offer much-reduced model sets, but otherwise have the same feature set. AmpliTube offers a range of export and sharing options including email, iTunes, SoundCloud, and more.

The following four specialty versions of AmpliTube all come in separate iPhone/iPod touch and iPad versions, and have similar features to the flagship AmpliTube, except Loop Drummer and the AmpliTube studio upgrade are not available on them. You can upgrade their recorders — to four and eight tracks for the iPhone/iPod touch and iPad versions, respectively. From a sonic standpoint, however, they rock. You can also add expansion bundles to the main AmpliTube app with the sounds from the specialty versions, which are:

- **AmpliTube Fender ($14.99):** This bundle contains a collection of five Fender amp models with matching cabinets, and six Fender stompboxes.

- **AmpliTube Orange ($14.99):** The Orange bundle gives you six officially certified amp and cabinet models from Orange, the legendary British amp maker, and also includes four stompbox effects.

- **AmpliTube Slash ($14.99):** This bundle offers six officially certified stompboxes and two amps and cabs from the top-hatted guitar hero. Speaking of guitar heroes . . .

- **AmpliTube Jimi Hendrix ($14.99):** The Hendrix bundle models five stompboxes, two amps, and two cabinets, all used by Jimi during some point in his career. Even cooler, you get presets that mimic the guitar sounds in most of his recordings.

Flying Haggis (db audioware, $6.99, iPad only, Audiobus compatible):
If you just want amp-and-effects sounds, and don't need extra features like recording, a metronome, a tuner, or models specific name-brand gear,

Flying Haggis, which was ported from the Mac/PC version, could be the choice for you. It offers an easy-to-use interface (see Figure 6-19), and a single generic-but-versatile amp model with Bass, Mid, Treble, Distort, and Drive controls. Six different cabinet models, with names suggesting what they're emulating, are available via button, as are four mic positions. Flying Haggis gives you six stompboxes, which are always open at the bottom of the screen, and include Gate, Auto-Wah, Phaser, Tremolo, Echo, and Chorus. Additional effects include Reverb and Compression. No tuner or metronome. No in-app purchases are available at the time of this writing.

Figure 6-19:
Flying
Haggis's
complete
set of
stompboxes
is always
visible.

Guitar Amp (Studio Devil, $4.99, universal app): Designed as a tube-amp emulator, this app is light on the features but heavy on the great sound. Three interchangeable amp and cabinet models are included (see Figure 6-20), and you can get some serious crunch out of this app.

Figure 6-20:
Guitar Amp
focuses on
tone rather
than fea-
tures.

There's only one effect, called Delay Box, which models several different types of delay effects, including Digital Delay, Analog Delay, and Tape Echo. Like Flying Haggis, it has no in-app purchases, tuner, or metronome.

GuitarTone (Sonoma Wire Works, $2.99, Audiobus compatible, universal app): This app provides three amps, three cabinets, and three effects (phaser, overdrive, and ambience), and then offers $4.99 in-app expansion packs consisting of 12 amps or 12 effects each (there are currently two amp packs and two effects packs available.) You could get by with the included amps and cabinets — although they have a lot of interesting ones available for purchase — but you're definitely going to need more effects, because some basic staples, like reverb, delay, chorus, and flanger are missing. So figure on spending at least $4.99 for one of the model packs. One of the unique features of GuitarTone is that it gives you the option to have one or two cabinets (and they could be different ones, if you want) in your setup. A mixer window (see Figure 6-21) lets you adjust the volume of each cabinet independently, and a Stereo Width control lets you dial in some fat stereo tones.

The app also features a *presetboard,* which is a preset switcher that looks like a pedalboard with 10 virtual footswitches. It's handy because it lets you switch between 10 of your favorite presets, without having to open a menu.

Figure 6-21: GuitarTone offers a dual cabinet setup with independent volume control from the Mixer window.

JamUp Pro XT (Positive Grid, universal app, Audiobus and Inter-App Audio Compatible): One of the heavy hitters of the guitar multi-effects market, JamUp Pro XT has an easy to use drag-and-drop interface, where you can configure your rig, and slide the components around to change the signal order (see Figure 6-22). Up to seven components can be active at a time, including an amp and effects. You can choose between 6 amps and 16 effects, which are included, and expand from in-app expansion packs.

JamUp Pro XT comes with a single-track recorder/mixer that can be expanded to eight tracks with a $4.99 in-app purchase. No additional effects are offered in the expanded recorder. Other features include a metronome, tuner, Live Mode, which offers a large display that can be easily seen from a distance onstage, an iTunes player with time and pitch controls, and a phrase sampler for layering loops.

JamUP Pro XT has a couple of unique features. One is its integration with *Bias* ($9.99), the company's amp designing app. If you've purchased Bias as well, you're given the option within JamUp Pro XT of editing the amp model in Bias, and from there you can easily swap out the components and design your own amp.

The other unusual feature is called Tone Sharing, which allows you to create, upload, and download custom presets, sharing them with the JamUp Pro community. You even get presets from a number of pro guitarists.

Positive Grid also offers the free *JamUp Pro,* which is similar from a feature standpoint, but has a smaller model set containing one amp and six effects.

Figure 6-22:
JamUp
Pro XT lets
you slide
components
around
at will to
change the
signal order.

All prices listed here can (and probably will) change at some point, based on either increases or sales. This information should guide you, but let your ears be your final judge on that app you wish to choose. You don't have to buy all of them — just the right ones.

Chapter 7

Connecting Your Mic to Your iOS Device

. . . .

In This Chapter

▶ Choosing the correct mic for your needs

▶ Selecting the correct audio interface for your mic and your iOS device

▶ Adding effects to your recorded audio

. . . .

*P*laying with new and innovative musical apps from the App Store can help you create all manner of music, and you'll no doubt spend hours doing just that. But iPhones and iPads can also record audio from the "real world," as well. In this chapter, we look at the wide variety of microphones available to you and how you can make them work with your iOS device to record what you play, what you sample, and what you choose to radically mangle within a sound effects app.

Note quickly here that this chapter doesn't really cover the internal mic for your iPhone or iPad. There's a reason for that — it just isn't that good, unfortunately. Sure, it handles your phone calls, voice messages, and inane questions to Siri, but you'll need a little more horsepower to record quality audio for your purposes. And if you're using an older iPod touch, you don't even *have* an internal mic. The good news is that you have plenty of options at a relatively low cost. So let's take a look at those options, which generally fall into two categories:

✔ Mics that connect directly to your iOS device

✔ Mics that connect to your iOS device through an audio interface

Using a Dedicated iOS Mic

The term *dedicated* refers to the specific purpose of the mic, not necessarily an undying love or affection. It's just a mic, after all. And in this case, it's a mic designed for the single purpose of connecting to your iPhone or iPad. It may look like a regular mic for most of the body, but the connection terminates in either a Lightning or a 30-pin connection designed to plug directly into the data port of your device, as shown in Figure 7-1.

Depending on the amount of money you spend, the audio quality of these mics can vary greatly. Remember that the higher the bit and sample rate, the better quality of audio you'll get during recording. Each mic also has unique sonic characteristics that can change the sound of your audio recording, so testing a mic before purchase is a handy bit of knowledge. And because all of the audio technology you need is built right into the mic, you'll need to look at those numbers when you make your purchase. But no matter what kind of mic you purchase, you'll notice a few common advantages and disadvantages, including the following:

✓ **Portability:** If you need to record something out in the real world (which means away from home or the studio, so that sentence could mean a whole lot of things), all you'll need is your iOS device and your mic. The mic gets power from your iPhone or iPad, and you can take it anywhere you need to go (as long as you remembered to charge your device first). This portability can be especially helpful if you're carrying other gear or travelling a long distance and don't want to carry a lot of extra weight with you.

Figure 7-1: The Apogee MiC makes valuable connections with your iPhone.

✔ **Operability:** To borrow a commonly used phrase, these mics just work. Because they were designed to interface with a specific kind of device, you can be pretty sure that you'll get a good connection and app compatibility from the start. There's always a little comfort in eliminating the unexpected from your recording plans.

Of course, you can *only* use your mic with your iOS device, because other interfaces won't use the same connection. So operability is both a blessing and a curse. But you can't have everything, can you?

✔ **Simplicity:** Just plug it in and go — that's all you have to do. Because the mic only works with iOS devices, you don't have to worry about any extra cables or boxes. You're good to go, right out of the box.

✔ **Only one mic:** While dedicated iOS mics are amazingly portable and functional, they can also be quite jealous in that you can only use one at a time. Since you only have one data connection, you can only plug in one mic at a time. Which means you can only record from one place at a single time. Hopefully you're the kind of person who finds a lack of options liberating, because you'll only get one way to record audio.

✔ **Battery life:** Always remember to charge your device fully before recording with your iOS mic, because your device will power both your apps and your mic. And because the mic already uses a data connection, you can't charge and record at the same time. Watch your battery meter and get to work — you're wasting time and energy!

Selecting an Audio Interface

Your other option when connecting a mic to your iPhone or iPad involves putting an audio interface in between your mic and your iOS device. Although this process does involve a little more equipment (and money), you do get a few more advantages than using a dedicated iOS mic, including the following:

✔ You can use a wider variety of mics, since you're not limiting yourself to a mic designed only for use with iOS devices.

✔ You can take advantage of preamps that allow you to boost and color the audio in more ways than a dedicated iOS mic allows.

✔ You can record using more than one mic at a time. The exact number of mics may vary depending on the inputs allowed by your interface, but that's up to you and your bank account.

Now, you will be carrying around more equipment, and you will also need to find an independent power source for the audio interface. That means finding a nearby power outlet, so your travel options are a little limited.

Again, you should always determine what you plan to record before buying any equipment. You should also plan on buying the highest level of audio quality you can afford. A 24-bit, 96 kHz audio interface represents the best choice at this point, although you can get away with 48 kHz if necessary. You should also plan on using at least one mic per audio source. For example, if you plan on just recording vocals and guitar (with a standard guitar jack), you can get away with two inputs and a single mic, like the Focusrite iTrack Solo interface shown in Figure 7-2.

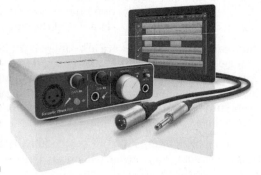

Figure 7-2:
Capture all the singer/songwriter you can on your iPad.

If you want to record a four-piece band, you'll need at least four inputs (and more than that if one of the pieces you plan on recording is a drummer). Plan ahead and make sure you get the interface you need before you shell out your money.

Should you plan on recording a standard drum set, you'll probably need at least four mics — one for the bass drum, one for the snare, and two to place over the drums for that overhead, all-kit sound. This setup may sound like an involved operation, but you're talking about a lot of parts to a single part of the band. And then you have to deal with a drummer, too.

Of course, before you buy anything, you should understand the components of the audio interface and why it's so important to stick that device in-between your chosen mic and your iOS device.

Understanding the components of an audio interface

Every audio interface contains a few common features. Different models may offer new and advanced features and lay out the controls differently, but you should be able to count on enough commonalities to get to work fairly quickly. Some of these common features are described in the following list:

- ✔ **Inputs:** Inputs allow you to plug in a mic (usually via an XLR cable). Simple, isn't it? You plug in the mic, and the interface takes that signal and runs it to the iPhone or iPad. If the interface contains more than one input, the interface delivers all of those mic signals to the iPhone or iPad as separate audio sources, meaning you can route that audio to your digital audio workstation and record each mic as a separate track (if the app supports multi-track recording, of course). We talk more about digital audio workstations in Chapter 10.

- ✔ **Preamps:** Before the interface delivers the audio to your iOS device, the audio usually goes through a *preamp.* The preamp boosts the signal of the mic to a higher level in all cases, and may allow you to alter the signal a little using EQ or compression and limiting, depending on the preamp model. Think of the preamp as tailoring your sound before you amplify it to its final recording level.

- ✔ **Headphone jack:** Plug in your headphones to hear the audio as it sounds before it hits your iOS device. Why not use the headphone jack in the iPhone or iPad, you ask? Well, because the audio you hear from the iPhone or iPad will be ever-so-slightly delayed, so you'll notice a difference if you're playing or singing and recording at the same time. Even a few milliseconds can make a huge difference, so hearing the audio in real time before you record it will help you get better recordings. You'll also be able to hear the audio without any effects you might be running on the iPhone or iPad.

  And sometimes you just want to play or record without anybody hearing, so that's valuable as well. Especially if you need to record and sing at the same time — using headphones helps to prevent feedback caused by recording and listening to speakers at the same time.

A little latency is inevitable — this is just the nature of digital recording. Your goal should be to record with as little latency as possible, and your recording apps will offer settings that allow you to reduce the amount of latency the app requires to keep everything running smoothly. Check the settings for the app and start recording at the lowest level latency possible, then bump it up as necessary to avoid stuttering or clicks as you record.

- ✔ **Outputs:** After the sound enters your interface and receives a little TLC from the preamp, you have to get the sound back out. Most interfaces give you the digital output (the cable that runs to the Lightning or 30-pin connector) and audio outputs (usually in the form of quarter-inch jacks you can run to your monitor speakers or a PA). Plug the digital output into your iOS device and the audio outputs to your speakers, and you're good to go.

Dedicated iOS interfaces and mic preamps

Even if you want to use your own specific mic, you can pick audio interfaces that connect directly to your iOS device. Different docks and interfaces give you the option to connect your iOS device directly and give you the best of both worlds. If you're buying an interface brand-new for your mics, consider looking at these devices. A side benefit is that these devices usually power your iOS device while you record, so you never have to worry about running out of juice during a recording session.

USB interfaces

Just because you already have an older USB audio interface lying around (because really, don't we all?) doesn't mean you can't necessarily use it in conjunction with your iOS device. You just have to perform a little research.

The key here is using a camera connection adapter. Apple may call it a camera connection adapter, but it really handles most class-compliant USB devices (so, in other words, you don't need to load additional drivers or software to make the device work). Apple just doesn't want to guarantee that it will work with all devices, so they hedge their bets with the approved camera usage. Savvy manufacturers use this adapter to make their own devices work with the iPad.

Understand that because you must use one of these devices to connect the USB interface, this option is only available to iPad users. And you aren't guaranteed to have the audio interface work — you'll have to check with the audio interface manufacturer to ensure it meets Core Audio and MIDI standards for iOS. But the advantage here is that compliant audio interfaces can move from iOS devices to your home computer by just removing the camera connection kit. Versatility is always good, and it helps you save a little money.

Recording multiple mics

We touched on it a little earlier in this section, but external audio interfaces give you the option to record multiple mics at the same time. This ability isn't really important if you're just recording one vocal or instrument at a time, but it does become a big deal when you want to record your garage band (in GarageBand or something else) and keep the audio tracks separate for later processing and mixing (covered in Chapter 10). A great deal of audio interfaces offer at least two inputs (although these interfaces usually offer one mic and one instrument input, and only one input uses phantom power), and many of those offer four or eight inputs with preamps. If you need more, you might be able to get a device to help you out, but you might also want to look at a larger solution (or a full-featured recording studio).

You'll also have to purchase enough mic cables and stands to account for all of the mics and inputs you plan to use.

Handling instruments, mics, and MIDI

Manufacturers don't just make audio interfaces with inputs designed only for mics. Because data connections are at a premium for iOS devices (there's only one), you might see multiple inputs that account for different kinds of devices, including instrument inputs and MIDI connections. These types of audio interfaces can help you put together a more full-featured recording option (allowing direct connections of electric instruments like guitars or basses and the ability to pass MIDI information between external MIDI devices and the iPhone or iPad). You don't have to have any of these extra features, but they can be helpful even if you're not going to use them immediately. Keep them in mind as you shop.

Understanding Mic Types

Recording engineers can point to multiple variations of different mics as the best mic for a situation, and some of those engineers might even agree with each other. But no matter which mic you choose to use, you can break down microphones down to three basic categories that serve different audio recording purposes. You don't have to own all three, but you should understand why you're buying the mics you buy and when you should use them for the best results.

We're not going to get into capsule design, wiring, and the inner workings of each microphone — you can dig deeper into this if you want, but know that there's a ton of technical information behind this, including electrical engineering knowledge and theory. Instead, in the following list, we look at the practical applications for each mic and what you'll need to do in order to make them work for you:

✔ **Dynamic:** Dynamic microphones work best in live applications, since they stand up well to high volume situations and tend to be more resistant to feedback. You can use them for both vocals and instruments, as demonstrated by the venerable Shure SM57 (instruments usually, although Lemmy uses one for vocals and we're not going to argue with him) and SM58. The joke is that you can use these mics to drive nails for the stage and then hook them up for the show later. These mics don't require any external power source, but it does help to run them through some sort of preamp to get a good signal (usually the preamps contained in the mixer at the live music venue).

✔ **Condenser:** Condenser microphones may provide a little better sound quality and more sensitivity, but these attributes tend to make them more suited for home or studio recording. These microphones also require an external power source, usually called *phantom power,* and send from the mixer or audio interface. Condenser microphones can range from a couple of hundred dollars to many thousands, depending on the audio quality and the size of the capsules in the mics. Larger capsules tend to handle louder and lower frequencies better than mics with small capsules. Finally, condenser microphones often offer more than one response pattern, making them versatile tools in the studio (see the "Understanding Mic Response Patterns" section, later in this chapter). Use a good preamp with condenser mics during the recording process to bring out the best of your sound.

✔ **Ribbon:** You've probably seen a ribbon mic in old films, where radio broadcasters talked into huge pill-shaped microphones about the latest news and crooners sang their famous tunes. Ribbon microphones literally use a magnetic ribbon to capture sound vibrations and transfer them to a recording device. Recording engineers prize good ribbon mics for capturing smooth and rich vocal tracks, and they can be very expensive. The problem is that ribbon microphones tend to be incredibly sensitive, and even blowing on them too hard can cause serious damage. Definitely restrict your ribbon mic use to a controlled studio environment, and pair it up with a good preamp.

Never use phantom power with a ribbon microphone. The extra voltage will fry the ribbon and render the microphone useless. Turn off all phantom power before you connect the mic and make sure you never turn it on, even accidentally. You won't get another chance.

Understanding Mic Response Patterns

All mics perform their assigned tasks a little differently, so it's important to know how the mics you use respond to external sound. That way, you can know which mic to use in any given situation.

Some mics can use multiple response patterns, depending on the situation. Use the correct setting for the right purpose, and you'll be just fine.

The following list describes the basic mic response patterns:

✔ **Cardioid:** Cardioid indicates that the microphones picks up sound in a roughly heart-shaped pattern, as demonstrated in Figure 7-3:

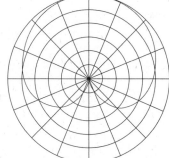

Figure 7-3:
A cardioid
mic pattern.

This diagram indicates that the mic pics up audio from the front and side or the mic, and it rejects sound from behind the mic. This pattern makes the mic suitable for recording a sound source from one direction, such as vocals or a single instrument.

✔ **Hyper-cardioid:** The hyper-cardioid mic acts similar to a cardioid mic, except more so. This response pattern is a little more pronounced, as demonstrated in Figure 7-4:

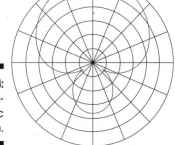

Figure 7-4:
A hyper-
cardioid mic
pattern.

These mics tend to be a little more directional and reject more sound from the sides of the mic, making them more useful for picking out a single source of audio amongst a large group of sounds. The mic also picks up a little more sound from directly behind the mic.

✔ **Super-cardioid:** The super-cardioid falls in between the cardioid and the hyper-cardioid. The super-cardioid is more directional than the cardioid mic, but it is less directional than the hyper-cardioid.

If you can get access to all three types of mics, test them on the same sound source to better understand their response and how you can use them in the real world.

✔ **Omnidirectional:** As opposed to the cardioid mic variants, omnidirectional mics pick up just about every sound occurring within their range. (See Figure 7-5.) No matter where you put this mic, it will pick up any sound happening around it. Think of the type of mics used in conference rooms, but usually sounding better. You can use these mics in good-sounding rooms to capture both the original sound of the instrument and the characteristics of the room.

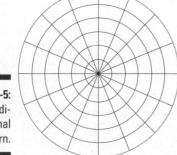

Figure 7-5: A omnidi-rectional mic pattern.

✔ **Figure-8:** Also known as bidirectional microphones, these mics pick up sound in two specific directions and reject sound from all other directions. Take a look at Figure 7-6 to understand how these mics work.

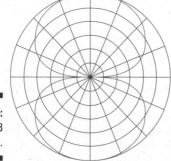

Figure 7-6: A figure-8 mic pattern.

These mics become most useful when you have to record two separate sources of audio and reject any other audio occurring around it.

✔ **The proximity effect:** Ever wanted to sound more like Barry White? Get closer to the mic! For all types of microphones except for omnidirectional, getting closer to the mic increases the bass frequency response of the recording. In other words, you get more low end the closer you get to the mic. Be careful how you use this effect — it can give you more bass in the right situation, or it can overload your recording and distort the low end (especially with plosive sounds, like the popping sound made by pronouncing the letter P). Listen carefully and use judiciously. More expensive mics might also include a low-cut switch that lets you eliminate excessive bass frequencies.

✔ **Phase cancellation:** If you plan on using multiple mics in the recording, you might notice that your sound becomes thinner when you listen to the audio from those mics at the same time. Without getting too technical, sound waves can cancel each other out by recording the same audio signal at different spots. If you notice this issue, move the mics and audio sources farther apart until you don't notice the situation. Some recording devices also let you flip the phase of a signal to avoid this situation.

For more information on dealing with mic placement and home recording, we recommend picking up *Home Recording for Musicians For Dummies,* by Jeff Strong (Wiley).

✔ **Other mics:** There are other types of mics, such as electret, pressure zone mics, contact mics, and more that you might encounter as part of your recording efforts. But these mics usually work best in very specific situations, and you might do better concentrating on the microphones listed in this section before branching out into these specialized types. Don't be afraid to experiment, but the listed mics should prove more practical in the short term.

So Which Mic Should I Buy?

As many as you can afford? Okay, that's not a helpful answer. But you should have a few mics available for your disposal at any time. Start with the Shure SM57 and 58 (or their equivalent with your preferred manufacturer) and branch out from there. You'll get a lot of usage from these dynamic mics in both live and studio situations before you find yourself needing to get additional microphones. And, of course, get a mic for every potential sound source you'll need to record at a single time. Then get a backup for each type you'll be using. Your bank account may hate you, but you'll be prepared for any situation.

Vocal Effects Apps

After you record your vocals, iOS devices provide a multitude of ways to alter those vocals to suit your tastes. Some tackle a single function (like the Antares Auto-Tune app for iOS — not that you need it, of course), while others combine several different effects together (such as the IK Multimedia VocaLive app). No matter which app you choose to use, you should know how these common effects work on vocals:

✔ **Compression/De-essing:** Compression (and more specifically, de-essing) controls the high and low volume peaks of especially expressive singers and brings everything into a more manageable volume level. This effect makes your vocals more consistent and helps it sit within the overall mix better. De-essing represents a specialized form of compression that removes the hissing sound known as *sibilance* from your vocals. Unless you want to sound like an evil snake, that sibilance must go.

✔ **Reverb/Delay:** Use these effects to make you sound like your singing in a concert hall, cave, or other large enclosed area. Judicious use of these effects can give your vocal a pleasing, full sound. Overuse of reverb makes your vocal performance echo-y and messy. Let your ears be your guide.

✔ **Equalization:** Equalization (or just EQ) helps take out too much high, mid, or low frequencies from your recording. Precise usage of EQ helps the entire sound of your vocals come through instead of just the most dominant frequency.

✔ **Chorus/Doubler:** This effect makes it sound like more than one of you is singing at the same time, like a duet or more. Use this effect to thicken up the sound of you singing by yourself.

✔ **Pitch Correction/Harmonization:** Although this category does include the much-maligned Auto-Tune effect, it can also be used to slightly change the pitch of vocals to tweak a performance slightly instead of totally re-recording the performance. Just don't use it to the point of annoyance.

Harmonization takes the original pitch of the vocal and adds a second performance of the vocal pitched higher or lower. This functionality allows you to create instant vocal harmonies during a recording or live performance. Just tell the app the *interval* (the distance between the original note and the synthesized note) and you're good to go.

Chapter 8

Performing with Your iOS Device

*B*ecause of their compact size and the powerful apps available for them, more and more iPads, iPhones, and iPod touches have been finding their way into musicians' live performance and rehearsal rigs. Guitarists use multi-effects apps featuring amp-and-effects models; keyboardists get powerful MIDI instrument sounds and can leave their laptops at home; vocalists no longer need to bring messy folders full of lyric sheets; and even some engineers use apps for controlling functions in their live mixers.

To accommodate all these live performance uses, manufacturers have been creating a slew of accessories to help musicians hold and connect their devices onstage. Let's dive into the world of iOS live!

Using Guitar Multi-Effects Apps Live

As detailed in Chapter 6, you can re-create the sound of a massive guitar rig right from your iPhone, iPod touch, or iPad, given the right apps and accessories. You have a couple of choices for how to bring these sounds to your stage rig: You can connect your guitar or bass into your iOS device and then direct the output of that device into either

✔ Your amp

✔ Your PA system

A number of different specialized audio interfaces are available that allow you to do either choice. Let's look at the former first.

Into your amp

With this type of interface, you can use your device as an effects processor onstage, giving you a large selection of stompbox-style effects between your guitar and your amp. You can change the sound of your amp by dialing in various amp models, set up presets with specific sounds for various songs, and more.

In order to plug into a guitar amplifier from your device, you need an interface that offers a 1/4" *instrument level* output, which is the same kind of output that's on your guitar.

The connection for this type of setup would be as follows (see Figure 8-1):

✔ Guitar connects into interface with 1/4" cable

✔ Interface digital output connects to iOS device with Lightning or 30-pin cable (depending on your device)

✔ Interface output connects to guitar amp with another 1/4" cable

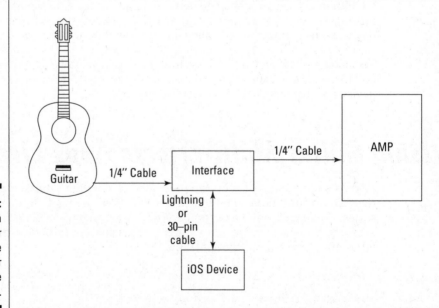

Figure 8-1:
Using a digital guitar interface with your iOS device and amp.

Here's how it would work:

- ✔ The signal coming out of your guitar's output jack goes into the interface.
- ✔ The interface's analog-to-digital converter turns it into a digital signal.
- ✔ The digital signal is sent into the digital audio input of your device's dock connector, and is made available to your multi-effects app.
- ✔ Your app processes it (adding amp modeling, virtual effects pedals, and so on).
- ✔ It's then sent back out through the digital output of your device and into your interface, where it's converted back to an analog, instrument level signal and sent to your amp through a 1/4" cable.

Sounds like a lot of steps, right? Actually, the time it takes for the signal to make the trip from your guitar's output through your device and into your amp can be measured in milliseconds. Too many milliseconds, however, and you'll experience distracting latency. Latency's slight delay is one of the impediments to using iOS apps, devices, and associated gear in this manner. Even the newest iOS device can experience latency when paired with an older interface, and vice versa. Older apps and iOS versions can also increase latency times. Although it's a measurable phenomenon, one's ability to put up with a small amount of latency is subjective. It bothers the heck out of some players while others can tolerate it better. All would agree, however, that the less latency, the better.

While we're talking about integrating iOS devices with guitar amps, we should point out that you don't necessarily have to plug the interface's output directly into your amp; you could also go out of it into effects pedals or a pedalboard and *then* into your amp, or make the order: guitar>pedals>interface>iOS device>amp.

One of the most flexible guitar interfaces for live use is Sonic Port from Line 6 ($99.95, see Figure 8-2). It gives you 24-bit, 48 kHz audio, plugs into your device through the dock connector, and offers a 1/4"guitar input, a 1/4" stereo output (for the sound coming out of your iOS device) that can be used mono into a guitar amp (guitar amp inputs are almost always mono). It also has an 1/8" stereo input so that you can connect say, a music player for backing tracks or practice tracks, along with an 1/8" stereo line/headphone output.

IK Multimedia, a company that's been a leading force in developing iOS apps and accessories like interfaces, has an interesting solution for integrating an iOS device into your live rig: iRig Stomp ($59.99, see Figure 8-3). This device is shaped like an ordinary stompbox and allows you to connect your guitar or bass to the input, send the signal to your iOS device (through the headphone jack, iRig Stomp uses the device's analog input), and also plug into your amp or your pedalboard. Because of its shape and size, it makes the process of integrating iOS into your live setup more convenient.

Figure 8-2:
Line 6's
Sonic Port
allows you
to play
through
your iOS
device into
an amp and
more.

In case you're confused by all the talk about line level and instrument level, let's clarify. These terms refer to the signal strength of the particular output type. Instrument level signals (also referred to as high-impedance or Hi-Z), which come from your guitar or bass, are weaker than line-level signals, which are what come out of the line outputs of gear like mixers, audio interfaces, and stereo receivers. Hi-Z signals might also introduce a little more noise and hum than balanced Lo-Z signals. Headphone outputs tend to be lower than line outputs but not by much. They usually have enough signal strength to be used for either application. If a signal level is too low for the equipment it's connected to, you won't get enough volume, and you'll have to turn it up to the point where it will be noisy. If it's too high, you'll get distortion.

Figure 8-3:
IK Multi-
media's iRig
Stomp is a
stompbox-
style audio
interface for
guitar and
bass.

Into the PA

The other option for connecting your iOS device live is to go directly into the PA system. The beauty of this is that you won't need an amp. Your entire guitar setup could consist of guitar, iOS device, audio interface, and cables. Other than your guitar, you could easily fit it all in a briefcase or backpack.

You would connect the line-level outs (or the headphone outputs) on your interface to the line inputs on the PA mixer. Depending on the interface you're using, you may have to purchase an adapter to make the output from your interface into one appropriate for the mixer's input.

When you plug your device into a channel of the PA, the output from your iOS device will be able to be sent through the main speakers (the speakers facing the audience) and the stage monitors (the onstage speakers for the talent to hear themselves).

One of the problems you may face with a direct-to-PA setup is that in order for you to hear yourself onstage, the signal from your "virtual" rig has to be sent to the monitors, and in most club and small venue PA systems, there's only one monitor mix. This means that everyone onstage gets the same mix out of their monitor. So why is that a problem? Well, you may want to hear your guitar nice and loud, but it doesn't mean that others in the band will, too. But with one monitor mix, you'll all hear it at the same level. It's not a deal breaker, but it is a possible complication with going direct into the PA. If the app and audio interface you use allows, you might consider sending a separate out to a separate powered monitor for your own use.

Controlling your apps remotely

Okay, so you can use your multi-effects app like a virtual pedalboard, but you can't control an iOS device with your feet, right? Actually, you can. At the time of this writing, the only wireless foot controller designed for iOS on the market, is the IK Multimedia iRig BlueBoard ($99.99, see Figure 8-4). This Bluetooth pedalboard allows you to change sounds, turn on and off effects and more, on IK apps like AmpliTube and SampleTank, and many other Core MIDI music apps. It also has inputs for an expression pedal (not included) so that you can control wah, volume, and other continuous controllers. (See Chapter 5 for more about MIDI controllers.)

Positive Grid, which makes the JamUp Pro XT app, among others, announced the BT-4 ($129) and BT-2 ($79). Both are wireless MIDI controller pedals, and they should be released by the time you read this. These will differ from the IK product in that they'll also function as audio interfaces and feature jacks for wired connection to your guitar, headphones, and your iOS devices.

Both the IK and Positive Grid products require that you run a dedicated app in the background, which converts the Bluetooth signal to MIDI, after the iOS device receives it.

Performing with Keyboard Apps

If you're a keyboardist, you have a wide world of great sounding MIDI instrument apps at your disposal, from sampled grand pianos to classic synthesizers and everything in between. If you currently use only one stage keyboard, which is your controller and sound source, then adding an iPad won't necessarily lighten your load, but it will give you a lot of additional sounds to choose from. However, if you carry more than one keyboard because you're using one for a controller and one for at least some of your sounds, perhaps an iOS device could free you up to shrink your rig a bit.

Getting set up

To use an iOS-based rig onstage, you need to be able to:

- Plug in a MIDI keyboard to the iOS device.
- Take the device's output to your keyboard amp or the PA.

To accomplish these tasks, you could use separate iOS MIDI and audio interfaces, but unless you already own one or the other, it's a lot more convenient to get an interface that handles both. Many of the dedicated iOS interfaces and USB interfaces covered in Chapter 7 would do the job nicely.

You would also need a MIDI keyboard controller of some sort, preferably a 76- or 88-key model, unless you're only playing synth parts or are trying for an ultra-mobile rig, in which case you could go for a smaller 25- or 49-key keyboard. That's up to you.

A typical setup would be like this: Your keyboard connects to the MIDI input on your audio interface. The interface connects to the iOS device via dock connector, and audio interface output connects to either a keyboard amp or the PA mixer (see Figure 8-5).

If you wanted to go for the low-budget setup, you could just use a MIDI interface, rather than an audio and MIDI interface, and take the output from the iOS device's headphone output to the amp or PA. The amp would need to have line inputs; the signal would be too hot for a high-impedance instrument input. You would need to use an adapter to convert the stereo 1/8" output to either a mono 1/4" output or a stereo pair of 1/4" outputs. It's also possible that a mixer would have RCA inputs, in which case you'd have to convert your cable to those instead using plug adapters, which are readily available via online retailers.

In either case, you'll be depending on audio from your iOS device's headphone output. This shouldn't be a problem from a sound standpoint, but because it's a mini jack it's not particularly robust, and your cable could get pulled out pretty easily if somebody stepped on it or jostled it. So take care how you set it up.

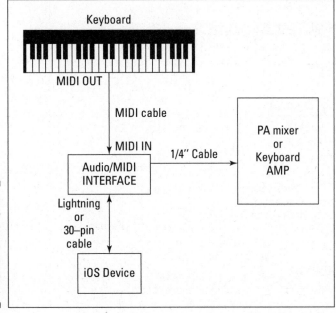

Figure 8-5:
Here's how you'd connect up an iOS-based keyboard rig live.

This alternate iOS keyboard setup would look like this: Your keyboard connects to MIDI In on MIDI interface, which is connected to the iOS device (most likely through the dock connector). The iOS device is connected to the keyboard amp or PA via its headphone out jack and adapter cables (see Figure 8-6).

If you're connecting to the PA, and don't have a stage amp, you'll face the same issues we talked about earlier for guitarists regarding the monitor mix. That is, it's hard to find a level for your keyboards in the monitors that you feel is loud enough for you to play correctly, but that won't seem too loud to others in the band.

Playing unique iOS instruments live

As we discuss in Chapter 5, instrument apps exist that eschew the keyboard paradigm, and use touchscreen-based input on an original user interface to produce their music. Chances are, such apps wouldn't be set up to respond to MIDI, because you couldn't play them correctly with a keyboard if they did. Wizdom Music MorphWiz and Normalware's Bebot – Robot Synth are examples of apps with user interfaces that rely mainly on touchscreen motions. To use an app like that onstage you'd have to play directly from your iOS device (you'd probably want it to be an iPad for the larger user interface).

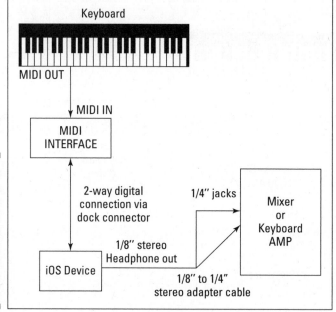

Figure 8-6:
Here's a setup with only a MIDI interface and using the device's headphone output.

If one of these iOS-specific instruments was all you were using for a performance, then you could either send your output directly from your iPad or through an audio interface, into an amp or the PA. Unless you're planning to hand-hold your device — which would be difficult considering it would have wires coming out of it — you'll need a special holder so you can mount your iPad to a microphone stand. We discuss those a little later in the chapter.

Reading Music and Lyrics Onstage

The iPad offers musicians an alternative to carrying physical sheet music and lyric sheets onstage with them. A growing number of score-reading apps are available in the iTunes Store. When you load all your charts and scores into such an app, you can conveniently organize and display them on your iPad, making custom setlists for your various gigs.

Sheet music readers

For reading sheet music or a chord chart onstage, it's best to use a sheet-music–reading app. Most let you import your own scores if they're in PDF form. Different apps give you various options for this — many offer more than one way to import. One common import method is iTunes File Sharing. Let's quickly go over the steps involved; they're the same for all apps that support this method:

1. **Sync your iPad to your computer using a physical cable connection.**

2. **Choose iPad from the iTunes window.**

3. **Select Apps.**

4. **Scroll down to the iTunes File Sharing window.**

5. **Select the app's name (in this case, GigBook).**

6. **Press the Add button in the Documents.**

7. **Navigate to the file you want on your computer.**

8. **Select the file you want and press Choose.**

Another way to import scores in many sheet music readers is by opening the file in another app and then using the Open In option, which can be used for email attachments, and from apps like Dropbox, GoodReader, Evernote, and more.

This would work as follows:

1. **Open the PDF in whatever PDF reader you have.**

2. **Look for the "sharing" icon (see Figure 8-7) and tap it.**

   This opens a window giving you choices for how or where you want to send it (message, mail, Twitter, print, and so on). One of the choices should be Open In.

3. **Tap Open In.**

   You'll see a menu of the apps you have that can open the file. One should be your sheet music app.

4. **Tap the sheet music app's icon to open the PDF in it.**

If your PDF is in the form of an email attachment, tap the icon for the attachment and you should see icons including your sheet music app. Tap your app's icon to open the file in it.

Fully featured sheet-music readers such as GigBook or forScore LLC's forScore app (see Figure 8-8) offer a variety of features, including the ability to annotate your score by drawing with your finger, organize scores into setlists, check tempos with a metronome, and lots more.

With your iPad onstage in a holder on your mic stand (more on these later in the chapter), your sheet music reader app opened, and your music arranged in a setlist corresponding to the one you're using for the show, you're ready to go. Turning the page in a score is typically achieved by swiping one direction or the other on your iPad's screen.

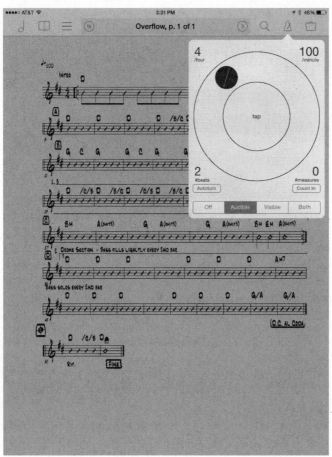

Figure 8-8:
The
forScore
app's metro-
nome is one
of its many
features.

One app, called Tonara, offers a "polyphonic music following" feature, which uses the iPad's mic to listen to the audio of your performance, and automatically turns the page when you get to the corresponding spot in the score. This probably is most useful for classical performances, where all the notes of a piece, from beginning to end, are written out.

Page turners

In most situations and with most sheet music reader apps, you have to manually turn the pages in your score. That can be problematic if you're playing an instrument and your hands aren't free to swipe your iPad screen. Luckily, several companies, such as AirTurn, PageFlip (see Figure 8-9), and BiLi, make

Figure 8-9:
The
PageFlip
Cicada, a
Bluetooth
page-turning
pedal.

page-turning systems that use Bluetooth to wirelessly send page-turn commands to a sheet-music–reader app running in your iPad. IK Multimedia's iRig BlueBoard, mentioned earlier in this chapter, can also be used for wireless page turning.

These devices come in the form of a foot-pedal unit with two or more pedals attached to it. When you pair the unit (in the Bluetooth sense) with your iPad, which is typically pretty simple, the Bluetooth page turner turns pages in any compatible app. Usually, one pedal is for page up, and another for page down. For a two-pedal unit, figure on spending somewhere in the range of $90 to about $150, depending on the brand and model. Not all apps support all pedals, so double-check before buying.

Setlist apps

You can also find a number of apps that let you create, display, and save setlists, and many also let you display song lyrics. Many setlist apps are available, and many of these also include lyric readers. For setlists, you enter song names and certain song info, and then you can rearrange the songs in whatever order matches your set. Strangely, some of these apps don't let you enter the key, which is, pardon the expression, a key item of information for a song in a setlist. Luckily, there's an easy work-around, which is to add the key right after the song name when you're entering it. So instead of entering in "Pop Goes the Weasel," you could change it to "Pop Goes the Weasel Bb."

When you have all your songs entered, you can create a setlist, and save it with information about the gig. Ideally, the app will have some way for you to organize the songs you've entered, either by keyword or by categorization, so that when you have sets from multiple projects loaded, you can still see the songs for only one, if you want to.

Here is a sampling of setlists apps available at the time of this writing (alphabetized by app name):

- ✔ **Metronotes (Grincheux, free):** You can't beat the price, and this app lets you enter song names and song info under separate band names, making it really easy to juggle multiple bands' song and setlist info.

- ✔ **Setlist Maker (Arlo Leach, $4.99):** A fully featured setlist maker for iPhone and iPad that also features lyric sheets and lyric sheets with chords, customizable performance layouts, and a lot more.

- ✔ **Setlists (Bombing Brain Interactive $9.99):** Create setlists and lyric sheets with this app, which gives you a great deal of control over the look of the lyric sheet, including background color, text color, and font size. It also lets you break up the lyrics into smaller sections, each on its on page, so that you can use a really large font. You can even use an AirTurn BT-105 for hands-free page turns.

- ✔ **SongSheet (Ghostdust, $6.99):** Not only does this app do setlists, but also lyric sheets with chords, if you want them. It features a WYSIWYG editor for creating chord charts (chords above lyrics, no bar lines or rhythmic notation), and lets you add unlimited songs and setlists.

Holding Your Device Securely Onstage

If you're going to use your iPad or iPhone onstage, you're going to need a holder or stand of some sort for it. Luckily, many companies now offer accessories designed to do just that.

For the iPad, the most popular types of holders attach to a microphone stand, and clamp around your iPad, holding it securely in place. Many allow you to position your iPad in either portrait or landscape orientation, and also offer adjustable viewing angles. Typically, you can clip such holders onto the same stand that's holding your mic. However, in some cases, it might be better to use a dedicated stand.

If you have an iPhone or iPod touch, the IK Multimedia iKlip Xpand Mini ($39.99) allows for mic-stand–mounting your device.

For most musicians, the stand-based solution is best. However, if you have flat space around you in your setup, you can also find many tabletop stands available. Some stands, such as the Peavey Tablet Mounting System (see Figure 8-10), can be stand-mounted or work on the tabletop, via a clamp.

Figure 8-10: The Peavey Tablet Mounting system gives you multiple mounting options for your iPad.

Make sure that the stand you buy is compatible with your model of iPad. When you start shopping around, you'll see that some of these stands are only compatible with certain models of Apple's devices.

Part III
Setting Up Your iOS Studio

In this part . . .

- ✔ Map out your recording goals so you can better pick the hardware and software you'll need.

- ✔ Explore the available digital audio workstation apps.

- ✔ Find out what type of app will work best for your recording needs.

- ✔ Get the scoop on monitors and headphones to find the right tools to reveal the best parts of your music.

Chapter 9

Planning Your Rig

*E*very good project starts with a plan. If you threw every ingredient in the kitchen into a single pot without following a recipe, you'd come out with . . . well, it wouldn't have a name, but it would be something very foul. But if you take the time to decide what goal you wish to accomplish and the tools you'll need to make that goal happen, you'll accomplish that goal (and you probably won'tend up with something very foul).

This chapter guides you through the process of outlining exactly what purpose your collection of gear and apps (known as a *rig* to those who regularly talk about musical equipment) will serve and what you need to make that rig take shape. Don't spend too much or buy equipment you'll never use — make a plan and follow through!

Getting the Gear You Need

This section gives you some insight into what you need to purchase in order to make your rig a reality. If you play multiple instruments or play different roles in your music-making career (such as a guitar player and an audio engineer), you might look at multiple pieces of equipment. But each heading below outlines the basics of the equipment you'll need to put together to make or record music.

Guitar or bass rig

You more than likely already own the guitar or bass you want to use as part of your guitar or bass rig. And, given the wide range of price and preference in these instruments, it's just not practical to tell you to buy a specific type of guitar or bass. And really, it doesn't make too much of a difference which instrument you choose to use — they more than likely use the same quarter-inch instrument cable guitarists and bassists played through for decades. So in this case, pick up your axe — it's ready to go.

Okay, so there might be a *slight* difference in instruments that use active pickups (that is, instruments that include a battery-powered preamp to provide an audio signal with a higher output volume) versus passive pickups (instruments that don't include that preamp). Although you can debate the tonal qualities of these pickups (and trust us, *plenty* of people do), active pickups do tend to provide more volume and will give you a little more sonic options (and less extraneous noise) during the recording process.

The interface

You will need to decide how you connect that quarter-inch cable to your iPhone or iPad, though, as Apple has yet to make that connection standard (don't hold your breath). The question now is what kind of connection you wish to use:

- ✔ **Headphone jack:** With this, your guitar or bass connects through an interface that plugs into the headphone jack of your iPhone or iPad.

- ✔ **Lightning or 30-pin connector:** With this, your guitar or bass connects through an interface that plugs into the data connection of your iPhone or iPad.

Generally speaking, the interfaces that plug into the Lightning or 30-pin connector of your device provide much better audio quality than interfaces that go through the headphone jack. Because of the way headphone jack interfaces must be wired to allow a headphone connection as well, you may experience some noise or feedback (depending on where you play and how you configure your audio) as you play or record. For casual playing or practicing, this noise won't make much of a difference, and software will offer you options for dealing with feedback. For example, AmpliTube includes a No Feedback switch you can enable to prevent feedback, whereas JamUp Pro XT advises lowering the iPhone or iPad device output volume to reduce feedback.

If you record audio through your headphone jack, you can only record at 16-bit/44 kHz resolution. This resolution will work fine for practice or live playing, but you may want to upgrade if you plan on recording master tracks.

However, depending on the interface you choose to buy, you may not be able to power or charge your device while you're playing. Power might not be an issue for an iPad you use only for playing and you remember to power it off between sets. But if you're using your iPhone at night while you've been talking all day, power could present a challenge. Nobody enjoys losing an audio signal right before the big solo in "Purple Rain" because you stayed on the line with Grandma an extra half-hour. So take a look at the following list as advice for the type of interface to purchase:

✔ **Casual practice and rehearsal:** Go with a headphone jack interface or a data connection interface (charging or non-charging).

✔ **Live performance:** Use a data connection interface that provides charging options.

✔ **Recording:** Use a data connection interface (charging or non-charging).

As you might suspect, data connection interfaces (such as the iRig Pro HD) tend to be a little more pricey than the headphone jack interfaces (such as the original iRig). But for live performance and certainly for recording, the audio quality outweighs the price issues.

The apps

This book covers this subject in much more detail in Chapter 6, but you'll also need to choose the type of apps you want to use as part of your performance or recording rig. Most guitar-based apps (like AmpliTube, AmpKit, and JamUp) provide amp modeling and effects (with the option to purchase many, many more) in one location. Depending on how the apps interface with Inter-App Audio or Audiobus, you can also chain together multiple apps to create your ideal signal path.

The pedalboard

Unless you're extraordinarily quick and can tap out settings on your iPhone or iPad between riffs, you need a foot-based controller to change settings while you're playing. The kind of controller you choose depends on how you need to interface with your device and what audio interface you use.

If you already use the data connector for your audio interface, try a wireless or Bluetooth MIDI pedal to connect with your device. Luckily, iOS 8 makes such Bluetooth connections possible. Also, if you use a device like the Focusrite iTrack dock, you could connect a USB controller like the Keith McMillen SoftStep pedal to the dock and control the apps via MIDI connections. Mapping the pedal controller to the app functions does take some time and effort to, but many apps use a MIDI Learn function that makes the control process easier. These steps vary depending on the controller, but they all follow the same basic pattern:

1. **Plug in the controller.**

2. **Start the app.**

3. **Engage the MIDI Learn function (process may vary depending on the app).**

4. **Tap the control onscreen you wish to manipulate with the pedal controller.**

5. **Press the control on the pedal controller you wish to use to manipulate the app.**

6. **Save.**

After you map all of your settings, you're ready to go.

The speaker (or speakers)

You may already use amp modeling software on the iPhone or iPad, but the end of your signal chain must make your signal . . . even louder. You can use something as simple as a pair of headphones or a full-on guitar or bass amp. But every rig must include something that makes the sound you create with your instrument and process with your device.

Use Figure 9-1 as a model for putting together your guitar or bass rig, and have fun!

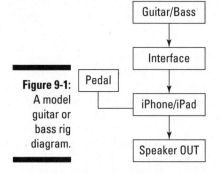

Figure 9-1:
A model guitar or bass rig diagram.

Synthesizer rig

This section goes over the devices you'll need to put together a synth rig based around your iPhone or iPad. Note that when we talk about synthesizers, we're talking about keyboard-based instruments from acoustic and electric piano simulators to more advanced synthesizers like the Moog or Fairlight. This rig centers around two different devices — the iPhone or iPad that acts as the sound-producing device, and the MIDI controller that tells the iPhone or iPad which sounds to make.

The apps

Don't get us wrong — you're still the central part of this whole rig. You make the playing decisions during the performance, and every sound that occurs happens because you made that sound occur. But in this case, the iPhone or iPad acts as the "brains" of this operation, in that it actually produces the sound you hear.

When you load a synthesizer app on your iOS device, you set up the instrument to be played by incoming MIDI commands. The iPhone or iPad receives the commands and produces the sound. Pretty simple, really. After you buy the apps you want to use, of course. And therein lies the dilemma — which apps do you choose for your rig?

Synth players constantly look for and create new sounds and *patches* (preset sound values that tell the synth which noises to make), and back when you had to buy entire keyboards to get those sounds, that required a lot of money. Luckily, these days, all you have to do is buy a few apps here and there. You can choose from a ton of synth apps, and you should always let your ears make the decision of what you play. But the most important quality you should look for in these apps is MIDI compatibility. The iOS operating system makes MIDI usage extremely easy, and any app worth playing will support receiving MIDI commands.

Some apps make MIDI functionality an in-app purchase, meaning you must pay a little extra to use MIDI with the app. Make your decision on the sound first, but note what you'll have to purchase to make everything functional.

So why is MIDI so important? Because playing the keyboard on an iPhone is cramped and unrealistic, and even the larger iPad screen size doesn't help that much. Some apps and effects (like Bebot, Lemur, or LiveFX) make creative usage of the touchscreen, but if you plan on playing keyboardlike sounds, you'll need a keyboardlike device.

The MIDI keyboard

If the iPhone or iPad represents the brains, then the MIDI keyboard is the body that does the actual movement and work in this operation. Although the keyboard doesn't include any sound-producing device of its own, it does allow you to play the apps on your iOS device as if the sounds did exist within the keyboard.

The advantage here is that a MIDI keyboard doesn't cost anywhere near what more traditional keyboards cost. You can purchase a decent keyboard for hundreds or thousands less, and the keyboard will give you a realistic playing experience. But before you make your purchase, know what you want to play and how many keys you'll need to play it.

Keys to the controller

Traditional piano keyboards provide you with 88 keys, spanning the full range of notes provided to keyboard players. However, many keyboards provide a smaller number of keys, and you may only need that number of keys to get by. If you're a trained pianist, anything less than 88 keys might feel small and incomplete. But if you need to get multiple keyboards into a smaller place or if you just think that a smaller controller will work for you, you can also purchase versions with 25, 49, or 61 keys.

The *type* of keys also makes a difference. Pianists may count on *weighted* keys for a realistic feel (and they pay more for this feature). Weighted keys provide some resistance when playing. Some keyboards even contain small hammers (just like real pianos) to help create the illusion of a real piano. *Semi-weighted* keys provide a little resistance, but not as much as their fully weighted counterparts. *Non-weighted* or *synth-action* keys don't provide any resistance when you press down, and spring action returns the keys quickly to the starting position when you let off the key. Synth-action keyboards also tend to be more portable and less expensive than other models.

Synthesizer keys can also provide *velocity-sensitive* keys that can detect the amount of force you use to press the key (from feather-light to giant-monster-fist-slamming). Some keys can also provide *aftertouch,* which lets you increase the amount of pressure you put on the key after you play the note and trigger different effects (such as filters or levels of distortion).

So how do you make sense of all these keys? You pick the type that works best for your playing style. If you want to just play piano with an easy-to-move rig, consider a full-size (88-key) keyboard with weighted or weighted hammer action. If you want to play synthesizer apps and receive a large amount of control over the notes and sounds over the time you play a specific note, get a smaller keyboard (easier to move, right?) with velocity-sensitive keys and aftertouch. Some players even use a 25-key keyboard for keyboard bass playing, where they just cover the low end of the song with the 2 octaves available on the keyboard. Tailor your choice of controller to the music you create (and how much weight you want to carry — remember that weighted keyboards obviously weigh more than other models).

Even if a keyboard has fewer keys, it usually include controls that help you *transpose* (move the pitches played by the keys up or down) the keyboard to play higher or lower notes. It's not as easy as just pressing a key on the full 88-key keyboard, but you'll be able to get the notes you need with a couple of clicks.

Other knobs, sliders, and pads

MIDI keyboards don't just give you control over what notes you play and how you play them. Today's offerings also include other controls you can use to create and alter sounds, from common fare to more outlandish options.

Most keyboards include pitch bend and modulation wheels, found on the left side of the keyboard. Use these wheels to raise and lower the pitch of the notes or modify the frequencies of those notes. Keyboards containing less than 88 keys usually also provide transposition buttons to move the available octaves on the keyboard up or down. From these common features, the controls become a little less . . . normal.

Some keyboards include knobs or sliders you can map to controls within the software. For example, you could use the knobs to alter controls on a synthesizer or raise or lower the overall volume of the sound. Remember that these controls don't actually produce sound, either — you'll need to tell the software which functions these controls . . . control. Some keyboards even provide pads you can strike, just like a drum machine or sampler. Depending on the software you control, you can use these pads to trigger drum sounds or lower notes.

We talk more about MIDI controls and mapping in Chapter 4.

The interface

You'll need a device between the iOS and the MIDI keyboard to handle a couple of different signals:

- ✔ The MIDI signal from your keyboard to your iOS device
- ✔ The audio signal from the iOS device to the speakers or headphones

A device like this plugs directly into the 30-pin or Lightning connector on the iOS device and provides connections for both MIDI and audio. You can use a dock like the one mentioned in the "Guitar or bass rig" section earlier in this chapter, or you can hook up a USB audio/MIDI interface to your iPad through a camera connection kit. The important concept to remember is that you need to purchase an interface that handles both MIDI and audio, not either one or the other. Unless you plan on listening through headphones, you need a decent device to play the audio. And you need to plug your keyboard into the interface using either a USB or MIDI (5-pin) cable. Think of the interface as the clearinghouse for all the instructions and signals travelling between your iOS device and the keyboard.

The pedals

If you're an experienced pianist, you'll want to purchase a sustain and damper pedal for your keyboard. Otherwise, you'll have no realistic way to simulate those aspects of the performance. MIDI keyboards can also accept expression pedals, which let you send a signal to the app to affect different kinds of controls, such as the speed of a Leslie speaker on an organ or a wah effect. Again, though, you need to use MIDI mapping to tell the app what the pedal controls.

The speakers

Like the guitar or bass rig earlier in this chapter, you'll need to provide either headphones or a PA system for the sound to come out of. Let your need of volume be your guide, and try not to annoy the neighbors. The good news is that, in a lot of live performance venues that already come with PA systems, you can just plug your rig in and go from there.

Use Figure 9-2 as a model for your synthesizer rig.

Practice switching apps on the iPhone or iPad to get between synths quickly. You'll need to know how switching apps affects the MIDI connection between the iOS device and the keyboard to ensure you don't encounter any surprises along the way.

MIDI data may follow a standard, but all music apps may not recognize or use certain types of MIDI data, such as CC messages that come from pedals. Make sure you know what your app and controller can do together before making any major purchases, and consult your manual and online resources frequently to get the most out of your rig.

Electronic music rig

The difference between putting together a rig for synthesizers and a rig for "electronic" music (after all, when you're running it through an iPhone or an iPad, isn't all music electronic in some way?) is slight. The interface remains pretty similar, and you'll still need a PA system to hear the music through. The big change involves the style of apps and the MIDI controller you use to control those apps.

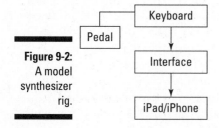

Figure 9-2:
A model
synthesizer
rig.

So what's the big difference?

Electronic music (at least in the sense of EDM, or electronic dance music) usually involves controlling a number of audio tracks or loops and modifying those sounds with different filters or effects. You can use a MIDI keyboard to control these apps, but you may find new and different MIDI controllers a little more suited for apps that play to the EDM crowd.

The apps

Check out apps like iMaschine, iMPC, and Novation Launchpad — these products can work on their own, but they can use specially constructed MIDI controllers (sometimes built by the app manufacturers themselves) to control which loops or sounds play at a certain time. Most of these controllers follow the 16-pad configuration (laid out in a 4x4 grid) made popular by the MPC sampler. Strike the pads to trigger a sound or loop, and strike the pad again to either continue the loop or restart it.

The controller

Now you get to play with some unusual toys — many manufacturers provide different kinds of pads and controls that allow you to manage your music software. All you have to do is plug the controller into the interface or the iOS device itself, and you're ready to go. The challenge here is telling the MIDI controller exactly which aspects of the apps to control. Apps matched with hardware by the manufacturer should match up instantly. But other devices, like the QuNeo from Keith McMillen Industries or even the Livid Guitar Wing (a guitar-mounted MIDI controller), may require a software editor to help plot out your MIDI controls. That kind of editor gives you a wide variety of available controls, though.

Another factor to consider is how you connect your controller. Most controllers connect through a dock or cable like MIDI keyboards, but some can use WiFi or Bluetooth connections to interface with your iOS device. For example, the Guitar Wing we mentioned earlier uses Bluetooth to communicate back to the brains of your rig, and you can add a WiFi connection to the QuNeo device to allow wireless communication.

Bluetooth and WiFi connections can make for convenient connections, but sometimes wireless means trouble. Long distances or environmental conditions can interfere with these connections, and dead batteries means devices stop talking. Make sure you test your connections before any live performance and keep everything juiced up. And if you're worried about people interfering with your WiFi devices in a live performance, you may want to go with Bluetooth LE connections for a little extra security (if available).

You may need to review the MIDI charts to see how these devices match up with the apps, but most apps give you the same MIDI Learn functionality we discussed in Chapter 4. It may take a little work, but you can get a control to work well for you.

Use Figure 9-3 as a model for your electronic music rig, and get the crowd dancing!

Recording rig

Up to this point, we looked at rigs that allow you to perform music or modify the sound you run through your iOS device. In this section, we look at the devices you need to put together in order to record live audio in your home or on the road. This task is a job in and of itself, so you don't want to plan on using the same iOS device to record while performing.

For this rig, the iOS device acts as both the controls and the destination for the recorded audio. You can manage the controls on the touchscreen, and the audio resides on the internal storage of the iPhone or iPad.

If you're buying a device strictly for recording, go ahead and spring for the iPad and get as much memory as you can afford. The iPhone is an extremely useful device, but you'll appreciate the additional screen size and lack of nagging cell phone calls while recording audio.

You ask your iPhone or iPad to do so much — record and play music, watch movies, listen to music, play games, read books, surf the Internet, and interact with the many, many apps you can download. But because you can perform all of these activities, your storage can get easily overloaded. And if you don't have the storage space, you can't record audio. Be sure you have enough room for recording (about 3 GB per recording session is a good model) before you get started. And don't count on recording to the cloud, as WiFi connections and app limitations make this a dicey (if not impossible) proposition.

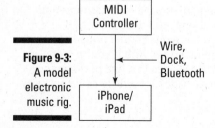

Figure 9-3:
A model electronic music rig.

The apps

The App Store offers some great apps you can use to record audio, including PreSonus Capture, Auria, Cubasis, and MultiTrack DAW. These apps follow the common design of presenting a virtual mixing board on the iPhone or iPad screen, so you should be able to take experience from recording on other devices or software onto your iOS device with little effort. And, if you're new to the game, you'll be working with apps that look remarkably like each other, so you should be able to look up the help you'll need remarkably quickly.

The interface

Most performing rigs just require a smaller audio interface that can output one or two channels of audio and maybe some MIDI commands. For audio recording, you need as many inputs as possible to allow you to record as many tracks as possible at the same time, especially if you need to record multiple performers at the same time. Eight inputs is a good place to start, and you can adjust up or down depending on your specific needs.

And, of course, you need the mics. We discuss microphones more in Chapter 7, but you need a decent variety of available microphones in order to be ready for every recording situation. Shure SM57s and SM58s are reliable options for vocals and instruments, but you might also think of a mic to handle lower frequencies such as bass cabinets or bass drums as well as a dedicated vocal mic.

You should probably also look at purchasing at least one or two DI boxes, which allow you to record electric instruments like guitars, basses, and keyboards without the need for a mic. Just plug the instrument into the box, plug the box into the interface, and you're good to go.

Most audio interfaces come with preamps that you can use to boost the signal for recording audio. The signal that comes from mics and instruments needs a boost to provide adequate recording levels, and some mics might need extra power (called *phantom power*) to function properly. If you plan on recording more than two or so mics or *line* inputs (the input coming from the DI boxes), you might need to look into purchasing additional preamps or using a combination DI/preamp, like the long-beloved SansAmp Bass Driver DI for bass guitar.

The controller

Recording rigs don't require MIDI controllers as much as performance rigs because you're able to directly access the screen instead of busying yourself with playing an instrument. Simply slide your fingers across the screen to modify the settings, and you're good to go. You can, of course, buy a controller if you find yourself needing to modify extra parameters beyond what you can use on the screen. For example, you could buy a foot pedal that starts and stops recording while you monitor the virtual faders on your mixer. But you could probably save some money here and skip the controller, at least when you start out.

So much of live recording revolves around where you record the audio. You can carry a bunch of gear with you, but recording next to a construction site will never produce great results. Mobile recording means finding the best possible site or minimizing what you must deal with at the time.

The diagram in Figure 9-4 displays four audio inputs, but note that you can use as many as possible.

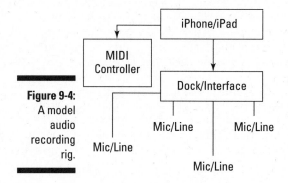

Figure 9-4:
A model
audio
recording
rig.

Deciding Whether to Go Fully Mobile

You're probably looking at playing or recording music on an iPhone or iPad for reasons that center around one factor — you can move this device around easily. You can take it anywhere, and even the equipment associated with making your iOS device a serious piece of musical equipment is pretty portable. Certainly, it's more portable than trying to lug around an entire recording studio or a vintage Moog synthesizer. Still, you need to take a look at your situation and decide whether making everything portable is the right decision for you.

If you're planning on just playing or recording at home, you probably won't need to make sure everything can move along easily. After all, you'll have your comfortable recording or playing environment, and you're good to go. But if you're planning on performing or recording in the field, you'll need to be able to carry everything along with you. iOS devices are pretty portable on their own, but you'll also need to make sure that anything that goes along with you (controllers, pedals, and other devices) can be easily carried. And don't forget about power — you'll need to carry devices to either charge the batteries or provide power as you play.

It all comes down to the purpose you want to accomplish. Always come at your projects with a clear goal, and determine whether you'll need to accomplish all of your tasks in the field.

Preparing a Gear Checklist

When you planned your rig, you took into account the major pieces of equipment you'd need to make your rig happen. Your iOS device was a given, and you planned for the controller and interface. But don't forget about the incidentals, either. Think of your gear checklist as your recipe for music, and you'll need to gather all the right ingredients.

The main course

You already know about these devices, but make sure you gather them and ensure they're ready to perform:

- ✔ Fully charged iPhone or iPad
- ✔ Any apps you want to use
- ✔ An audio interface
- ✔ MIDI keyboard or MIDI controller

Side dishes

These devices can vary depending on what you want to accomplish, but you'll need to keep them around to be fully functional. You just can't have a meal without them. These devices include:

- ✔ Control pedals
- ✔ Microphones
- ✔ Headphones
- ✔ Speakers (if you're not playing through a PA)
- ✔ Instrument and mic cables

Your 1/8" headphone connections may work well for practice or home listening, but live performances and professional recording studios require quality audio interfaces and cables. Don't skimp here.

Your picnic basket

You can't just grab all of these items and go — you need to transport and protect these devices as you move around. Before you head out, always buy the proper cases and supports for your devices, such as:

- ✔ Case for the iPhone or iPad (you may have to take your device out of these cases to put them into docks, but it's worth the extra protection.)
- ✔ Case for the MIDI keyboard or controller
- ✔ Stands for your iOS device and MIDI keyboard or controllers
- ✔ Cases for microphones and headphones
- ✔ A case or bag for your associated cables
- ✔ Mic stands for your microphones

Dessert

This category covers anything that you carry around with you for your own purposes, like guitar picks and small things like that (that never seem to be around when you need them). You could call them garnishes or spices or something like that instead, but we prefer dessert. And who wouldn't prefer dessert, really?

Chapter 10

Working with Digital Audio Workstations and Other Recording Apps

To be fair, recording studios never had to be huge, expensive affairs, even before the advent of inexpensive digital recording technology. Sure, you could walk into multimillion-dollar facilities in Los Angeles, New York, Nashville, London, and many other famous locations. But some of the most important records in history came from smaller locations, like Sun Studio in Memphis or J&M Recording Studio in New Orleans. The point here is that, with the right motivation and knowledge, you can make great recordings just about anywhere.

Digital music gives you the ability to take technology and tools previously reserved for recording studios anywhere you need to be to make those recordings possible. This chapter takes a look at the most common, versatile, and powerful recording tool in music today — the *digital audio workstation* (hereafter referred to as DAW, because that's what the professionals call it, and because it's easier to type). This type of app provides the tools you need to record, mix, and export your music. This is still basically the same recording process used in those large studios — you just need a lot less equipment to make it happen.

Using DAW Apps

If you do a little research, you'll find a multitude of DAW apps available for you. Before you get intimidated by all of those possibilities, recognize that each DAW offers pretty much the same tools, give or take a little functionality here or there. The main difference is the workflow and user interface — that is, what it looks like and how it responds when you interact with it. Some apps try to keep everything basic and simple, whereas others toss all of the available tools at you and let you run everything like an expert. And, of course, there's the price difference — for better audio quality and more recording options, you're likely to pay a little more money. Still, even the most expensive DAWs for iOS devices top out around $50, which is significantly less that their computer-based counterparts.

If you plan on collaborating with other musicians, find out which software they use. You can sometimes share file types between different DAWs, but using the same software makes transferring files so much easier.

Let's take a look at what common functionality DAWs share and what purpose they serve in recording your music.

If you want a more specific starting point, a number of companies offer versions of their flagship DAWs as iOS apps (such as GarageBand and Cubasis, which we cover in the "Surveying the Major DAW Apps" section, later in this chapter). If you're already familiar with the big brother of the iOS DAW, you might find a friendlier transition to the little brother.

A multitrack recorder

The entry point for each DAW involves recording multiple tracks of audio, preferably at the same time. The amount of tracks may vary from app to app, but the overall point of the DAW is to bring together multiple audio sources into a single file. You also want to record the audio on separate channels so that you can better modify the audio later as necessary. Just assign the inputs from your audio interface to each track in the multitrack recorder so that you capture each piece of audio on a separate track.

Depending on the functionality of the DAW, you may also be able to set a metronome (also called a *click track*) to set the tempo for your song, and DAWs that use virtual instruments may also let you set a key and time signature to help everything stay in sync as you record. These settings can be especially helpful as you add external loops or MIDI to your songs.

Note that there's a difference between the amount of tracks you can record at one time versus the number of tracks you can record at all. The amount of tracks you record at one time depends on the number of inputs your audio interface includes. However, even if you only have a couple of audio inputs, you can still record up to the maximum number of audio tracks available to your DAW (such as 48 tracks for the Auria DAW app). You just have to assign the audio input to a new track and start the recording over again. At least you don't have to wait for the tape to rewind each time. And, of course, the age of the device, the version of iOS, and the amount of effort you ask from the processor for effects and instruments affect the number of tracks you can record as well.

The mixer

Whenever anybody thinks of a recording studio, the mixer is usually the first thing that pops into mind. All the knobs, the levels, the meters — the mixer brings all of the audio together into a single track. You'll have to provide your own group of people standing around the mixer, looking intently and slightly bobbing their heads in the tried and true dance of the recording session.

This section of the DAW allows you to modify a few aspects of the audio you record with the multitrack recorder. Each track you record gets its own slot on the mixer, also called a *channel strip*. The channel string includes the following controls:

- **Volume:** The volume control is often represented by a vertical slider called a *fader* — move the slider up to fade the audio in, move the slider down to fade the audio out.

- **Pan:** This is often represented by a knob that helps you move the audio around the stereo audio field. Turn it left to make the audio louder in the left channel, and turn it right to make the audio louder in the right channel.

Okay, so it's possible to record audio in 5.1 and even 7.1 channels right now, but people still mostly listen to music in stereo recordings (reserving 5.1 and 7.1 channels for video, games, and other multimedia applications). In this book, we stick strictly with stereo.

- **Solo:** This is often represented by a button that lets you listen to only that track during playback.

- **Mute:** Mute is often represented by a button that prevents you from hearing that track during playback.

- **Record:** This is often represented by a button that enables that track to receive recorded audio.

Back in the days of recording on tape, the Record button prevented the engineer from accidentally recording over a track — because after that happened, the track was forever gone. Digital recording offers the benefit of the instant undo for errors like this, but it's still a good idea to watch when you engage and disengage this control to keep from accidentally recording over your existing audio.

- ✔ **EQ:** EQ is often represented by knobs that allow you to emphasize or reduce the levels of certain frequencies on a track, like taking annoying high frequencies out of a recording.

- ✔ **Aux:** This is often represented by knobs that allow you to add a certain amount of a specified effect, such as reverb or delay, to a recording. You might also see Aux controls referred to as *sends,* because the controls route (or send) audio through different effects.

Some DAWs will add more controls, such as compression and *limiting* (tools that even out audio signals or prevent them from exceeding a specified volume level), but that depends on the app you buy. Ultimately, though, each DAW will provide the controls listed in this section as a matter of basic functionality. Those controls might not appear in the same way — Auria does a good job of virtualizing what a mixer looks like in real life, whereas GarageBand lays the controls out in a more horizontal manner. After you learn the basic concepts, you can transfer that knowledge from app to app fairly quickly.

The effects section

Not every recording needs a ton of effects — some of the best recordings in history came from a single mic and a tape machine. And you can certainly make that happen with your iPhone or iPad and a single mic as well. But some of the best recordings in history also include judicious use of effects during the recording process to make parts stand out. And some recordings just threw out all the rules and put some weird effects on there just for the heck of it. It ended up working, and there you go. Good music sounds good, but using effects can help you bring out the most in your good music.

Most DAWs offer a basic set of effects you can use to modify the sounds of your recordings:

- ✔ **Reverb:** Short for reverberation (musicians and engineers hate saying the whole word when a cool abbreviation will work), the reverb effect makes the audio sound like it was recorded anywhere from a small room to a majestic cathedral.

✔ **Delay:** This effect creates an artificial echo that you can modify from a quick "slapback" (think early Elvis songs) to a sound ping-ponging back and forth in the stereo field.

✔ **Compression:** As mentioned earlier in this chapter, compression raises the volume level of a recording's quiet parts and lowers the volume level of a recording's loud parts. Overall, compression makes an audio track more even and simpler to manage while mixing.

✔ **Limiter:** The limiter does just what the name implies and prevents an audio recording from exceeding a specified volume level. Use it to keep tracks from getting too unruly.

Some DAWs also offer chorus, phaser, flanger, distortion, and other effects usually associated with individual instruments, but again, that depends on the model. The effects we talked about earlier are more commonly used on all tracks during the recording and mixing process, so you're more likely to see them in the DAW as opposed to emulator or performance apps.

DAWs can integrate two different types of effects:

✔ **Insert effects:** These apply to a single track and are usually placed at the track level. These effects can apply only to that specific track.

✔ **Auxiliary effects:** These can apply to multiple tracks at a same time. You can use the aux controls we talked about earlier in this chapter (in the section called, "The mixer") to dial in the precise level of the effect you want to use. Auxiliary effects also let you use a single instance of an effect instead of multiple insert effects, sparing some processing power for other use.

Insert effects usually apply to effects that you use on single track for more effects, like distortion or a flanger. Auxiliary effects work better for effects that can apply to multiple tracks at the same time. For example, you can use a reverb to make all the instruments sound like they were recorded in the same room (even if they weren't recorded in the real world), and you can dial in different amounts of the effect to suit your purposes. A little less reverb on the lead vocal makes it seem closer to the listener, whereas a little more reverb on the drums puts them farther in the background (where you may want to keep the drummer, anyway).

Finally, some DAWs will include a final stage of effects with a master compressor or limiter that applies to the overall stereo mix. This feature may not be as common as some of the other effects we've looked at so far, but it can be extremely helpful in evening out the levels on the entire track and finishing your final product. We talk more about this kind of effect in Chapter 20.

Integrating DAWs with MIDI

DAWs can handle more than just recording digital audio from the real world, though. Today's digital audio workstation seamlessly mixes actual audio and MIDI information to help you create all the tracks you need, even if you don't have all of the actual instruments (and could play them well if you did).

Recording MIDI

Recording MIDI information involves a process similar to recording audio, but the actual results are a little different. What you're recording isn't actually the audio; it's the performance information — the volume and velocity levels, the notes, the duration of the sound, and much more. After you have that information down, you can assign that information to just about any software instrument the DAW can access. So if you start out with an electric piano track and want to see what it might sound like with a clavinet or a spacey synthesizer, just change the instrument. MIDI data also takes up a lot less room than recorded audio.

And because you can modify MIDI performance data after the fact, you can click into the MIDI data within the DAW and change the notes or other performance data to fit what you want it to sound like. Every DAW that records MIDI allows you to modify that data, like changing text within a word processor.

MIDI control

Some DAW apps also let you control MIDI devices outside the app (and outside of your iPhone or iPad). A MIDI clock helps multiple MIDI devices stay in sync by sending control messages. Depending on what functionality you have available, you can keep everything you track and record in sync, as opposed to press play on several different devices and hoping for the best. The app can send this information via cables, Bluetooth, or WiFi, depending on how you have your rig configured.

MIDI control surfaces

You already have access to the controls for your DAW right on the screen, which is pretty convenient, really. But you might need to add a little control to your DAW. Maybe the iPhone or iPad has to be across the room, or you have a preferred control surface you like to use during recording because it feels right. Most MIDI keyboard controllers also include knobs and transport controls (like Play, Stop, Fast Forward, and Record) on them as well, and you can use those controls to do everything from the keyboard instead of having to reach over to the iPhone or iPad to perform an action there.

Keeping all important controls close to you makes the entire recording process easier, even if you're not performing at the same time. Make use of as many physical controls as you can get your hands on. Those controls are probably larger and easier to interact with than anything on your iPhone screen, anyway.

Make sure the controls you need to use map to the app correctly before you get started with any major recording or performing activities. Some controls will automatically connect, whereas others may need some additional settings within the app.

Surveying the Major DAW Apps

Again, by no means do the apps we look at in this section cover the entire spectrum of DAW apps available within the App Store. Even some "best of" lists include more than double the number of apps we cover here (although these apps are certainly on those lists). But the apps we discuss here cover the vast majority of the functionality DAWs should offer, and you'll get the knowledge you need to make your own DAW choice after learning about these apps.

Recording audio is probably the only function most DAWs have in common — from there, the interfaces and methods can vary greatly. Although this section focuses on recording audio, each DAW will offer enhanced functionality or other options (like recording MIDI) that can sway your decision. Pay attention to all the details before making your final choice.

Anyway, why wait any longer? Let's dive in and get to recording!

GarageBand

This DAW probably lives on every musician's iOS device because of its price point — free. Now, when we write "free," we mean that only a *version* of GarageBand is free. You can get the app on your iOS device for free, that is, but the free version doesn't necessarily give you all the features that come with the full app. GarageBand indulges in the brand new reality of the app world — *freemium*. You get the app for free to get it on your device, and then you get to make in-app purchases to round out everything the app has available. At the time of this writing, that price is about $5 (plus applicable sales tax in your area) for all of the instruments and loops that come with the GarageBand app. And, if you owned a previous version of GarageBand (you lucky long-time Mac user), the content and instruments come for free.

Because the price point for the full version of GarageBand is so low, we discuss the full version of the app here. And because we took a closer look at the virtual instruments in GarageBand in Chapter 4, this section concentrates only on the audio recording capabilities of the app.

Tap open the GarageBand app and tap My Songs to see the screen in Figure 10-1. This screen displays a demo song and any other songs you've recorded (although this screen is pretty light if this is the first time you opened the app).

Tap the plus sign in the top-left corner to start a new song. Swipe the screen until you see the Audio Recorder shown in Figure 10-2.

GarageBand on the iPhone looks a lot different than on the iPad. Don't be thrown off-course if your screen looks a little different than the screenshots you see here.

After you open the Audio Recorder, you can lay down an audio track using the controls at the top of the screen. If you plugged in an audio interface, you'll see the meter react to whatever audio comes through that interface. If you're just using the iPhone or iPad itself, GarageBand routes the audio through the device's internal microphone.

You always get better audio through an audio interface. If you're recording anything else than scratch audio to capture a basic idea, use a proper audio interface.

Figure 10-1:
Creating
your first
song in
Garage-
Band.

Figure 10-2:
Audio
Recorder
in Garage-
Band.

As with most good DAWs, GarageBand lets you adjust the incoming level of audio. Tap the icon that looks like the end of a cable just under My Songs to see the options listed in Figure 10-3.

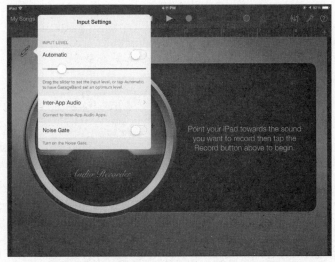

Figure 10-3:
Setting
recording
options in
Garage-
Band.

You can either adjust the slider to control the amount of incoming volume or move the switch above the slider to let GarageBand set its own interpretation of the best volume level. You can also select another app to record audio from using Inter-App Audio (we discuss Inter-App Audio more in Chapter 16, but you should know now that this kind of audio routing provides additional flexibility when recording audio, so having that feature in a DAW is a good sign). The Noise Gate feature shuts down audio when it falls below a certain level, which helps eliminate background noise or buzz from a distorted amp. Just make sure you don't set the gate too high, or you may lose the beginning or end of your audio performance.

After you record your audio, you can apply a variety of effects to it. The options displayed in Figure 10-4 may come across as a little cartoonish, but they do offer you some control so you can customize how the effect works with your audio.

For the guitarists, GarageBand also allows you to run your instrument through an amp simulator instead of the Audio Recorder. Swipe through the available options until you see the Guitar Amp and tap it to see the screen shown in Figure 10-5.

You record audio the same way in Guitar Amp as you do in Audio Recorder, but you can add simulated pedal effects by tapping the pedal icon on the right side of the screen. The tuner icon appears next to the pedal icon, and you can use it to tune up your guitar before you start recording.

Always tune your guitar before recording. It's the right thing to do.

Figure 10-4:
Adding a
little extra
to your
recorded
track.

Figure 10-5:
Cranking up the amp in Garage-Band.

When you're done recording your track, tap the sequencer icon (right next to the microphone icon in the toolbar at the top of the screen) to see how the tracks in your song lay out, as shown in Figure 10-6. In this case, the screen shows several different tracks already laid down — it's like a cooking show displaying a pre-prepared dish that way.

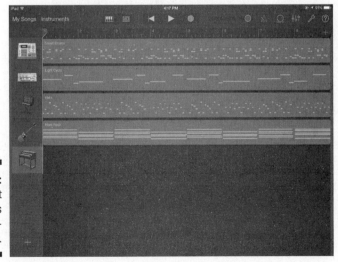

Figure 10-6:
Looking at the tracks in Garage-Band.

Swipe right on the tracks to see volume level, solo, and mute controls. You can also tap the mixer icon in the top-right corner to see additional track controls, like panning and master effects (such as echo and reverb). The drawback is that you can only adjust the volume of one track at a time.

GarageBand allows you to record in sections. These sections default to eight bars, but you can change the length of these sections manually, or you can set the section to be the length of the first piece of audio you record. After you record a section of a song (such as a verse or chorus), you can add another section by tapping the plus sign in the top-right of the screen, as shown in Figure 10-7.

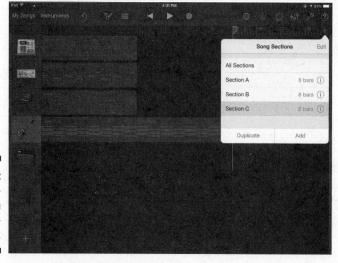

Figure 10-7:
Adding sec-
tions within
Garage-
Band.

Record other tracks from there, or double-tap your existing tracks to copy and paste them between sections.

So GarageBand may not look like a traditional mixing board or tape machine, but it does provide the basic DAW functionality you need to capture audio tracks and basic song structure. It can also handle a multitude of virtual instruments like keyboards, strings, guitar, bass, and drums. Finally, GarageBand includes a hefty set of audio and MIDI loops that you can use in your own songs, either as parts or idea starters. You can also purchase Apple Loops and transfer them to your iPhone or iPad using iTunes to transfer the files. With all of these features, you can arrange a fully formed recording right from your iPhone or iPad.

After you get your song arranged, GarageBand lets you export and send the song to a variety of sources, from SoundCloud and YouTube to file storage services like Dropbox. Depending on the apps you use on your iPhone or iPad, you may also be able to send the song to another app (such as an audio editor) for additional work. Of course, if you own a Mac laptop or desktop computer with GarageBand or Logic Pro X (the pro-level DAW software also available from Apple), you can export the track to that program for additional recording or editing. In a lot of ways, GarageBand functions as much as a sketchpad as a full-fledged recording app.

Cubasis

Cubasis shares GarageBand's status as a smaller counterpart to a larger DAW app on the computer side of recording technology. In this case, Cubasis comes from Steinberg, the same company that makes Cubase and Nuendo audio recording software. From there, though, GarageBand and Cubasis go in radically different directions. Cubasis offers a more traditional DAW interface that's familiar to anybody who's ever used a computer-based DAW. Cubase's more-traditional interface also includes a great deal more flexibility and power, as do Cubase's features:

- ✔ MIDI and audio recording

- ✔ Built-in audio and MIDI editing

- ✔ Virtual sampler and synthesizer instruments based on Cubase offerings

- ✔ Audio and MIDI loops

- ✔ Multiple tracks and master audio effects

- ✔ Automation for parameters, including volume, pan, and filter effects

- ✔ Track, mixer, media, and instrument views

However, Cubasis outshines a lot of the competition by offering 24-bit/96-kHz audio and the ability to freeze audio tracks to improve recording and playback stability (by preventing any changes during playback, the processor spends less time and effort on those tracks), and potentially unlimited tracks of MIDI and audio. Professional producers use freezing to lock in their basic sounds and tracks early to save time when finishing a recording.

Cubasis technically allows you to add as many audio or MIDI tracks as you wish, but that doesn't necessarily mean you'll be able to keep adding tracks on tracks without noticing performance issues. Although Cubasis doesn't cap the number of tracks, it will slow down to the point of stalling if you put too many tracks in the project. Pay attention to the performance of the track and use your track judiciously.

Put simply, if you require the full functionality of a DAW on your iPad (that includes the automation and routing capabilities that implies), Cubasis presents an amazingly strong option. Cubase users also should take a long look at Cubasis, because you can transfer projects from Cubasis to Cubase.

For all of this functionality, though, you do pay a little more than GarageBand. At the time of this writing, Cubasis goes for about $50. But for that extra investment, you get a much more intricate, customizable DAW.

Cubasis makes recording audio rather simple. Get started by opening the app and tapping a template to start from. Cubasis makes several different templates available to help get you closer to starting your project.

Everything in Cubasis revolves around the menu bar at the top of the program. Take a look at Figure 10-8 to see how a typical Cubasis project appears.

Tap the +Audio button to put in an audio track. Our pre-baked project looks like the one shown in Figure 10-8, but your screens will vary.

Tap the Record Enable button under the Mute switch for the audio track you wish to record, then tap the Record button to actually start recording audio within the app. Cubasis differs from GarageBand here in that you don't record audio in sections in Cubasis — let the audio record as long as you wish, and press Stop when you finish. You can record shorter sections of audio by setting loop points in Cubasis, but all activities take place within the single frame of the Cubasis project you record in.

Figure 10-8:
Laying down tracks in Cubasis.

After you're done recording audio, you can actually dig down into what you just recorded by double-tapping the audio clip to open the sample editor, shown in Figure 10-9.

Within the sample editor, you can make small corrections to the clip you just recorded so you get things just right (without having to re-record the track):

✔ Remove audio around the section you wish to keep (or erase a section in the middle)

✔ Fade the audio in or out

✔ Reverse the audio (checking for hidden messages?)

✔ *Normalize* the audio (that is, make the highest point of the recording the maximum limit, raising the overall volume level of the track)

From there, you can leave the audio where it is or save it to the MediaBay section of Cubasis to use later in another project.

This section only scratches the surface of the power of Cubasis — the instructions for this DAW could probably fill a small book of its own to help you figure out everything you can do with the program. Cubasis rivals what comparable computer-based apps can do, and you only need to spend $50 on it to get a fully portable DAW that can handle most audio projects. Toss in the extensive virtual instruments and MIDI implementation, and you've got a powerful songwriting and recording tool.

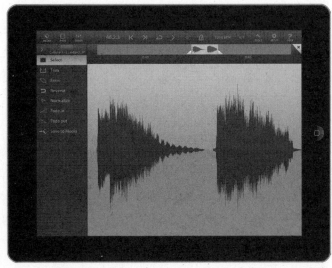

Figure 10-9:
Getting
closer to
your audio
in the sam-
ple editor.

Auria

Auria comes in two flavors — the full version and the LE version. The only real differences between these two versions are the number and quality of audio tracks each one can record:

- ✔ The full Auria app can record up to 48 audio tracks per project (at 44.1 kHz, 48 kHz, and 96 kHz).
- ✔ The Auria LE app can record up to 24 audio tracks per project (at 44.1 kHz only).

Appropriately, the Auria LE app costs half as much as the full app ($25 vs. $50), but both versions offer solid performance and access to name-brand plug-ins from companies like PSPaudioware and Drumagog. When we say "access," though, we mean you'll have to pay extra for them. The app itself includes a few plug-ins, but you'll end up paying extra for the additional toys.

The term *plug-ins* refers to bits of software that manufacturers (or third-party software programmers) write to function within a larger piece of software. It's like buying an additional compressor or EQ to use even though your mixer console already includes that functionality. You just want to use the device for a different or better effect. Same with software, although the software tends to be a LOT cheaper. The term *plug-ins* appears more with computer-based DAWs than on the iPhone or iPad because iOS doesn't really lend itself to supporting familiar plug-in formats like AU or VST. On iOS devices, you can use Inter-App Audio or Audiobus to simulate this process (and we discuss that more in Chapters 16 and 17), but programs can make plug-ins available via in-app purchases like Auria does.

Some Inter-App Audio effects can consume a ton of processor power in older devices. Always test your recordings first, and don't be surprised if highly intensive effects like reverb or delay brings the process to a screeching halt.

Auria dedicates itself to recording audio well, and as such doesn't include any MIDI tracks or virtual instruments. However, you can route other virtual instruments and synthesizers into Auria via Inter-App Audio functionality, so you can still access external synths if you wish. Auria will route this audio to one of the tracks and record from there.

Auria also permits you to import and export projects for use with other computer-based DAWs, such as Logic and Pro Tools. With this flexibility, you can either completely record and export projects from your iPad, or you can start on your iPad and move projects back and forth between your computer and iPad.

Auria pops you right into the mixer window when you start a project, and the mixer looks exactly like a mixer — no surprises there. (See Figure 10-10.)

All of the familiar controls line up in a virtual channel, so you can change them before, during, and after your recording session. And the process for recording audio is pretty simple:

1. **Select your audio inputs for all of the tracks you want to record.**

2. **Tap the Record Enable button for each track you wish to record.**

3. **Tap the Record button in the main toolbar at the top of the screen.**

4. **Tap Play to actually start the recording process.**

5. **Tap Stop to stop recording.**

Auria also records per song instead of sections like GarageBand, so you might find this DAW useful if you plan on recording song-length tracks instead of sections. Of all of the choices you have, Auria functions most like a traditional recording studio, so your level of familiarity with that environment might translate well if you choose to use this program.

After you complete the recording, you can tap the Edit window icon in the top-left corner of the screen to see how the tracks you recorded lay out in a standard sequencer view (just like you see with GarageBand and Cubasis — it's a common view). Check out Figure 10-11 to see how the Edit window appears in Auria.

Figure 10-10:
The Auria
mixer view.

You can then move the clips around, trim and edit, and generally manipulate them like you can with any other audio app.

Auria also includes subgroups, which allows you to combine the audio signals from similar sources (such as drums and percussion) and using a single virtual fader to raise and lower the volume and effects levels for everything within that group. For those who have used busses on mixers before, subgroups will be a familiar and welcome sight. You can use subgroups to simplify a lot of the mixing process later.

Choosing the Right DAW for You

So armed with all the knowledge this book can provide (in addition to the research your insatiable curiosity no doubt demands), how do you bring your search to completion and welcome the DAW of your dreams to your iOS device?

Well, it depends.

No matter which DAW you choose to use, spend the time necessary to learn all the tips and tricks that go along with it. Even if you use a simple tool, the complete knowledge of how to use that tool will help out way more than just toying around with a complicated piece of equipment.

But let's take a look at the most common factors involved in a DAW hunt and how you might respond to them. It's more accurate than shaking a Magic 8 ball and hoping for the best, at least:

✔ **Your device:** Most full-featured DAWs exist only for iPads — you need the extra screen space to make full use of what the apps can offer. When in doubt, look up the app from your iOS device and see what's available.

✔ **Features and functionality:** Simply put, how much horsepower do you need? Are you planning to record full tracks on your iPad, or will you be using your iPhone as a scratch pad for tracks you plan on re-recording later? If you're experienced and want to do more on your iOS device, take a look at the larger, more full-featured apps. If you want to go the easier route, go ahead and look at the smaller, more inexpensive apps. And check out reviews of the app — a little extra knowledge and real-world experience go a long way.

✔ **Virtual instruments:** If you need some synthesizer or sampler options as part of your songwriting and recording process, Auria will require external synths and instruments patched in via Inter-App Audio or Audiobus. Comparably, if you're only recording audio, buying Cubasis will get you a bunch of tools you might not otherwise need to use.

✔ **Audio quality:** To record 24-bit/96-kHz audio, you need both an interface and an app capable of functioning at that level. Be sure that the app you purchase can handle what you want to do.

✔ **Audiobus and Inter-App Audio support:** At some point, you may want to patch other synth or processing apps into your DAW for additional recording or processing. This level of support should be pretty common among DAWs, but read the fine print before you make your final decision.

We talk more about Inter-App Audio and Audiobus in Chapters 16 and 17, respectively.

✔ **Price:** It all comes down to what you can afford, doesn't it? To be fair, the jump from $5 to $50 isn't too major, but that depends on your budget. Do what you need to do. And there are plenty of DAW options out there — this section may cover a common option and a couple of heavy-weights, but apps like Capture, Multitrack DAW, and FL Mobile Studio HD bring a great deal of functionality at a lower price tag. The three examples in this chapter serve as examples and not necessarily recommendations (although they are fine apps).

Using MIDI Workstation Apps

The line between traditional DAWs and MIDI workstation apps lies squarely on recording audio — DAWs can handle recording multiple audio tracks, and MIDI workstation apps work mainly with virtual instruments and MIDI tracks. That doesn't mean you can't create full productions using MIDI workstation apps. Indeed, it's probably easier to work with these apps on an iPhone or iPad because you can record and produce with just the device and some headphones (and a MIDI keyboard or controller, if you feel inclined to beat on something).

These kinds of apps can take many different forms, but they generally fall into a few categories.

- **MPC-style apps:** The Akai MPC (Music Production Center) helped produce some of the most iconic hip-hop tracks in history (from Boogie Down Productions to J Dilla, whose personal MPC now resides in the Smithsonian), and that interface translates well to the single screen of the iPad. Akai licensed its own version of the MPC to the iPad, and other apps like the iMaschine and the Novation Launchpad (shown in Figure 10-12) emulate the multiple-pad configuration.

  These apps let you use pre-defined samples or audio you can upload separately to create loop-based productions. You can usually set the pads to play a single time upon being pressed (sometimes called a single-shot) or to loop automatically based on the tempo settings of the app. You don't actually lay down tracks as you would in a DAW, but you can record these loops as a performance and create songs as you go.

- **Multiple-device apps:** Apps like SampleTank from IK Multimedia may also include pad-based screens like the MPC-style apps from the preceding bullet, but they also include different input devices and instruments. You might use the pads to input drum sounds, then switch over to a keyboard to play piano or other key sounds (as shown in Figure 10-13).

  Some other apps, such as Korg's Gadget or Retronym's Tabletop, actually let you drag and drop devices into different tracks and route audio from each device through effects into a main mixer. Again, you won't actually lay down audio tracks like a traditional DAW, but these apps give you access to a wealth of other instruments, and you can get your songs together for either completion or export to an audio DAW for completion with vocals or "real" instruments.

- **Retro synths and sequencers:** If you have some great affection to the sounds and machines of early electronic music, you can still take advantage of these designs on your iPad (there are just too many tiny knobs and switches to these apps to really work well on an iPhone). Apps like the Korg Electribe and Propellerhead Rebirth let you use *step-based sequencing* to create a song. Just tap a button to make the app play the specified drum or synth sound on a selected beat. As you can imagine, this kind of recording works best with short phrases and loops, but it's possible to put together complete recordings using just these apps alone. Given the possibilities on your iPad, though, these apps work best as part of a larger arsenal, and most apps of this type work with Inter-App Audio and Audiobus (which we talk about more in Chapters 16 and 17).

Figure 10-12:
Tap a pad and make some music with the Novation Launchpad.

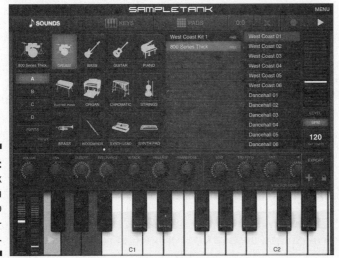

Figure 10-13:
SampleTank gives you access to many different sounds.

Recording with Loopers

If you've seen any solo artist perform within the past ten years, chances are you've seen that artist play with a looper. These devices let you play or sing phrases and automatically loop that audio to play back as you continue to play or sing a different line over those loops. Whether it's the advancement of technology or the realities of the costs of touring and the need to fill more space with fewer people, loopers allow you to explore your compositions in new and different ways.

And, of course, iPhones and iPads can handle this functionality with ease. The only drawback is that you usually have to provide some hardware to go along with your looping performance, such as:

- **An audio interface:** Although you can loop using the internal microphone, your vocals will sound better using an actual microphone. And, of course, you need some form of interface to play your chosen instrument into your iPhone or iPad.

- **Some kind of MIDI foot controller:** If you're playing an instrument, both of your hands are likely busy actually playing and therefore unavailable to trigger the starting and stopping of audio loops. A foot controller lets you trigger those loops while you continue to make the magic happen.

The process itself is pretty easy:

1. Start playing or singing.

2. Start recording right at the beginning of the phrase you want to loop.

3. Stop recording right at the end of the phrase you want to loop.

4. Play over that loop, or repeat recording as necessary.

In reality, you need to practice starting and stopping to get as precise as possible when looping. A little space at the beginning or the end of the loop can through the whole process off, and making a little mistake may mean you'll need to re-record the loop.

Let's take a little closer look at looping audio using the Loopy HD app.

Explaining Loopy HD

First, here's how Ryan personally uses Loopy HD — it's a fairly common setup, common to a bunch of solo performers:

✔ His bass guitar plugs into his audio interface.

✔ The audio interface takes a USB connection from his MIDI foot controller.

✔ The audio interface passes this audio and MIDI information to his iPad.

✔ The iPad loops the audio and sends it to the audio interface outputs (either speakers or headphones, depending on where he is at the time).

When you fire up Loopy HD, you see a screen like the one shown in Figure 10-14.

You can set the tempo and time signature manually here if you want, but Loopy HD will also infer these settings from the first loop you record. You can also swipe across this toolbar for other actions:

✔ Set the metronome settings.

✔ Add, subtract, multiply, or divide the amount of bars in your loop (default starts at four).

✔ Set the inputs you wish to use for recording.

✔ Start, stop, and check the audio levels for incoming audio.

Before you get started, tap Settings to make sure you make sure you configure the app properly. You don't need a ton of loops in this case (a lot of bass tracks recorded together tend to make the overall effect kind of muddy), so tap General and select six tracks, as seen in Figure 10-15.

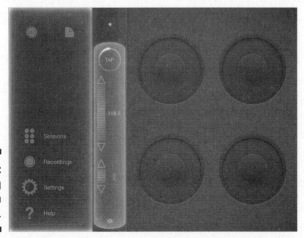

Figure 10-14:
Getting
loopy with
Loopy HD.

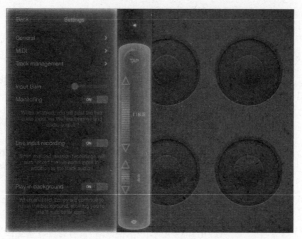

Figure 10-15:
Choosing
the number
of tracks in
Loopy HD.

You then tap MIDI and set up key bindings for your MIDI foot controller. Sound complicated? Not really — it's just a matter of tapping the right control at the right time:

1. **Tap MIDI to see the scene in Figure 10-16.**

2. **Tap the arrow next to the Control Input you wish to configure.**

   We picked iTrack Dock iTrackDock1.

3. **Select the action you wish to trigger (such as Record Loop).**

4. **Select the loop you wish to affect (either Selected Track or a specific track).**

5. **Tap the button on the MIDI foot controller you wish to control that action to see the screen in Figure 10-17.**

You'll have to repeat this action for each control on your foot controller, but this process gives you the ability to customize your controller for exactly what you need. The foot controller performs the following actions:

1. Record loops on tracks 1-4.

2. Adjust volume on tracks 1-4.

3. Pause playback.

4. Stop and reset playback.

Depending on your controller and looping needs, you can set up controls as you need. You might dedicate buttons to move control to different tracks as opposed to controlling specific loops at a time, or you might need to clear and re-record tracks as you go. Loopy HD really adjusts to your recording and looping needs.

From the Setting screens, you can also adjust the input volume, decide whether you want to monitor the audio through the iOS device as you record, record the audio input as you record with loops, and allow Loopy HD to function in the background as you route in audio from other apps using Inter-App Audio or Audiobus.

You'll need an audio interface to take advantage of any extended monitoring or audio routing functionality, such as if you want to send loops to different speakers or mixing configurations.

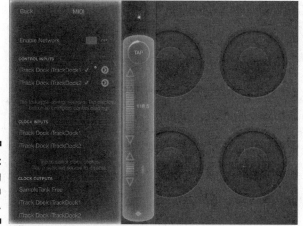

Figure 10-16:
Configuring
MIDI in
Loopy HD.

Figure 10-17:
Binding
MIDI con-
trols in
Loopy HD.

Finally, tap Track Management to see the screen in Figure 10-18.

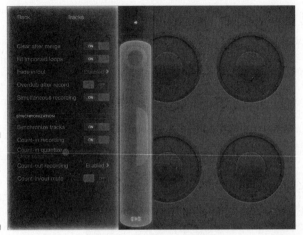

Figure 10-18: Track Management in Loopy HD.

This section allows you to control how you import audio into loops and synchronize loops as you record. We tend to leave these settings on their displayed defaults, but you might want to use count-ins if you want a specific tempo or a click to get you into recording.

Looping audio

Now that you have everything configured, let's have some fun! Recording the loop is terribly easy — just tap the middle of the track to start recording (or use your foot controller). Tap it again to stop recording and let it play back. An orange loop demonstrates a track recording live audio, and an orange cursor shows the amount of time before that tracks begins recording audio. You'll only see the cursor on loops recorded after the first loop. You can then record more tracks until you're satisfied. It's really that simple.

After you record a loop, you can perform a multitude of actions on it. Follow these steps to try some of these actions:

1. **Move your finger around the loop to increase or decrease the volume, as shown in Figure 10-19.**

2. **Swipe across the track to re-record or clear the track, as shown in Figure 10-20.**

3. **Start and stop the loops by tapping the center.**

4. **Twist the loop around using two fingers to change where the loop starts.**

5. **Record more loops as you wish.**

Everything you loop goes into a session with a time and date stamp as the title. Tap the Sessions button in Figure 10-14 to see these sessions, where you can rename them or save them as new sessions.

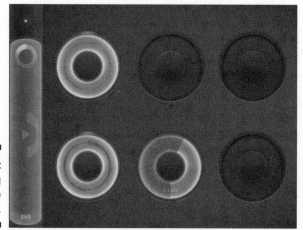

Figure 10-19:
Adjusting
the volume
in Loopy HD.

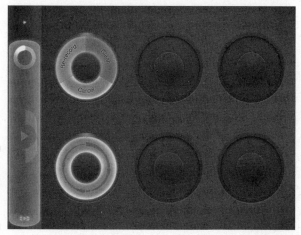

Figure 10-20:
Starting
over in
Loopy HD.

When these sessions are in place, you can make full songs out of them using the Record button (see the upper-left corner of Figure 10-14):

1. **Tap Record.**

2. **Manipulate the apps as you wish.**

3. **Play or sing over the loops as you go — by turning on the Live Input Recording setting shown in Figure 10-15, you don't have to loop this audio.**

4. **Press Record to stop.**

You can then export these recordings for listening or further manipulation.

Loopy is obviously a powerful, powerful tool for looping (either live or in the studio), and you can spend a lot of time customizing it to your needs. Loopy HD is less than $5, so have fun with it!

You don't have to sync the loops — change the settings in Loopy HD to let them run free and see what interesting music comes out of your experiments!

Remixing Apps

Suppose you already recorded your tracks, but you want to add a little spice to them when you play them back. Or you want to take a bunch of your tracks and record them into a single track, DJ style. Remixing apps like Remixer, djay, or Traktor let you cue up two tracks at a time, sync the tempo, and let you mix and loop to your heart's content. Take a look at Figure 10-21 for a quick view of Traktor for iPhone.

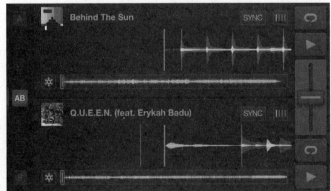

Figure 10-21: Traktor on your iPhone.

After you load the tracks, you can manipulate times, effects, and EQ, and record your mixing for export to other services, like SoundCloud. Functionality may vary on apps from device to device, but you'll basically be able to mix, alter, and record to your heart's content. Note how in Traktor you can hit the Record button to capture your mix. (See Figure 10-22.)

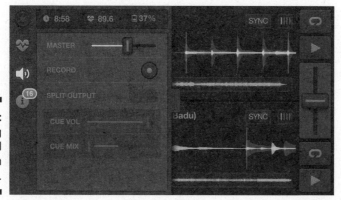

Figure 10-22: Recording the virtual 1s and 2s on Traktor.

The important thing to note here is that these apps don't actually create tracks as much as they let you mix audio together into your own mix file. This functionality might allow you to create a virtual mixtape of your own songs for distribution or as a gift to appreciative listeners. You don't have to solely be a DJ to make use of this brand of app.

Be careful when using tracks you didn't create yourself — depending on how litigious the artists and record companies you "borrow" from are, you could face headaches down the road.

Chapter 11

Monitoring with Speakers and Headphones

Recording your audio isn't just about the best apps and recording equipment you can afford (and the inspiration to actually create the songs, of course). You need to hear the audio during and after the recording to make sure you get everything recorded correctly. The "during" part of recording helps you make sure that everybody who is recording tracks (even if it's just you) stays in time and tempo with the backing tracks and doesn't get too loud or too soft. The "after" part lets you mix and master the audio properly so others can share in your recordings.

In this chapter, we talk about choosing the two most important tools you'll use to hear your recordings — your monitors and your headphones. You learn what differentiates monitors from everyday speakers, how you should set them up, and when you should use both the monitors and the headphones. Set your volume to a nice, even level and let's get started!

Deciding If You Need Speakers

In a perfect world, we would have left the words "Deciding If" off of this section's heading — because to accurately and faithfully reproduce and evaluate any recorded audio, you need a good pair of monitors (along with maybe a subwoofer, but definitely the two monitors). These monitors provide the correct stereo details in the stereo field and let you make decisions on the levels of your audio during mixing and mastering. Larger speakers, headphones, even car stereos and earbuds play a role in mixing your audio. But for your main listening work, you need a good pair of monitors.

However, this truly isn't a perfect world. And you're working with a mobile studio in some cases where monitors just aren't practical. If you want to mix a song after a gig and have it up on the Internet within a matter of minutes, you're not going to be able to get back to an acoustically perfect environment and listen on your good monitors. Or maybe you live in an apartment where the slightly noise earns you a heap of grief from your next-door neighbor. Or maybe you just can't afford a good pair of monitors; although you certainly don't have to have the five-figure monitors you might see on high-end recording sites, even lower-end monitors can set you back a little bit. Read through the following sections, evaluate the situation, and make the decision that works best for you.

Speakers are the best way to evaluate audio in most every case, so make an effort to work with them whenever possible. And pay attention to how the room around those speakers affects the sound. Even the best speakers will sound terrible when placed incorrectly in a small, boxy room.

Studio monitors versus consumer speakers

Studio monitors and consumer speakers look the same in a lot of cases, and most include the *tweeters* (high-frequency speakers and *woofers* (low-frequency speakers), so what's the big difference? Why should you look specifically for studio monitors instead of grabbing the bookshelf speakers from your stereo or running your mixes through your home theater system? The difference lies in hearing the best possible scenario versus the truth.

Consumer speakers are designed to make the records you hear sound good. They work with your stereo system to play back pleasing sounds with the amount of bass or treble that sounds best to you. You just put on the recording, sit back, and take in the music.

Studio monitors don't include features designed to make music sound good. Instead, they accurately reproduce the frequencies on the recording, even if those frequencies don't sound good at all. If your recordings have a boomy, unfocused low end, that's what the monitors play back. If you have a mid-range frequency that's way out of control, or if your singer's *sibilance* (hissing "s" sound) or *plosives* (explosive popping "p" sound) are too present, the monitors let you know. Whatever happens with the audio, these monitors tell you the truth about your recording, ugly warts and all. Pros often describe them as *flat* — the lack of coloration or EQ enhancements makes them good reference tools.

But that's okay! That's what you want to hear! Your audio has to be ready to play on a variety of systems, from the best high fidelity systems to the crappiest of earbuds, and you want your songs to have a fighting chance on every system you come across. The only way to ensure you get everything right is to make sure you mix it right the first time, and that includes:

- ✔ Proper balance in the stereo field

- ✔ Proper levels for each audio source

- ✔ No overloading of high, mid, or low frequencies

- ✔ Proper level for the overall track

When you get the mix correct using the unflinching, unyielding truth of studio monitors, you can make sure it works well for other methods of playback as well.

 Although studio monitors give you the most accurate version of your recording, you should keep different playback methods around for reference as well. Many a recording or mixing engineer has taken his or her test mixes out to his or her cheap car stereo to make sure the mix sounds good on bad systems as much as good systems.

Connecting studio monitors through your audio interface

Studio monitors come in two different configurations:

- ✔ **Active or powered:** These monitors contain their own *power amps* (amplifiers that supply the electrical power to move the speakers, as opposed to preamps that get the signal ready to be amplified).

- ✔ **Passive:** These monitors require a separate power amp to provide the power necessary to amplify the signal.

Most audio interfaces don't provide enough power to drive passive monitors, so you'll definitely need to match those with a separate power amp. The ultimate decision rests with your ears. Although many professionals prefer to choose their power amp and their monitors separately in order to better manage the components within their system, powered monitors provide the convenience of packaging everything together (and making sure your power amp doesn't accidentally overdrive your monitors into blowing a speaker).

The configuration in Figure 11-1 shows how you would hook up powered monitors to your audio interface. Most interfaces use either ¼" or RCA connections, and you would run one cable to each monitor.

Start the left monitor in the first jack — audio interfaces set mono or left monitors as the first output.

After you make the connection, use the volume knobs on the monitors to raise or lower the volume.

Figure 11-2 shows how you would place a power amp in-between the audio interface and your monitors.

After you get everything wired up, use the volume knobs on the power amp to control the level of the monitors.

Active or passive, ensure that your monitors maintain the same volume levels on the left and right sides. Good monitors often use *trim* controls to help you fine-tune volume and EQ levels.

Figure 11-1: Your powered-monitor configuration.

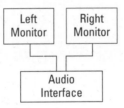

Figure 11-2: Your passive-monitor-and-power-amp configuration.

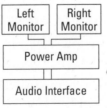

Understanding how room acoustics affect sound from your speakers

The type of monitors and volume levels present only part of the picture when it comes to listening to your audio on your monitors. Where you listen to your monitors makes just as much difference as the monitors themselves. If you listen in a big room with high ceilings, the tracks will sound different than if you listen in a small, boxy room with a brick wall directly behind you. You may not have a choice as to where you listen to your tracks, but you can come to understand how the environment affects that sound and to compensate for poor acoustics as best you can.

Sound can come at you in multiple ways, from *direct sound* (audio that travels directly from the speakers to your ears) to *primary reflections* (audio that bounces off of one surface and then goes to your ears) and *secondary* or *tertiary reflections* (audio bouncing off of two or three surfaces). All of these sounds arrive a little later than direct sound and may emphasize different frequencies than the direct sound. You don't have to understand the physics of it all, but you do need to know that these different factors will color your audio and how you can try and control those factors.

Compensating with near-field monitoring

Most of what you hear described as studio monitors are *near-field* monitors, or monitors that use small speakers designed to provide accurate sound and frequency reproduction at close range. Put simply, near-field monitors provide the best sound just a few feet away from the speakers so you can listen to them at a desk or monitoring environment. Yamaha made probably the most "famous" near-field monitor when it manufactured the NS10 model. The speaker wouldn't necessarily make anything sound "good," and you wouldn't include it in your stereo system at home. But many, many studios used this model (no longer in production, by the way) because if the engineer could make audio sound good on those monitors, it would probably sound good on anything else.

Near-field monitors let you hear an accurate version of your recorded sound at close distance so you can mix and master effectively. Most studios use near-field monitors for work and a larger set of speakers (more like your home stereo or PA system) for playback to clients or other listeners.

Placing your speakers

When you accurately place your near-field monitors, you get a full representation of the frequencies in your recording as well as a good idea of the stereo field. Again, because different rooms handle sound frequencies differently, you have to handle each unique situation differently — with a lot of trial and error, unfortunately. However, a few rules can help you get your monitors into the right position and create the "sweet spot" where everything comes together:

✔ Keep the same distance between each monitor and between each monitor and where you will sit and listen.

✔ Measure that distance using the center of the woofer in your monitor.

✔ Keep the monitors at ear level, not above or below.

✔ Mount the monitors on anything *except* directly on the desk at which you're doing your work. Instead, use speaker stands or isolation pads that raise the monitors off your desk.

✔ Keep your monitors from sitting too close to any big, flat surfaces (including close walls or big desks) that could cause bad reflections of sound.

Figure 11-3 shows the optimum configuration of monitor placement and seating. The distance can vary depending on the environment, as long as you keep each side of the triangle the same distance.

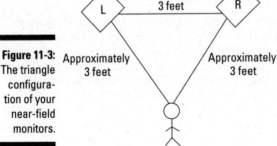

Figure 11-3: The triangle configuration of your near-field monitors.

After you get the monitors set up, turn the speakers toward your listening spot and play some music you know well through your monitors. Adjust the speakers until you get to the right stereo spread and frequency response (in other words, where everything sounds the best). If you can bribe a friend or family member to help you, have him or her move the monitors while you listen and direct. Otherwise, get ready to move back and forth a little bit as you get everything correctly settled.

Putting up acoustical treatment and configuring your mixing room requires a great deal of professional attention and methods (there's a reason professional studios spend so much time, effort, and money constructing control rooms), so don't be disappointed if you can't make the perfect listening environment. Your goal should be to get everything as good as possible, then recognize if you're getting too much of one frequency or another and learn how to work with it.

Using dedicated iOS speakers

Depending on how you configure your listening environment, you may want to have a set of speakers used only by your iPhone or iPad. You could be using these for reference (just to see how the music sounds on those speakers), or you may need something a little more portable to move around and play back recordings outside of your normal listening environment.

Speakers designed specifically for iPhones and iPads carry some benefits with them:

✔ They directly connect to your device.

✔ They usually use their own battery or are powered.

✔ They may use docks that power your iOS device.

For all of these benefits, you should note that these speakers will not function well as near-field monitors. They provide decent playback sound, but they're not designed for the rigor of true studio monitoring. Instead, use these speakers where you just need to listen to your audio in remote locations.

Some dedicated iOS speakers use Bluetooth technology to stream audio directly from your iOS device to wireless speakers. And everything is better without having to hook up wires, correct?

Well, it depends.

Bluetooth does make hooking up speakers and your iOS devices a little more convenient to move and place without dealing with a rat's nest of wires, but you do end up using more battery life. Your iOS device must use more power to use the network connection, and the Bluetooth speakers must use the network connection on their end *and* power the speakers. So the price for that portability is shorter battery life or the need to connect to some sort of power supply.

And then there's the audio quality. Bluetooth audio for cell phones is nothing new, but would you regularly listen to audio on the same earpiece you use for your phone calls (let alone try any type of mixing or performing)? Any time you have to begin a sentence about audio with "It could be worse . . .," you aren't dealing with the best possible scenario. Wired audio still provides better audio fidelity over Bluetooth connections, so you'll want to use wired connections wherever possible. Bluetooth may provide advantages when you have to place speakers in different locations where wires aren't practical, but you'll notice a difference from regular wired connections.

Choosing the Right Type of Headphones

Now that you've made your studio monitor purchase, you can focus on your headphones. You need a good pair of headphones (or 'phones or cans or whatever you want to call them) to mix audio correctly, because they allow you to focus in on smaller details of the recording (and actually hear the audio when you're recording and can't use speakers). And hey, your iPhone came with earbuds, so you're ready to go, right?

Sadly, it's not that easy. And you really should only use earbuds for phone calls and get something better for listening to and recording music, but we'll get to that.

This section takes a look at all of the different types of headphones you can purchase, how they should be used, and which kind you should purchase to complete your listening and recording environment.

And seriously, ditch the earbuds for everything except making sure your music sounds the best it can on those inferior devices.

Common headphone models

So many different types of headphones — you've seen them all over the place, and maybe even engaged in frantic Internet debates about your favorite model. Despite all of the varieties, they all trace back to a few common designs.

Over-ear

Over-ear headphones are the biggest member of the headphone family. The cups of the headphones completely enclose your ear and sit directly on your head (usually with an adequate amount of padding). Depending on how expensive the model you buy, you could also notice different features like detachable cables (perfect for when you or your dog fray the cable and you need to buy a new one, saving you the cost of an entirely new pair of headphones), larger *drivers* (the speakers in the headphones), and different headbands and swivels that let you use the headphones in different ways.

Over-ear headphones usually use 1/4" plugs to connect with more professional recording equipment (or at least an adapter to get to the correct connection). This type of headphone shows up most often in recording studios or audiophile home listening environments.

On-ear

On-ear headphones don't enclose your ear, but they do use larger speakers than earbuds or in-ear headphones, obviously. They can give pretty good sound, but they can't insulate your hearing completely from the outside world the way that over-ear headphones can.

Closed-back

Closed-back headphones completely enclose the ear cups, and prevent sound from leaking out and outside noise from leaking in. These monitors usually show up in the recording studio, where you need to prevent any external sound from coming through microphones. You might also see these headphones in use where you encounter a bunch of excess noise (like behind a drum kit) and you need to focus on a different sound source (like the click track that keeps the entire show in sync with any backing tracks or light shows).

Open-back

Open-back headphones don't seal off the cups like closed-back headphones do, so you can hear what's going on in the outside world while you listen to music. Of course, that also means the outside world can hear what you're listening to at the same time, so maybe keep the volume down, OK? Save your ears!

Open-back headphones also allows less sound reflection inside the ear cups, usually giving you better sound reproduction for overall listening needs. That sound quality depends on where and how you listen, of course, as well as the quality of the headphones you purchase. All other things being equal, though, you can usually count on open-back headphones to sound better than closed-back headphones at the same price point.

Semi-open

Semi-open headphones provide a little more enclosed environment while still allowing some sound in and out. This configuration tries to have the best of both worlds, but you should always let your ears be the ultimate judge.

Earbuds

Seriously — earbuds are everywhere because they're less bulky than over- or on-ear headphones, and you can include them with every iPhone at a fairly low price point. They are convenient for use anywhere, and they usually include a microphone and volume control on one of the wires so you can carry on conversations or adjust any call volume as needed.

Notice we keep on referring to *calls,* though. Not music. You *can* listen to music on earbuds, obviously, and plenty of people do. But earbuds simply do not give you the best audio reproduction you can hope for. They're good for hearing how your music sounds on tiny speakers, but that's about all they're good for. Keep a pair around for reference, but don't use them for anything else. Good music is worth so much more.

In-ear

In-ear headphones may have the same size as earbuds, but there is a world of distance between earbuds and in-ear headphones. Although earbuds rest near (and frequently fall off of) the opening of your ear canal, in-ears go directly into your ear canal. Because of this design, you get better sound reproduction than out of earbuds.

Depending on how pricey you want to get, you can also get custom-molded in-ear monitors that fit perfectly within your ear canal and can include multiple drivers for better sound. This process usually requires a trained professional to make the models, but the extra money is worth it. Professionals often use in-ear monitors onstage in place of the large, loud wedge monitors familiar to anybody who's seen a live rock show. The custom fit helps isolate external sound and provide the sound you need for performance.

Noise cancellation

You may notice that some headphones offer noise cancellation, which actively blocks the outside noise and lets you focus on the music you want to listen to. This feature usually requires active power (some kind of battery) and a microphone that picks up the outside noise and uses that signal to cancel out the audio by flipping the phase of the signal. Hence, any outside noise is blocked and you just get the good stuff.

Although this feature comes in really handy (blocking out the entire world on airplanes or public transportation can be mandatory sometimes), noise cancellation doesn't really help you while you're recording or performing. Noise cancellation technology is designed to prevent noise, not enhance listening or guarantee totally accurate playback. We're not saying you should never use these headphones — we have to travel, too. But you shouldn't necessarily reach for these headphones for mixing or other specific listening. Generally, you should try to keep as simple a path between your audio source and your speakers or headphones as possible. Save noise-cancelling headphones for the highway and the airports.

Wireless or wired?

Headphone wires can be a pain, and there's nothing worse than listening to something and having your headphones yanked off or out of your ears. Or catching a cord on a doorknob and getting yanked back. Or even damaging the wires and having to buy an entirely new set of headphones.

Wireless headphones eliminate these concerns, but have the same old concerns about wireless technology that we address in the section, "Using dedicated iOS speakers," earlier in this chapter. The sound quality of wireless headphones still isn't up to snuff for professional applications, and you end up using a lot more power to make the connection. Unless you're moving around a lot and need to keep your iOS device in your pocket while you move, go ahead and get the wired version to keep the sound quality up, at least until the wireless audio quality catches up. You'll end up spending a lot less money, as well.

If you looked at Ryan's desk, you'd see about four pairs of headphones:

- ✔ His wonderful high-end listening headphones.
- ✔ The headphones with mic he uses for audio and video conferences.
- ✔ His decent-quality in-ear headphones for mobile listening.
- ✔ The earbuds Apple included with his phone, just in case everything else breaks and he can't leave his desk to get everything else fixed. And for quick reference for recordings, of course.

It's okay to have multiple headphones to do multiple jobs, budget depending. No one pair can handle all the different environments.

Studio headphones vs. consumer headphones

Much like the quality differences between monitors and speakers, there's a significant difference between studio headphones and consumer headphones. Studio headphones provide the tools necessary to monitor and mix recorded audio with full frequency response, whereas consumer headphones are designed to make music sound as good as possible.

Studio headphones stand out in two crucial areas, as outlined next.

More expensive

Yes, studio headphones are more expensive than their consumer counterparts. It costs more to build headphones that can stand up to the extended use demanded by professional listening. Also, professional headphones are usually designed to be fixed (as opposed to the disposable nature of consumer electronics — just throw it away and buy another one!). Replaceable cables, cup padding, and drivers mean that you can keep your headphones around longer. You come to rely on good tools, and you want to keep quantities around as long as possible because you can trust what you hear.

You may pay a little more money for studio headphones, but the investment is worth it.

Note that more expensive doesn't always mean better, though. You can get good studio-quality headphones for the price of some brand-name consumer electronics headphones. Again, consumer headphones don't provide clear, uncolored, unaltered audio — they alter the audio by adding more bass or emphasizing other features. Although they may sound good, they can't be trusted for mixing or recording. Always check your headphones for studio quality when spending your money.

More accurate

Studio headphones represent a crucial part of your recording and monitoring workflow — they let you listen to exactly what your audio sounds like and decide how you need to change that sound to make it right. Headphones give you the added benefit of being able to focus on small details of your recording, better than even your monitor setup could provide. With the right monitors and headphones, you can switch back and forth between your headphones and monitors to get everything right. A good pair of headphones can tell you everything you need to know about your audio.

Part IV
Your Recording Workflow

Find out how to record audio in a DAW on your mobile device at
www.dummies.com/extras/ipadandiphoneformusicians.

In this part . . .

- ✔ Choose between recording live versus recording one track at a time.
- ✔ Establish the right resolution and recording quality for your project.
- ✔ Capture audio recordings as they happen with the best possible results.

Chapter 12

Recording Live or Layered?

It's always easier to record audio when you have great musicians playing great material. But whether or not you're working with quality performers playing great songs, you still need to figure out the best way to actually get the audio into your iOS device. To get everything working correctly, your strategy should involve a combination of recording techniques, gear, and a little bit of magic.

In this chapter, we take a look at the advantages and disadvantages of recording audio — recording one track at a time (layering) and recording everything together at one time (live). You learn which techniques work best and when to use them — you need to be good at both to capture as much good audio as possible, but each technique has its time and place.

Weighing the Pros and Cons of Layering

When you record one or two tracks at a time with the intention of going back over and recording additional tracks later, you *layer* tracks and put together entire songs in a step-by-step process. Usually, this process involves laying down tracks in a specific order, so you can lock in the *form* of the song (the correct order of verses, choruses, and bridges) for other instruments and get everybody on the same page. Here's the basic outline of the process:

1. **Record the drums or percussion along with a *scratch track* (a draft not meant to be kept) to outline the form of the song.**

2. **Record the bass line.**

3. **Record any remaining rhythm instruments, like guitar or keyboards.**

4. **Record any lead instruments, like guitar or brass and woodwinds.**

5. **Record any lead vocals.**

6. **Record any backing or ad-libbed vocals.**

7. **Record anything else the song needs, such as auxiliary percussion or wacky sound effects.**

You don't *have* to record everything in this order, of course. Maybe you want to record a lead instrument as part of the initial tracks to ensure all the other instruments leave enough space for the special parts. Otherwise, you could have a bunch of players performing their fills at the same time and making everything too busy and complicated. Or maybe you have to record drums last because (surprise) the drummer showed up too late and you didn't want to waste everybody's time. So you use the metronome in your DAW as a click track so you can go back and record drums later. Ultimately, the order you record your tracks is up to you and your circumstances. But the preceding list gives you a logical order in which to record your tracks for good results at the end of the project.

So now that you understand the basic concept of layering tracks, you can move on to the advantages and disadvantages of using this technique to get your audio recorded.

When you layer your tracks, always use some kind of click track or metronome in the background. Keeping a steady tempo means other players better lay down their tracks when their turn arrives. Although it may seem a little machinelike at the time, it solves a lot of problems down the road. It also prevents you from having to do too much work quantizing or stretching audio later in the process.

No method is perfect all the time — use whichever method works best for the recording situation you find yourself in.

Getting better control over quality

When you only record one track at a time, you can focus all of your attention on that track and make sure you get the perfect representation of what you're trying to record.

When you have a whole band playing at the same time, you've got a lot of things going on at the same time. You're trying to manage multiple microphones, multiple headphones, and multiple tracks. When you just have one or two people recording at a time, you can devote your entire attention to the factors that influence the track and make sure you get the environment as perfect as possible. And, because you're not doing too much at one time, you can probably take a little extra time and re-record tracks as you need to, ensuring the perfect track goes down to tape — er, memory.

The key factor is not to spend *too* much time tweaking each possible track — it's possible to micro-manage a track into lifelessness as you constantly go back and redo a part to get it just right. If you're unsure about what you really want, have the player (you or whoever is playing) record two or three takes so you have options later. And remember that you can always try different effects and EQ options later, after the track is recorded. Get the track you need, but don't make the player keep going and going until you're both tired and frustrated with the entire situation. Nothing good comes from that.

When you have the takes you need, you don't have to limit yourself to a single good track. You can *punch in* on tracks and record parts of an otherwise good track over again, making a take that much better. You can also *comp* (short for compile) several tracks together into a single perfect track. We talk about this kind of editing more in Chapter 19, but you should know now that recording multiple tracks and layering them together makes these techniques available to you (and makes them fairly easy to accomplish).

Layering requires less gear

If you're going to take your recording process one track at a time, you don't have to invest in bunch of gear that you'd need to capture the performances of a bunch of musicians at one time. You won't need an audio interface with multiple inputs, and you won't need several microphones and preamps that must be used at the same time.

This situation benefits you in a few key ways:

- You won't lay out as much money in equipment.
- What money you do have can go toward better quality gear, instead of a number of lower quality units.
- You can develop more and more familiarity with the gear you own, letting you understand how it works and what you need to change to make different instruments sound good.

Music technology manufacturers recently recognized the importance of the second point on this list and started developing high-end audio interfaces for use with both computers and iOS devices that provide only a few inputs (anywhere from one to four), but do so at 24-bit/96-kHz resolution with an extremely small and mobile footprint. This kind of interface lets home recordists get excellent audio quality while recognizing the realities of their recording situation and not selling inputs these buyers never need.

And, of course, you'll save a bunch of time and effort by using extremely familiar audio gear in your recording. Certain preamps or interfaces may lend themselves to one type of instrument or another, but you can make any mic or instrument sound better with quality gear used properly. The layering recording method lets you use your cash strategically to buy the best quality gear you need and make the music you hear in the best possible fashion you can.

Play around. Experiment. Whatever you want to call your process, you should do it to make sure you know how your gear responds in different situations. The more knowledge you have, the better you can respond to any recording situation that might occur.

You won't get as "live" a feel

Both hobbyists and professional have been recording in layered sessions for decades — basically, ever since multi-track recording first became a possibility. Until the late '60s, nobody could record on more than four or eight tracks at a time, period. If you wanted to record more parts than that, you were forced to overdub over these tracks or *bounce* tracks (combine several tracks into a single tracks) and then record new tracks into the vacated space. So layering is nothing new, and musicians made masterpieces using this method.

But certain genres lend themselves to live recording more than others. Sure, a producer creating abstract electronic dance music can do whatever he or she needs to record tracks and have it sound okay, but a bluegrass group feeds off of the interplay of the musicians in a live performance. The players might be able to deliver their parts one at a time, but the unfamiliarity of the situation might take something away from the performance. The performance isn't wrong, but it isn't necessarily right, either. Live performance might just deliver something better because of the normal circumstances in which the players create their music.

In this situation, you need to take a look at the overall picture and decide whether you're going to get the best result by layering tracks one at a time and getting "perfect" takes versus letting whatever happens happen and possibly including some mistakes in the overall best try at recording. You may have to experiment more with mic and musician placement, but ultimately the situation that makes the best recording is the best technique to use at that time.

Choosing to Record Multiple Simultaneous Sources

The first part of this chapter took a look at making your recording one track at a time. But after perusing all of the information in that section, you still think that method doesn't really apply to your project. And you're probably right — you know your project, and there's probably a good reason you're leaning towards doing it all live. Let's take a look at some of the most common reasons and see if they help justify your reasoning.

You only get one shot

The best reason to record everything live revolves around situations where layered recording just won't work — you're recording something that only takes place one time, so you need to get everything down while you can. This situation applies most in live events, where everything takes place in front of an audience as part of a show. You can't reproduce moments like these, and any attempt to do so would feel . . . inauthentic ("Mr. Hendrix, could you please try your version of the national anthem again and maybe throw in this ending instead?"). When circumstances dictate live recording like this, you must be ready to record it all as it comes along.

You need to capture live interaction

Electronic music, hip hop, and other genres that use a lot of technology and production lend themselves to record layered tracks. But other genres, like jazz, bluegrass, or improvised music, demand a more live feel. The interaction of the players matters as much as the songs they play, because so much of the recording depends on where those improvised decisions take the song. No version of a song sounds the same as the next. Therefore, you need to record everything at the time it occurs.

You and the players feel more comfortable

The best music comes from confident and comfortable players (including you) who know exactly what they're doing and are ready to play rehearsed material they know well. Or not — maybe the musicians need to feel a little pressure when they record for motivation. Or maybe you need to record in a specific location where layering tracks just won't work. But whatever the situation, live recording may give you the best results when it works best for those involved in the recording.

You make these kind of decisions based on experience, so don't be quick to take on live recording in situations where you're not familiar with the players or the circumstances. Be realistic about what you can accomplish in a live recording situation.

So suppose you've decided to take the plunge and record your tracks live. Congratulations! You've set yourself up to both capture some magic and deal with some additional headaches. The good news is that you're not treading unfamiliar territory — multitrack recording in the field or in the studio is a tried-and-true procedure practiced for decades, and the tools have only gotten easier to use. Pair those new tools (such as your handy iOS device and audio interface) with some tested recording techniques, and you'll be able to put together some fantastic sounding recordings.

Choosing and connecting a multiple-input audio interface

You already know that you're going to record your audio to your iOS device, so the next step involves getting the correct audio interface and making sure it work works with your iOS device. This process involves either making a direct connection to your iOS device or using the camera connector to connect your audio interface with your iPad.

There's a reason we write iPad specifically when talking about the camera connector. Apple only guarantees the connector works with the iPad and not the iPhone (not even the latest and larger iPhone models). Anything is possible, but because we can't say for certain that the connector will work with your iPhone without jailbreaking (and we don't recommend that), it's best to stick with the iPad if you need to use the camera connector. In fact, for live recording in general, it's best to stick to iPads, given the hardware advantages and wider availability of DAW options.

Docks

Docks provide a tailored experience for iPads that connect between two or four audio inputs directly to the iPad, along with a headphone connection and a main volume control. When using a dock, you get both an instantly available connection to your iPad as well as integrated controls packaged into a single piece of equipment. That's an advantage — you know what you're getting and you can count on a usable audio interface. Take a look at the dock in Figure 12-1 as an example of what you can look for while shopping around.

Figure 12-1:
The
Focusrite
iTrack dock.

Docks also provide power for your device while you record, so you don't have to worry about battery life during the recording process. You do need to remain close to a power outlet during the recording, but you'll have to do that when you use any larger audio interface, anyway.

The issue with docks appears in the first sentence of the first paragraph in this section. Even the largest docks only make four inputs available, so you don't get a large number of simultaneous audio tracks to record. Four tracks might work for a small folk group, but a loud rock band with a full drumset will certainly need more than four inputs. You can use a dock to record live audio, but it restricts the kind of live audio recording you can perform.

Manufacturers design docks for specific models, and you may notice that future iOS devices may not work when they get larger or smaller than what the dock allows. Don't count on a dock working with anything except the specified iOS device for which the dock was built.

Audio interface and camera connector

Would it be more appropriate to call the iPad camera connector a USB adapter? More than likely. After all, the camera connector works with more than cameras — you can use it to connect other devices to your iPad, and everything will work just fine. At issue, though, are the types of devices that work with the camera connector. Apple permits only a few audio and MIDI devices to work with the camera connector, and those devices must use a couple of standard protocols. Figure 12-2 displays an audio interface approved for use with the iPad via a camera connector.

Figure 12-2:
The
Focusrite
Scarlett
18i20, a
Core-
Audio– and
class-
compliant
audio
interface.

Core Audio

Apple developed Core Audio to help audio interfaces and software function correctly with iOS and OS X (the operating system for Mac desktop and laptop computers). Luckily, you don't have to get too technical with Core Audio — just check that your audio interface is Core Audio–compliant when you purchase it and you'll be good to go. That compliance indicates that the drivers and software that power your audio interface will work with iOS, although it's best to do your research and to make sure the interface will work with your iOS device and apps.

Class compliance

The other compliance you need to check for is *class compliance.* This compliance indicates that the audio device uses the software present within iOS to function in connection with your iPad. Because you don't normally get the chance to install driver software for external hardware on an iPad, you need to make sure any device you try to use is class compliant. You might be able to skate by with other audio interfaces, but we certainly can't guarantee the success rate for this kind of operation.

On the list

Even if the audio interface shows Core Audio and class compliance, do your research before you buy it. Check the Internet for reviews and complaints about the model you wish to purchase and ensure you don't see any problems coming down the road. Some devices just don't work properly with iPads, and you need to make sure any decisions you make come with the proper amount of background information. Make sure you also check the supported iOS version — some devices might be too new for older iOS versions or not yet have the proper drivers for the newest version.

Powered

Make sure the audio interface you plan on using comes with some kind of external power supply, as recording on the iPad means you'll be using a lot of battery power to make everything run. Without that power supply, you run the risk of watching you iPad go blank right in the middle of a song.

Additional equipment

Because the iPad offers only a single connection, you'll only be able to physically connect your audio interface to your iPad. That limitation isn't a problem for your headphones or monitors, because you listen through your audio interface during recording anyway (otherwise, you might hear latency between the actual audio and the slight delay you'll hear through the iPad). However, if you want to use anything else (like foot controls), you'll need to make that connection through Bluetooth or via MIDI (if your audio interface provides MIDI inputs and outputs).

Making the connection

The actual connection process couldn't be simpler, but the diagram in Figure 12-3 illustrates that process just in case.

After you make the connection, you can test to make sure the audio interface actually works with your iPad:

1. **Plug in the audio interface.**

2. **Turn the audio interface on.**

3. **Open your preferred DAW app.**

4. **Open the settings for your preferred DAW app.**

5. **Check the audio setting and make sure you can see the audio interface you wanted to connect to your iPad, as seen in Figure 12-4.**

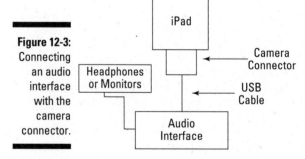

Figure 12-3: Connecting an audio interface with the camera connector.

Figure 12-4:
PreSonus
Capture Duo
displays the
connected
audio
interface
right on the
front page.

If you don't see the audio interface hooked up to your iPad, try any of these different solutions.

✔ Unplug the connection and reseat it.

✔ Turn the audio interface off and back on.

✔ Reboot the iPad (turn it all the way off and back on). You could also perform a hard reboot, where you hold both physical iPad buttons for eight to ten seconds until the reboot occurs.

After you get everything up and running, test to make sure that all of your channels work correctly before you record your final product. Plug in all of your mics, enable Record for all of your channels, press Record, and see what happens. You want to be sure that audio goes to the proper channels without glitches or problems, and that your iPad's audio doesn't stutter or drop out while you're recording. You must be realistic here — even though Auria offers a full 96 tracks of audio when you link two iPads together, you more than likely cannot record 96 tracks of audio at the same time. That's just too much (really, what do you need 96 simultaneous inputs for anyway?). Record some audio you don't care about to be sure everything moves along smoothly, and then you can move on to your most important recordings.

Ensure that you force quit any other apps during recording to keep background functions from interfering with your recording. Unwanted notifications or other processes can really muck up an otherwise beautiful moment. If you record on an iPhone, enable airplane mode to keep unwanted calls or texts from interrupting as well.

Purchasing a headphone amplifier

If you plan on recording multiple performers at the same time, you need to make sure that all of them can hear themselves properly. Each audio interface usually comes with one or two headphone jacks so the person actually recording the audio can hear the tracks being recorded. However, if you have to run headphones for more than yourself, you need to look into a separate headphone amplifier. This device routes the signal from the audio interface to multiple headphones, providing separate volume controls (and maybe even mixes depending on the number of outputs you can route from the audio interface to the headphone amplifier).

You'll want to run an output to the headphone amplifier and not use the headphone jack output, for a couple of reasons:

✔ The headphone jack already runs through an amplifier and could cause unwanted distortion in the signal.

✔ You might need to use that jack for yourself, depending on where you physically place the headphone amp.

Figure 12-5 demonstrates how to hook up the headphone amp to your audio interface.

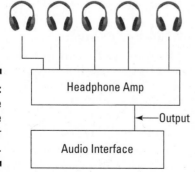

Figure 12-5:
A sample headphone amplifier connection.

If the headphone amplifier accepts multiple outputs from the audio interface (again, depending on the price and feature set), you might be able to provide different mixes from the audio interface to the headphone amp. That way, the drummer could hear more bass, and the pianist could hear less vocals. These setups vary greatly on the hardware you purchase.

When purchasing your headphone amplifier, keep the following things in mind:

✔ You need as many headphone jacks as you have performers.

✔ You need to save money to buy headphones.

✔ You need to also purchase enough cabling to connect the headphone amp and provide extenders to let the headphones go to where they need to be for proper recording.

The good news is that you'll be connecting audio using normal audio cables, so you don't need to worry about compliance issues. Just plug them in and go.

Combating potential leakage

When you're recording multiple tracks at the same time, you're going to deal with audio leakage. Simply put, you can't keep audio signals intended for one mic from going into other mics. It's a fact of life — sound moves through air without regard for direction, and any mic recording audio in the same area will pick up a little bit of everything in the background. But you can take some steps to help reduce that leakage so that when you go mix later, you can raise or lower audio signals without background noise causing problems. For example, you'd like to raise the backing vocals a little, but you can't because the drums come through on that mic as well, and there's no comfortable level that makes everything sound good.

Keep mics as far away from each other as possible

Audio obviously grows quieter as it travels over distance, so putting as much distance between mics just makes sense. Position the performers away from each other as much as possible (without putting them too far apart, obviously — they'll still need to see each other).

Use directional mics

If the mic rejects sound directly behind it or to the sides, use those mics on instruments to keep the signal strong and the background noise to a minimum.

Put the amps in other rooms

If you're using a headphone monitoring system, the players can hear each other just fine. Put the amps in different rooms or enclosures to knock down the background sound and better isolate the audio you need.

Record direct

Bassists usually record to the track using a direct box and not an amp, but you can use this option for guitars or even for electronic drums (if you use them, of course). With all the amp simulators available to you, recording instruments directly helps you lay down tracks without worrying about background sound bleeding into them.

Simply baffling

If you've got the money or the crafty nature to build one yourself, you can make portable sound baffles or barriers that help reduce the sound waves that hit the microphones you use to record. These movable panels help you shield these mics and allow only the audio you want to hear to go through the mic.

If you've ever seen drummers behind a large Plexiglass shield onstage or in the studio, now you know why they used that. The Plexiglass lets the drummers see the rest of the performers while keeping the drums and cymbals from overwhelming other performers in their mics.

Vocal booth

You could always put the vocalist (or soloist, like a trumpet player) in a booth to make sure those important lyrics or melody notes get captured independently. Just make sure the booth sounds okay (not boxy or dead) and that the performers can still interact with each other during the performance.

Overdubs

As a last resort option, you can always try to go back and re-record individual parts after the recording is done. Of course, overdubs are time- and personnel-dependent, but know that quite a few "live" recordings you've heard probably had at least one or two tracks edited (or "punched up") to make them sound better after the initial recording took place. A little studio magic to make things better . . .

Before you start your live recording, rehearse once or twice and make sure the sound you're getting is what you want. You might have to move mics, instruments, amps, or even pieces of furniture to make sure everything sounds okay. Spending a little time before you begin recording makes mixing and mastering later a less frustrating and time-consuming process.

Chapter 13

Getting the Best Recording Quality

• •

In This Chapter

▶ Understanding the basics of digital audio resolution

▶ Keeping your signals clean with plenty of headroom

▶ Practicing proper track management

▶ Making enough room for all of your audio tracks

• •

Audio formats come in so many different files and formats, each with its own specific advantages, disadvantages, advocates, and detractors. Do a little research on a specific type of audio, and you're bound to find a wealth of opinions on both sides of the debate. So how do you sort everything out? Well, you start with some basic principles and work your way out from there.

In this chapter, we establish the basic principles for digital audio that you should keep in mind while recording any audio, and then we delve deeper into your available tools to choose the right ones for the project. It just seems like you're drowning in audio options. Grab on to your audio lifeline, though, and everything will be just fine.

Understanding Audio Settings

We already looked at bit depth and sample rates in Chapter 1. And when you're dealing with your audio recordings, you can choose from a multitude of options. Bit depth can vary from 16-bit to 24-bit, whereas normal sample rates range from 44.1 kHz all the way to 192 kHz.

Now, traditional CD audio quality stands at 16-bit, 44.1 kHz. And that's what your iPhone or iPad headphone jack plays back as well. Finally, the Music app on your iPhone or iPad only handles files using this standard as well.

But you can find other options out there. For example, you could pair a set of HD headphones with an app like the Onkyo HF Player to hear 24-bit, 192 kHz audio on the go. And, of course, you can always listen to HD audio on other devices, from your home computer to your audiophile stereo system.

So with all of these options, what's the best option to choose? Start with the principle of recording at the best level you and your hardware can possibly handle, working your way down from there.

Why 24-bit is better

Theoretically speaking, 24-bit audio allows you to record with more *dynamic range* than 16-bit audio. Dynamic range means the decibel level between the highest audio peak and the lowest audible audio level (before you just hear noise — think the tape hiss of a cassette or something similar). 16-bit audio gives you a decent amount of range (around 93 decibels), but 24-bit audio gives you a much better ranger (around 115 decibels). Think of this as a better, more detailed audio fader on your mixer. Your levels get more room with better dynamic range, and you'll have more headroom (which we talk about in the section later in this chapter called, appropriately enough, "Clearing a little headroom").

24-bit audio also provides more detail in your recordings than 16-bit audio. The greater bit depth allows your recording to capture more information about the audio signal — it's the difference between taking a picture of a sports car versus taking a picture of a late-model crimson Ferrari with all the options. So between the better detail in the recording and the greater dynamic range, 24-bit audio is always the best option when possible. On the flip side, if your iOS device doesn't carry a lot of storage space, 24-bit recordings might take up too much room. Know how much room you need before you begin recording.

Even with the highest possible audio recording, you still need high quality devices on which to listen to your tracks. This step is where the investment in your monitors and headphones pays off.

44.1 kHz, 48 kHz, or Higher?

If you want to get *super* technical, the human ear can only hear certain frequencies. That's why your dog or cat always responds to higher-pitched frequencies that you have no chance of hearing. In order to save storage space and effort, digital audio standards set the frequencies for storage at what human beings are thought to perceive. In the case of CD-quality audio (16-bit, 44.1 kHz), that ceiling tops out around 22 kHz. Any frequencies generated above that level during recording simply aren't captured. For the purposes of that recording, those frequencies don't exist.

The highest frequency you can record is always half of the sample rate, otherwise known as the *Nyquist* frequency. This probably won't be a question on *Jeopardy!*, but it's good to know. As the sample rate goes up, so does the Nyquist frequency.

So if that's the absolute limit of human hearing, then why bother to record any higher? Well, because there's some debate as to the highest level of human hearing. Maybe it's a little higher than 20 kHz, and retaining that information could make a huge difference. Also, the additional detail at higher sample rates makes the audio you can hear more detailed and rich. Sample rate is similar to frame rates for video — the more frames per second you can create, the better the video appears to the human eye.

Audio levels and digital distortion

Whenever you hear a recording engineer or live sound engineer talking about *audio levels,* that person is referring to the general amount of volume for each vocal or instrument in the mix. During a level check, the engineer seeks the optimum volume for that audio source to ensure that it gets heard without overpowering the other tracks or distorting the speakers and sounding awful. So a good soundperson won't just slam all of the faders to the max, throw up some metal horns, and walk off for some beer — he or she pays close attention to the meters (and their ears) and sets the levels to provide the best possible output for the listeners.

Take a look at the Auria mixer shown in Figure 13-1 for a visual representation of audio levels.

Without getting too technical about the numbers next to the mixer (and why they're negative up to zero with very little room above zero), you should know that those numbers represent the amount of voltage (measured in decibel units — we know, it's complicated) used to amplify those sound levels. Your goal is to use those faders to achieve the correct levels for each sound source to make the best mix possible (we talk more about mixing in Chapter 20). In this case, each mixer channel has a meter next to it indicating the level of the track during playback. Because you're mixing in the digital world, you never want that signal to go above 0 dB. At that point, you encounter digital distortion, also known as clipping.

Figure 13-1:
Taking
a look at
audio levels
in Auria.

If you've used analog gear before, you might be comfortable letting the meters peak above 0 dB on occasion for a full, good-sounding signal. But that's the analog world, where a little bit of analog distortion may sound pleasing to the ear. In the digital realm, you get harshness. Unless that's the effect you're going for, best to avoid this particular issue.

The proper way to get good quality audio into your mixer involves *gain staging.* Gain staging involves starting with the highest possible audio level from the equipment you're recording and maintaining that level through any equipment until it gets to the mixer. When talking about iOS equipment, it's fairly easy to achieve proper gain staging. Plug the device into your audio interface, play or sing until you get the proper signal on your audio interface preamp (again, a good strong signal without distortion), then route that audio signal into your recording or audio processing app.

Each preamp and audio interface may use different controls to communicate audio levels back to you, but red usually means too loud, and you're usually given a knob to turn the audio up or down. Typically, play or sing until you see solid green on the knob without seeing red. Turn up until you see slight amounts of red, then turn back down.

When setting these levels, you want to leave some room for quick transient peaks. For example, the initial crack on a snare drum may cause the audio level to peak quickly, but the sound level dies out quickly. Or maybe hitting a loud strum on a guitar during an otherwise placid fingerpicking routine can cause a quick spike in volume. You want to make sure that you get a solid audio signal while still allowing room for the unexpected bursts of high volume.

Most recording apps display meters for peak audio and RMS audio. Peak audio shows the highest possible audio level, whereas RMS audio shows the average level of audio over a given amount of time. You need to use both levels in mixing, but peak audio helps you avoid bursts of audio that can cause distortion.

Your takeaway principle here is that before recording, you need to get the maximum amount of volume on the track without any distortion. That involves getting a good signal from the instrument, the preamp, and any other device in-between you and the recording app. Too low of a signal might allow external noise to creep in, whereas too much signal might result in distortion. And make sure the volume allows for the occasional peak in audio. You'll probably end up turning down the signal a bit from here for the final mix, but it's a good idea to have a strong audio level and work down from there (as opposed to trying to boost bad levels and possibly introducing noise into your mix).

Clearing a little headroom

Remember when we said to leave a little room for peak levels in your tracks when setting your audio levels? You should, because you just read it, but it bears repeating. But leaving a little extra room doesn't just help you avoid distortion and transient audio peaks. It also leaves you a little room for modifications later, like cutting or boosting EQ levels or accounting for additional signal from effects you might want to try during the mixing process. And it gives you a little room for dynamic levels — you let the audio levels come across naturally instead of constant loudness fatiguing your ears.

This *headroom* basically means your audio signal sounds good and natural without slamming into digital distortion. You also allow room when mastering to perform any modifications you need to make without pushing the audio level into clipping. We talk more about mixing, mastering, and exporting in Chapters 20 and 21. Just keep this principle in mind — until you have completely mixed and mastered your track, you need to leave enough headroom to allow for more work. Don't paint yourself into an audio corner.

So what is the optimum audio level to mix to for adequate headroom? It depends — in the analog world, mixers would set their tracks to an average of -6 dB on their mixers, but that was with a great deal of headroom "baked into" their analog mixing consoles. For digital consoles, that "baked in" level doesn't exist, so you need to mix further down. Depending on the app you use (remember, judge both by the meters and your ears), you might want to start out around an average -20dB to -15dB and work from there. That level gives you enough room to work with, make your changes, and then master and export your tracks to a decent audio level.

Managing Your Audio Tracks

The best part of digital recording is that, in most cases, you can keep layering and layering tracks on your recording. Need another shaker track? Slap it in there! Want to try a detuned guitar for a different rhythm? Put it on in and delete it later if you wish. The worst part is that you have to keep . . . track of all of these tracks. We all know that, in the beginning, you're going to keep recording tracks (and then probably deleting them later).

Obviously, every track should have its own name so you can make sure you know exactly what you're dealing with when you record. And you should always save your tracks right after you record to make sure you don't lose any data. But that's just the basics of what you need to do when you lay down tracks. By working a few more principles into your recording workflow, you can make sure that you keep all of your options open and eventually create the best possible recording you can create.

Track notes

Why are we bringing up paper? This is the digital age! Well, you don't *have* to use paper for the track notes, as you could switch over to a notes app or write a Google doc with the notes. But the important concept here is that you should write down what you record on what tracks each time you record, and maybe include any specific settings you change as you go. For example, you could write an entry like "11/5/2014 — recorded bass to track 4, set EQ at 100 kHz to -2 dB." You could also look up "tracking sheets" via the Internet (using your search method of choice) to see what the pros use. Whatever method you choose, make sure your notes include the following information:

- ✔ Name of the song
- ✔ Filename of the project you record your tracks into

✔ Your name

✔ The name of any musicians involved (even if it's just you)

✔ The time and date you made the recording

✔ Spaces for each track, including track numbers and what you recorded per track

It may take a little more time, but it helps you down the road when you try to figure out which tracks belong where and which songs you want to work with.

Using incremental saving can save you from disaster

So every time you make a change in your recording, you save the track. That's great news — that way, you'll never lose the most recent track changes you made. Now, suppose you want to go back to a previous version of the song you recorded a few days ago, because the track just seemed a little better before you changed up the guitar track? If you've just been saving to the same version of the project, you may not be able to backtrack to the previous versions and work from there.

A good way to manage your track saving involves saving in *increments* — that is, saving different versions for each day or every time you make modifications. For example, you record a song with the project name MyNewAwesomeTrack. You could continue to save the project under the same name, but again, that doesn't help you if you want to backtrack and start from a previous save point. To ensure that you can always go back, utilize the Save As functionality, as shown in the Korg Gadget screenshot in Figure 13-2.

Instead of automatically saving the file to the same project, use Save As to change the project name to MyNewAwesomeTrack11052014. This name allows you to identify the project as your new awesome track, but it also allows you to know when you recorded the track, and you can go back to that separate project later if you wish. Couple that naming convention with your well-kept track notes, and you're ready to navigate your project version quickly and easily.

Making safety copies

Making *safety* (backup) copies may seem like a huge hassle. You make a copy of the file regularly, and you may even run an automatic backup like Time Machine. So you're covered, right?

Figure 13-2:
Save As in
the Korg
Gadget app.

Before digital technology, recording engineers had to physically create analog tape backups for every recording. No matter what you have to do to make backups, it's probably easier than dealing with a heavily edited multi-track tape with multiple edits and a bunch of nervous, nervous musicians.

Nope, sorry. That's incorrect, and you may lose your music recordings.

So much trauma can occur to your iOS device. You can lose it, you can break it, you can drown it — any one of these accidents or incidents means everything on that device is gone. Services like iCloud, Dropbox, and Google Drive may help, but cloud storage may still go out of service or accidentally lose your files. Cloud developers are humans, too, and you can never beat human error.

So how do you make sure your files remain safe and sound?

Redundancy

Multiple copies of a file mean that even if one source goes down, you still have another copy somewhere else. When one source goes down, another source still has the information you need. So how many copies do you need?

You probably only have so much storage space, so you can't just keep making copy after copy. Plus, if you just put the copy on the same location as the original file, you're not really backing anything up. If that location goes away, you've lost the original AND the not-so-effective backup.

The 3-2-1 rule

You probably see this rule applied more for sensitive computer data, but in this case, your music *is* sensitive computer data. The 3-2-1 rule outlines the minimum effective backup strategy for your music:

- ✔ 3 separate copies
- ✔ 2 different formats (such as iOS device storage and a separate flash drive)
- ✔ 1 offsite location (meaning somewhere away from home, such as cloud storage)

Take a look at Figure 13-3 for a visual representation of the 3-2-1 rule.

Note that the flash drive represents a separate format than the iOS device, and the cloud service counts as an offsite source that you could access in case you lose both the flash drive and the iOS device.

You can also use an external hard drive as a form of backup if you can move the files to the drive from iTunes. Just remember to choose an SSD drive instead of a normal hard drive when possible — fewer moving parts and quicker data transfer means better backup.

Multiple cloud services also act as valid backup sources, because they aren't likely to go down at the same time. However, if you lose network access for any reason, no cloud storage solution will help out. If you do a lot of work outside of network range, cloud storage may not present the best solution for you.

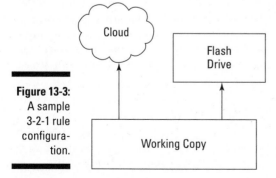

Figure 13-3:
A sample 3-2-1 rule configuration.

Cloud

Flash Drive

Working Copy

Storage constraints and the size of audio files

Considering the number of backups you need and the ever-increasing possibilities of improving audio resolution, audio file sizes continually increase. Wonder why the amount of storage iOS devices increases (beyond the improving technology, of course)? It's because we need them — better programs and better quality audio require a little more room to operate.

Audio file size

When you record audio, you record in uncompressed files to ensure that you work with all of the data you record. Those uncompressed files sound great, but they do take up quite a bit of room:

✔ A minute of 16-bit, 44.1 kHz mono audio takes up a little over 5MB of storage of space.

✔ A minute of 16-bit, 44.1 kHz stereo audio takes up a little over 10.5MB of storage of space.

✔ A minute of 24-bit, 96 kHz mono audio takes up a little over 17MB of storage of space.

✔ A minute of 24-bit, 96 kHz stereo audio takes up a little over 34.5MB of storage of space.

Start multiplying the multiple mono or stereo tracks within a project, and you can see the storage size soaring ever upwards.

How do you manage these large projects? And what happens with your iOS device when you fill up all the memory? Follow some strategies below to free up the space you need.

Back up off of your device

You can probably get away with keeping only the files you're working on your device to free up some space. For the projects you completed, you can move the files off to another source. For example, GarageBand lets you export your projects to your computer through iTunes. You can do so by following these steps:

1. **In GarageBand, tap My Songs.**

2. **Tap Select.**

3. **Tap the Export icon.**

4. **Select GarageBand.**

5. **Sync your device to your computer.**

6. **Save the file from your iTunes to your computer (and then to wherever else you need to store it).**

Plenty of other apps offer export options like this, especially those apps that pair with other computer-based apps (such as Cubasis and GarageBand).

Use the cloud when possible

If you save the files to your cloud drives (and those drives are accessible from the app, like Dropbox), you can make enough room on your device to store the audio. Watch your Dropbox storage limit, but otherwise you should be good. And use WiFi to make your cloud transfers to avoid eating up your cellular data plan.

Buy the largest storage you can

This strategy hurts your wallet, but if you plan on recording a great deal of recorded audio, you might as well get the most possible storage on your iOS device. 128GB doesn't represent a ton of storage for recording audio (where recording studios regularly deal with terabytes of data), but it gives you a good start.

Never rely on compressed audio formats for storage, and never delete your project files. You should always keep uncompressed (AIFF or WAV) copies of your final product and create compressed files from those copies. Otherwise, you risk losing resolution with your songs. And if you delete your project files, you can't go back in and remix or alter your recordings. You're forever stuck with the mix you last saved. And although you eventually must put your project behind you, keeping the raw materials around can help you in the future.

Chapter 14

Recording in the Field

· ·

In This Chapter

▶ Choosing the appropriate recording app

▶ Evaluating stereo microphones

▶ Maximizing the audio quality of your recording

▶ Correctly deploying your microphone

· ·

*Y*ou can't always break music down into component tracks and mix them to your heart's content, whether in the studio or on location. Sometimes, you only get one chance to make a recording, and you must make that recording using your iOS device and a single mic. The process of recording becomes really simple at that point — just aim your mic the correct way and tap Record. Everything that leads up to that point determines whether you correctly record the performance or not.

In this chapter, we take a look at the apps you need to make a proper field recording, as well as the equipment you need, and how to position your microphone to get the best results. Find a place next to the soundboard and get going!

If you're recording your own performance, feel free to breeze right by this warning. If you're recording random soundscapes for your own productions, you can move on as well. But if you're recording a performance involving music that you do not own the copyright for, be absolutely sure that you secure the permission of the artist or artists before you even *think* of trying to record. Most artists who allow this type of recording make their permission known publicly, but others do not permit this type of recording for a variety of reasons (including not wanting to have the material spread for free over the Internet or wanting you to experience the show with your own eyes and ears and not through the filter of your iPhone). Please be respectful of the wishes of the performers when it comes to recording.

Surveying Field Recording Apps

The first step to putting together quality field recordings involves choosing the correct app. Field recording apps differ from DAWs in that they don't concentrate on virtual instruments or multi-track recording. You lay down your audio in stereo tracks, usually at a pretty high resolution (depending on the kind of mic you invest in — more in that in the section "Deciding on Stereo Mics" later in this chapter). Some apps just record the audio files, whereas others provide audio editing functionality and other features. Take a look at the following five apps for a better idea of what field recording apps have to offer.

RØDE Rec

RØDE makes high quality mics first and foremost, so the apps they offer probably act more as accessories to their smartphone-based mics than as standalone recording apps. That said, RØDE Rec (and the free-and-less-functional counterpart RØDE Rec LE) offers some solid features:

- ✔ Up to 24-bit, 96 kHz audio (with their proprietary mic, of course)
- ✔ In-app audio editing and looping
- ✔ Built-in EQ, dynamics, and normalization
- ✔ Export to several different sources in many lossless and lossy formats

RØDE Rec allows you to get to the recording easily. Just follow these steps:

1. **Open the RØDE Rec app.**

2. **Tap the + icon at the bottom of your screen.**

3. **Tap Record and watch the waveform (as shown in Figure 14-1).**

4. **Tap Record again to stop the recording.**

You can tap Record to bring in more audio, or you can tap Play to listen back. Tap and hold the waveform to *scrub* the audio (listen as you move the waveform back and forth to hear the exact spot where you want to make an edit).

How and where you edit your audio depends on what you record, but RØDE Rec provides the tools you need to accomplish your task.

Figure 14-1:
Recording in
RØDE Rec.

Zoom HandyRecorder

Zoom also provides their app as a companion to their iOS mic, but they offer a full version for free. The app opens right into the record screen so you can get to work, as seen in Figure 14-2.

Just tap the Record button to start your audio recording, and tap Stop to stop it. Very simple. Zoom also offers in-app EQ, reverb, and mastering effects along with audio scrubbing, but not in-app audio editing. After you're done recording, you can send the file via email or share it to your SoundCloud account.

If you're going to record audio for an extended period of time, tap the lock icon on the Zoom app. This prevents you from accidentally stopping or pausing the recording before you want to.

If you use this app in conjunction with Zoom's mic, you can use the mid-side stereo recording technique to manually work with the stereo field, such as widening or narrowing the field to your taste. Check out the "Deciding on Stereo Mics" section, later in this chapter, for more information.

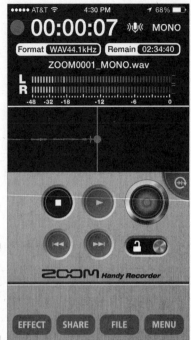

Figure 14-2:
Recording
in Zoom
Handy-
Recorder.

Tascam PCM Recorder MKII

This app provides very similar functionality to the Zoom app — a clean interface with easily recognizable controls. And like the Zoom app, it opens ready to go on the main control screen, as shown in Figure 14-3.

The scrub functionality doesn't show a waveform like the RØDE and Zoom apps, but you can still move your finger along the bar shown below the meters to review the file. The Tascam app also offers a lock button similar to the Zoom app. However, you don't get the ability to record in audio above 16-bit, 44.1 kHz resolution, and Tascam does not offer an iOS-dedicated microphone at the time of this writing. Still, you can't really argue with free.

Hindenburg Field Recorder

The full app costs almost $30 and positions itself as a professional tool for journalists and broadcasters. This app represents itself as the mobile version for a desktop app, but you can do just about everything you need within the app itself. The app opens into the main record screen, as shown in Figure 14-4.

Figure 14-3:
Recording
in Tascam
PCM
Recorder
MKII.

Just tap the Record button to start the recording, but don't expect the recording to stop when you tap the button again. In this case, tapping the button adds a marker to the recording but allows the overall recording process to continue. Markers identify a significant point in the audio file, such as the beginning of a song. To pause the recording, you must slide your finger over the switch at the bottom. From there, you can restart the recording when you wish or move to another file. Hindenburg only records at 16-bit, 44.1 kHz resolution as well, which makes sense when you consider that the main purpose of this app involves recording audio interviews. However, the robust audio editing capabilities of this app make it a very versatile tool for field recording.

If you want to give Hindenburg a try before you purchase it, download the free version of the app and see what you think. You might find it worth the effort to audition the app before you shell out full price.

Voice memos

The iPhone comes with a built-in app to record audio (shown in Figure 14-5), although the app works best as a quick way to record notes to yourself as opposed to a fully functional recording app.

Figure 14-4:
Recording in
Hindenburg
Field
Recorder.

Tap the Record button to start and stop recording, and tap the Crop icon to trim or delete the file. We mention this app as a possible last resort for quick jobs, but don't count on it being a full-featured recording app.

Plenty of fish in the sea

You'll encounter a great many recording apps in the App Store, but this overview should give you an idea of the features you should look for when choosing your app:

- ✔ Superior audio quality (above and beyond 16-bit, 44.1 kHz if possible)
- ✔ In-app audio editing capabilities
- ✔ Recording in WAV or AIFF files with the option to compress after the recording completes

Figure 14-5:
Recording
with the
built-in
Voice
Memos app.

Deciding on Stereo Mics

Field recording implies that you're moving around, possibly without access to a power source for an extended period of time. Therefore, the mics we talk about in this section connect directly to the data connector of your iOS device (either 30-pin or Lightning connector). You can purchase mics that connect directly to the headphone jack of your iOS device, of course, but these mics cannot provide the same audio quality that the data connector microphones can.

Some mics, like the Blue Spark, connect to the iOS device via a Lightning or 30-pin connector via a cable and not directly to the iOS device. This cable can make a difference if you need to hold the device and listen to the audio while you're placing the mic in a different location. Otherwise, the microphones discussed in this section attach directly to the iOS device.

Stereo condenser

The stereo condenser faces the audio source and records in stereo. Most microphones of this type, such as the Blue Mikey, can rotate on a base to better face the audio while you view your iOS device screen.

XY mic

This microphone, such as the one manufactured by RØDE, actually looks like two microphones pointed in different directions at a 90-degree angle to each other. Recording engineers use the X-Y pattern to record in stereo all the time, and this technique comes built in with the device.

Mid-side

Some microphones, like the Zoom iQ5, use the mid-side stereo recording technique to record audio. This technique uses one mic to record the main audio signal and another mic to capture audio to the sides of that main audio signal. This technique allows you to customize the width of the stereo field to suit your tastes, from a close focus to more spacious stereo field. The mid-side recording technique also guarantees that if (for some reason) you need to listen to the file in mono, you'll be able to hear everything with correct levels and clarity. This feature might not make much of a difference for people who listen on headphones or decent audio systems, but it could help if you're trying to ensure that everything can be heard without *phase* issues. With phase issues, sound waves from the same source arriving at different times may cause cancellation of some frequencies, resulting in hollow or similarly bad-sounding audio. Mid-side recording helps you avoid some of these issues.

Recording with the Best Possible Audio Quality

Remember that recording engineers and amateur tapers alike have captured many magic moments using technology that, although considered state-of-the-art at the time, would not merit a second look from today's audiophiles. You can make great recordings with great technology, but you need to know a little (or more than a little) technique to get your technology into the right place. The advice in this section helps you get your iOS device prepared for the best possible audio you can achieve.

Highest possible audio resolution

Remember that you always want to start with the highest possible audio resolution you have available and work down from that original recording for compression purposes. Go with 24-bit in any case, and work with the highest possible sample rate (probably around 96 kHz) you can while still leaving enough room on your iOS device to actually store all of the audio. You might need to clear some space by deleting some apps or extraneous files before the recording begins, but the results are worth it.

Maximize the signal-to-noise ratio

Field recordings must contend with several possible disruptions, from random environment noises like wind or falling rain to the loud drunk who *just won't be quiet* during the quiet parts of the recording. Whatever the unwanted sounds are, your goal is to find the spot as far away from those sounds as possible while still getting a clean signal from what you are trying to record.

How do you accomplish this task? Put on the headphones, start recording, and start moving around. Keep the microphone pointed at the source you're trying to record (if possible, maybe during a soundcheck or something) and move around until you find the perfect spot. Most cases are obvious (man, that's a loud generator!), but a little footwork here and there can be quite helpful.

Setting up close to the source

Remember that sound levels dissipate the farther they travel from the source. Also, certain frequencies tend to carry farther that others. That's why when you walk away from a show, you more than likely hear the low bass and the reverberations of the vocals or lead instrument. The low bass frequencies tend to spread over a long distance in all directions, and the lead vocals or instrument tend to have the most power behind them. If you set up where that's all you can hear, that's all you're going to get.

That said, you also don't want to set up too close to the stage. Why, you ask? That's pretty close to the source, and the title of the section talks about setting up close to the source! Well, getting too close to the stage isn't the source of the audio. The PA speakers are the source in most cases, and even if you're at a place that doesn't use a PA, certain frequencies take a little room to develop as well.

If you're recording an unamplified source (one without a PA), try to get within a few feet of the performer, but not too close to them. For example, if you're too close to a singer in a beautiful church, you may miss some of the wonderful natural reverb that church provides. Find a spot that works best, close but not too close, and you'll be ready to go.

If you record different locations (at the stage and at the soundboard, for instance), those locations will have audio slightly out-of-sync (since sound arrives at different locations at different times). You might need to do a little work after the recording to sync everything up.

If the mic includes a windscreen, go ahead and use it. This simple accessory prevents the sound of wind blowing across the mics from ruining your recordings.

For amplified sources, the best location is actually very close to the soundboard. Think about it — the person determining how the performers sound stands at the soundboard and makes decisions of what to raise and lower to make the overall sound the best it can be. Getting close to that location gives you the proper balance and sound levels to capture the entire performance without requiring too much work after you complete the recording.

A line recording from the soundboard may provide a clean sound for the instruments, but it might not give you the best possible sound of the live event. Sound engineers use the soundboard and PA to amplify the sound, but they also use it to reinforce elements of the performance that might not carry as well. Therefore, the soundboard may over-emphasize those elements over other parts of the performance. A good stereo mic picks up the crowd noise and other extraneous elements, but it also covers the entire spectrum of the performance at the sound levels set by the sound engineer. Note that larger venues will put more signal through the soundboard and get a more complete version of the performance, though. Try to get both signals, if possible.

Proper Mic Techniques

Your ultimate goal to successful field recording involves getting your microphone in the correct position to capture everything you need. The actual stereo recording type of the mics in this chapter are predetermined by the device you choose to use. This section focuses on getting your mic in the right place to record the audio.

Center up

Point the mic directly at the center of the audio source you want to record. Especially for stereo microphones, you want to make sure the center of the mic points at the center of the audio source to make sure the stereo field shows up properly in the recording.

You also want to make sure that you center yourself up when you point the mic at the audio source. If you're over to the far right and point the mic from there, the right side of the field will dominate the rest of the recording. This may not matter too much if you're next to an extraordinarily loud PA speaker, which drowns everything out anyway. But for stereo recording, you need to be as close to the center of the listening environment as possible.

The Stereo Mic Tools by Engineered Stuff app provides some information on where to set up stereo mics, and you can set the app to match the mic configuration you use. You can even use the bombsight function to view the live scene and tell you where to set the microphone. The app doesn't evaluate the actual sound levels for you, but it does give you information that can guide you to the proper microphone placement.

Raise it up

If you've been to certain types of concerts, you may notice some extended poles raised high above the soundboard. These poles hold mics and recording devices at a higher level than the audience. This practice serves a few different purposes:

- ✔ It puts the microphone at the same level as the audio source (remember, most shows put bands up on raised stages, and the drums might even be on a higher riser).
- ✔ It keeps the microphone away from people who might bump, touch, or otherwise disrupt the microphone.
- ✔ It keeps the mic away from the drunk *who won't stop talking.*

In the case of this chapter, that means putting your device up on a pole as well — nobody ever said good recording wouldn't involve a little risk. That said, plenty of strong mounts and rotating microphones can help you get the best possible recording.

Don't put your device up too high — you risk the safety of your equipment, and you won't be able to interact with the device if necessary. Be careful that you also don't block anybody's sight lines. Let everybody enjoy the show.

Keep it stable

For whatever mount you use, make sure the device and the microphone stay in place without moving around. Especially when dealing with stereo microphones, moving the microphone around causes problems with the stereo field.

Watch your levels

As always, make sure that your audio levels don't peak or distort during the recording. It's best to leave a little room to ensure that peaks don't cause problems with the recording. Test in a sound check if possible, and *ride the fader* (adjust the gain on the microphone during the first recording) if not possible. You might not be able to catch everything, but finding the best possible level and leaving a little headroom gives you good results.

Always charge your iOS device fully before any taping, and put the device in airplane mode to avoid unwanted interruption during the taping.

Part V
Using Multiple Apps Together

In this part . . .

- ✒ Take audio and transfer it back and forth between your apps, just like text in a word processor.

- ✒ Use Inter-App Audio to bring one app into another and connect instruments, effects, and other audio into one single audio chain.

- ✒ Use Audiobus to make connections between all compatible apps on your iPhone or iPad.

- ✒ Work with other audio connection possibilities as part of your creative process.

Chapter 15

Working with Multiple Apps Together

In This Chapter

▶ Running audio apps in the background

▶ Moving audio from one app to another

▶ Managing audio tracks using AudioCopy

*Y*our iPhone or iPad may look like it's only running one app at a time, but that point of view hides what's really going on in the background. At any moment, your apps may be working in the background, taking in additional data or monitoring your location to provide assistance when you call on the app again. Or, in the case of audio, you could be playing several different audio apps at the same time. You can work with an app in the foreground, but apps can also function in the background.

This chapter takes a look at how you can use multiple audio apps at the same time using background audio. You also see how you can take the audio generated by one device and move it to another via the AudioCopy app. Don't limit yourself to just one app at a time — make the most of what your iOS device can do!

Using Background Audio

We guarantee you've already used background audio before. Even if you never enabled a specific setting in your iPhone or iPad allowing background audio to function, this feature makes it possible for you to listen to your Music app (or any other app that lets you listen to music) while you check your email, update your social media, browse the Internet, or do one of the thousands of other things you do with your iOS device. Background audio provides the soundtrack without disrupting your other activities.

Enabling background audio

Background audio comes enabled automatically for the Music app, but other apps require a little more effort to get it working (if the developers allow for background audio at all, that is — some apps can't perform this task). For example, take a look at the steps to enable the background audio function in Figure:

1. **Tap Settings.**

2. **Scroll until you see the settings entry for the Figure app.**

3. **Tap Figure.**

4. **Scroll until you see the Background Audio switch.**

5. **Move the switch to On (as shown in Figure 15-1).**

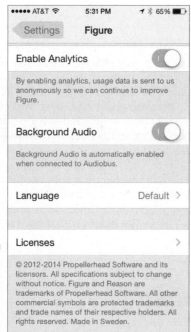

Figure 15-1:
Enabling
background
audio in
Figure.

When you enable this feature, you can start playback in Figure, then move on to other apps and do something else. You must go back into the app to stop or change the audio, but the actual playback continues until you tell it to stop.

Background audio also makes some special adjustments in the case of apps that record audio, like Loopy HD. Notice the red bar at the top of the screen indicating both the name of the app and the activity it currently performs, as shown in Figure 15-2.

So how many audio apps can you run in the background at one time? Theoretically, you don't really encounter a limit. While writing this paragraph, we looped some audio through Loopy HD, then started a song in Figure, and wrapped it all up by opening GarageBand and playing some keys. What results did we come up with? A glorious, cacophonous mess. But you can load several different apps using background audio and make whatever noise you need. Older devices, iOS versions, and apps may struggle a bit with a lot of apps, so be sure to test and evaluate before you take it to the stage. Now let's take a look at some more practical uses for multiple background audio apps at the same time.

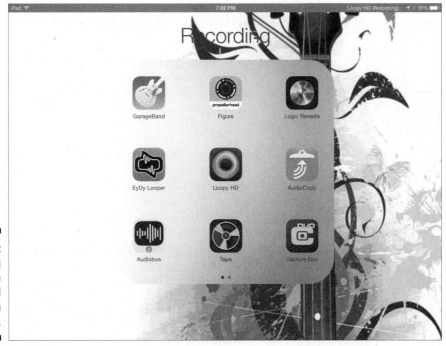

Figure 15-2:
Recording
in the
background
with
Loopy HD.

Rehearsal

Guitar or bass players can turn an iOS device into a valuable tool for learning and reinforcing songs to add to a set list by following these steps:

1. **Plug your instrument into your audio interface.**

2. **Plug your audio interface into your iOS device.**

3. **Start your amp simulator of choice.**

4. **Back out of your amp simulator and load up a track you want to learn in the Music app.**

5. **Start playback in the Music app, then play along.**

You can make sure you hear both the track and your playing as well by modifying the volume sliders on either the amp simulator or the Music app. Use the physical volume switch on the iOS device to control the overall volume of both apps.

From that basic setup, you switch to your PDF or ebook reader to look at sheet music or a chord chart for that song. And for those using virtual instruments, just replace the amp simulator with the synth app of your choice.

 Keep the app you need to interact with the most in the foreground, so that you don't constantly have to switch back and forth between apps during your rehearsal time. Your attention should be on your instrument, not your iOS device.

 If your audio app goes silent when you put it in the background, check the settings for the app and make sure you enabled background audio for that app.

Playover

Features like Inter-App Audio and Audiobus (discussed in Chapters 16 and 17, respectively) allow you to route audio through different apps, but you don't need to use those apps to layer the sound from one app over another. Simply start playback in one app (like a drum machine app), then switch to another app and begin working with that app. You don't get the functionality of being able to record the overall audio product or make use of any effects, but you do get things moving. And sometimes, saving time gets you where you need to be.

Working with non-Audiobus-compatible apps

Not every audio app you might want to work with will use Inter-App Audio or Audiobus. But if you want to work with these apps, you can enable background audio and have them play in the background. This scenario depends on using apps that can use background audio, of course, but this functionality is an integral part of iOS app development and should be easily available for you.

Copying and Pasting Audio between Apps

You probably see copy and paste associated more with word processing than with audio. But why limit perfectly good functionality to simple words? When you work with audio on your iOS device, you can take audio you record from one app and move it seamlessly to another audio app using integrated iOS functionality and the benefits of the AudioCopy app.

Moving audio between apps

The simplest operation for AudioCopy involves taking audio recorded in one app and moving it to another. You don't actually open the AudioCopy app to do this — the functionality comes integrated within the apps themselves. Let's take a look at moving audio from the Korg iMS-20 app to Loopy HD.

First, take audio recorded into the iMS-20 app and tap AudioCopy to copy it, as shown in Figure 15-3.

Now switch over to the Loopy HD app and hold down the center of one of the loops until you see the menu displayed in Figure 15-4.

You'll see several options in the side menu that opens in Loopy HD, but you want to choose the top option of General Pasteboard, as shown in Figure 15-5. The General Pasteboard isn't part of the AudioCopy app, but you're using AudioCopy technology to move the audio from one app to another.

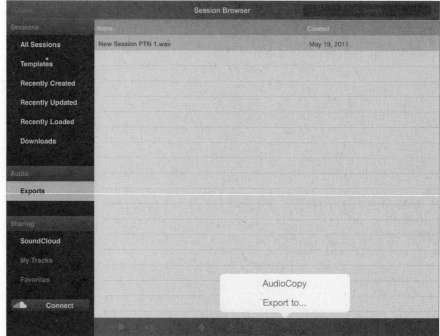

Figure 15-3:
Using
AudioCopy
to get audio
out of the
Korg
iMS-20.

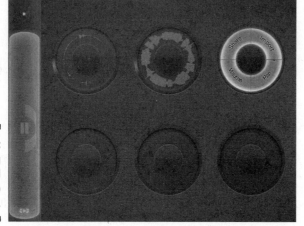

Figure 15-4:
Importing
copied
audio into
Loopy HD.

The copied audio appears in the loop, queued up and ready to go.

The methods of copying and pasting audio from one app to another will depend on the apps, of course, and the behavior of these apps will differ. For example, the Korg iMS-20 app can only produce audio for copying — it cannot import audio from other sources. Loopy HD, meanwhile, can both import and export audio. This example gives you the basic idea about moving audio between apps, though. The controls may change slightly, but the general workflow stays the same.

Record Audio into AudioCopy

The AudioCopy app itself lets you record audio directly into the app for later use elsewhere. And the controls couldn't be easier. Just open the app and tap the Record button in the upper-right corner of the app to see the screen shown in Figure 15-6.

After you record the audio, a file named by the time and date of the recording appears in the My Recordings section of the AudioCopy app, as shown in Figure 15-7.

Editing copied audio

Once you record your audio, you can do some additional work to get it ready for use in another app. Tap your new recording and then tap the Edit icon to pull up the edit screen for the recording. When you tap the waveform for the recording, you'll see a blue field that shows the start and end points for the audio you wish to work with, as shown in Figure 15-8.

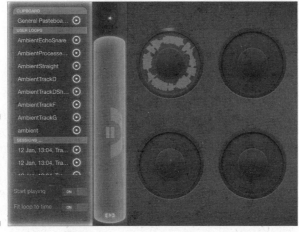

Figure 15-5:
General
Pasteboard
equals
AudioCopy
in this case.

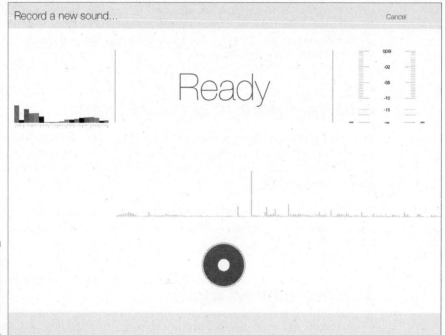

Figure 15-6:
Recording audio directly into AudioCopy.

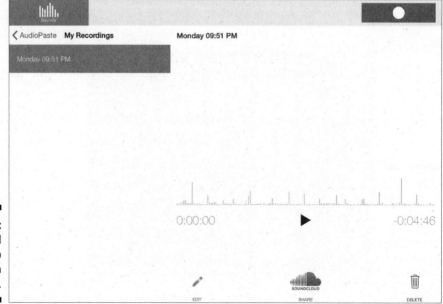

Figure 15-7:
Your brand new audio recording in AudioCopy.

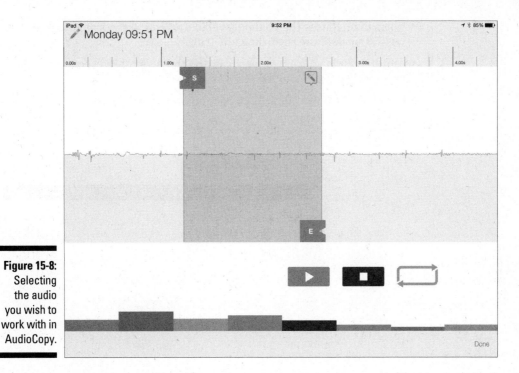

Figure 15-8:
Selecting
the audio
you wish to
work with in
AudioCopy.

Move the points to wherever you want on the audio recording — you can highlight the entire file or a small section. And once you decide on your chosen audio, tap the pencil icon in the upper-right section of the highlighted audio to pull up the menu shown in Figure 15-9.

We talk more about audio editing in Chapter 19, but take a look at the tools AudioCopy offers when you get to the editing process:

- ✔ **Cut:** Removes the audio from its current location for use elsewhere.

- ✔ **Copy:** Copies the audio for use elsewhere.

- ✔ **Duplicate:** Adds a copy of the highlighted audio directly after the location of that highlighted audio.

- ✔ **Delete:** Removes the audio from its current location.

- ✔ **Discard Ends:** Removes the audio from either side of the highlighted section.

- ✔ **Fade In:** Lowers the audio at the beginning of the highlighted section to zero and gradually fade it up to full volume.

- ✔ **Fade Out:** Gradually fades the audio at the end of the highlighted section to zero.

✔ **Normalize:** Raises the volume level of the overall recording so that the highest peak of the recording hits 0 dB.

✔ **Amplify:** Slide your finger vertically on the highlighted section to raise or lower the volume of the recording.

✔ **Reverse:** Plays the highlighted section backwards.

For a free app, AudioCopy offers a ton of useful audio-editing functionality.

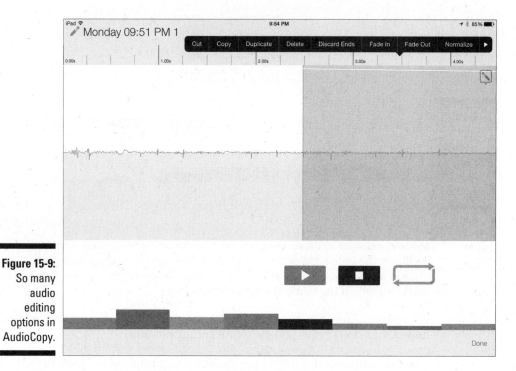

Figure 15-9:
So many audio editing options in AudioCopy.

Pasting audio from AudioCopy

Once you record audio from the AudioCopy app, that file becomes available from AudioCopy for all compatible apps. You can also import audio through the iTunes application on your computer by following these steps:

1. **Connect your iPad to your computer.**

2. **Open iTunes on your computer.**

3. **Click the iPhone or iPad icon at the top of iTunes to access your device.**

4. **Click Apps.**

5. **Scroll down until you see the File Sharing screen (if you have a lot of apps, this might take a few seconds).**

6. **Select AudioCopy.**

7. **Drag the audio file from your computer over to the File Sharing screen, as shown in Figure 15-10.**

8. **Sync your iPhone or iPad with your computer.**

   After the sync finishes, you'll see your file in the AudioCopy app, as shown in Figure 15-11.

Figure 15-10:
Moving
audio files
from your
computer to
AudioCopy.

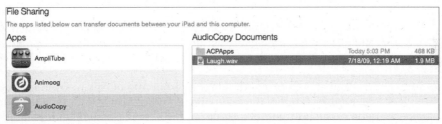

Figure 15-11:
The trans-
ferred audio
file, living
in its new
residence
on your iOS
device.

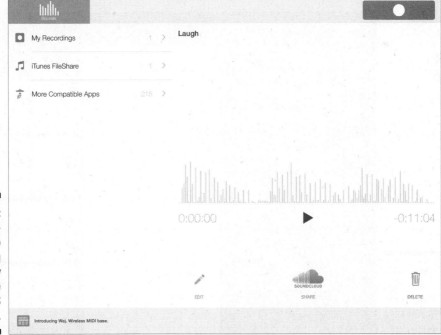

When you complete the transfer process, you can move audio from the AudioCopy app using other compatible apps. For example, you can load the audio as a sample within Retronyms Tabletop (we talk more about Tabletop in Chapter 18) by following these steps:

1. **Open Tabletop.**

2. **Add a Gridlok touchpad sampler to your session.**

3. **Tap the pad to which you wish to add the sample.**

4. **Tap Load under the Pad Controls heading.**

5. **Tap AudioPaste.**

6. **Select the sample, as shown in Figure 15-12.**

After you add the sample, you can manipulate it using the controls on Gridlok and other effects available within Tabletop (seriously, read Chapter 18 for some good information).

You can also export audio directly from AudioCopy to your SoundCloud account by tapping the audio file in AudioCopy and tapping the SoundCloud icon in the bottom-right corner of the screen (logging in to your account if you haven't done so already).

Figure 15-12:
Adding a sample in Tabletop via AudioCopy.

Chapter 16

Using Inter-App Audio

In This Chapter

▶ Learning the basics of Inter-App Audio

▶ Setting up nodes and hosts within Inter-App Audio

▶ Understanding how apps work with Inter-App Audio

*A*ll of the apps on your iPhone or iPad exist as separate entities and probably make great sounds all on their own. But musicians never satisfy themselves with a single instrument or a pre-packaged sound arrangement. Why would they give us all of those knobs and switches and keys if we weren't supposed to play with them? In "real life," you can always patch together different sounds and effects to get the sound you want (or make a hellacious racket, whichever you choose). Why not do that in iOS as well?

In this chapter, we take a look at how Inter-app Audio works and how you can configure it for your own uses. The functionality may differ from app to app, but the net results are the same — you make the apps you want work together to realize what you want to play.

Understanding How Inter-App Audio Works

Apple offers Inter-App Audio (IAA for short) to app developers as a way of routing sound from one app to another. Apps exist in the iOS world independent of each other, and up until a few years ago, there was no easy way for audio apps to play with each other. Audiobus came along in 2012 as a standalone app to help route audio from one app to another (and we talk about Audiobus more in Chapter 17), but it wasn't until Apple released iOS 7 that audio routing functionality became part of the core workings of an iOS device.

That last paragraph should tip you off that you need to run either iOS 7 or iOS 8 to make use of Inter-App Audio. If you're still on iOS 6 for some reason (such as an older device that won't upgrade or a specific version of an app that you need to stick with), use the Audiobus functionality (and upgrade when possible).

Though the App Store holds many, many different types of apps, IAA recognizes only two kinds of apps based on their functionality:

✔ Nodes

✔ Hosts

Every IAA-recognizable app sorts out into one of these two categories. Even if an app can act as either node or a host, it can only act in one of those roles at a time. However, apps can include multiple nodes, depending on how the app developer implements IAA.

Nodes

Nodes provide either audio input or process audio via IAA to a host app. Most times, nodes include synth instruments that generate sound (think Animoog, Thor, or one of the other synth apps we've looked at up to this point) and effects apps that modify sound provided by another app in some way (such as effects plug-ins or the effects provided by an amp simulator).

Each node sorts out as one of the four following types:

✔ **Generator:** This type sends audio to the host app, but does not accept MIDI or note information. The generator type basically starts and stops audio at the same time as the rest of the host app.

✔ **Instrument:** This type accepts MIDI commands from and sends audio to the host app.

✔ **Effect:** This type accepts incoming audio and returns it to the host app.

✔ **Music Effect:** This type accepts incoming MIDI commands and audio and returns audio to the host app.

Although an app can act as more than one type overall, it can only act as one type at a time.

Take a look at the instrument node apps available to GarageBand (a host app) in Figure 16-1.

You can patch any one of these apps into GarageBand as its own track. For instance, patch Thor in to GarageBand and use that app as the synth source for a pad in your new track. Thor then stands by the drum loops and real audio you recorded into the song via GarageBand and comes together in your song.

So why does Loopy HD appear so many times in Figure 16-1, even if there's only one instance of the app on your iPad? The Loopy HD development team created the app to provide several different audio outputs, including the main stereo out and individual loop outputs. For example, you could just patch in a specific instrument or vocal loop to the host app for recording. This app demonstrates a perfect example of how different app developers implement IAA.

You can also patch in some effects if you wish, as seen in Figure 16-2.

In this case, you can patch an effect in between the instrument node and the host node. Depending on the effect you choose, this patch could involve a virtual pedalboard from AmpliTube or JamUp, or maybe an experimental granular processing app like GrainProc. Your setup all depends on what your host node permits.

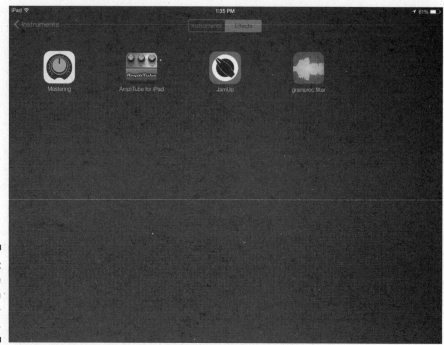

Figure 16-2:
Effect node
apps within
Garage-
Band.

Hosts

Speaking of *hosts,* let's take a look at the other part of the IAA relationship. Hosts receive the audio processing of the nodes and usually record that output as part of a larger project. That is why GarageBand makes an appearance in this chapter — Apple developed IAA, after all, and it makes sense to have a DAW act as a host for IAA. That said, plenty of other apps can act as host apps (like the Cubasis and Auria apps we look at in Chapter 10).

Check the app listing on the App Store before you buy it to see whether it works with IAA. Although Apple provided IAA as a standard, each app must implement it on its own. Unless that app specifically supports IAA, you won't see it show up in a host as usable.

Creating an Inter-App Audio Session

Let's create a sample track in GarageBand using IAA to provide a synth and a little love from additional effects. The steps below take place within Garage-Band, which allows a node for the original audio and a node for the effects.

First, open your GarageBand project and scroll through the Instruments list until you see the Inter-App Audio Apps choice shown in Figure 16-3.

Tap the icon and you see a screen similar to the one shown in Figure 16-1. Let's pick Nanologue, an interesting synth app with enough controls to satisfy your tweaking urges (also, it's free). When you tap the icon for Nanologue, your iOS device immediately shows the interface for that app, which you're probably familiar with already. What you might not have seen earlier is the small Inter-App Audio menu that lies dead-center in the app, as shown in Figure 16-4.

Pull down on that menu tab to see the fully expanded menu in Figure 16-5.

This menu lets you control the following actions, from left to right:

✔ Rewind the project to the beginning.

✔ Play the project.

✔ Record new audio to the project.

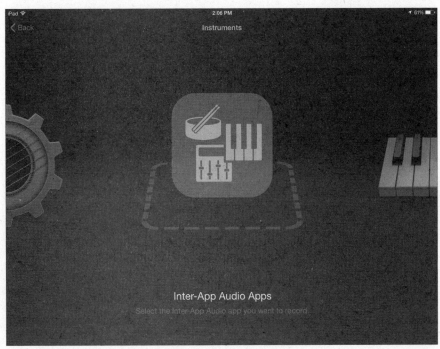

Figure 16-3:
Initiating
Inter-App
Audio
within
GarageBand
(without any
hazing).

Figure 16-4:
Inter-App
Audio within
Nanologue.

Figure 16-5:
The Inter-
App Audio
menu.

You can also review the following information:

✔ The current time position of the recording

✔ The BPM of the project

Every IAA implementation looks a little different. Work with your individual apps and check out the documentation to understand what's possible with your specific features.

Tap the GarageBand icon to go back into GarageBand. Now tap the guitar cable icon next to the Nanologue icon to see the menu in Figure 16-6.

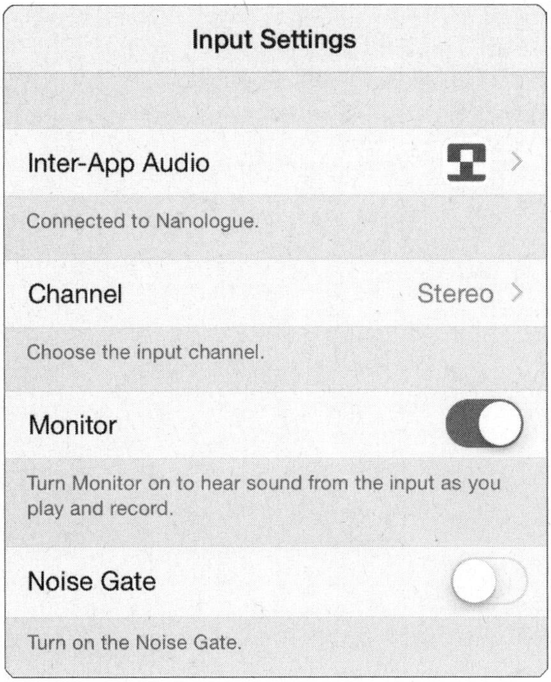

Input Settings

Inter-App Audio   >

Connected to Nanologue.

Channel   Stereo >

Choose the input channel.

Monitor

Turn Monitor on to hear sound from the input as you play and record.

Noise Gate

Turn on the Noise Gate.

Figure 16-6: Inter-App Audio settings in Garage-Band.

Make sure the settings appear correct for the app you record. In this case, we're okay with the stereo track and being able to monitor the audio as we play and record. We'll leave the Noise Gate off because we're recording directly from a virtual synth, but we'd probably turn it on if we were recording a live audio source, such as a guitar on a high gain setting where the app generated a lot of noise when not actually receiving a guitar signal. Tap the Nanologue icon to go back to that app when you complete your settings.

Controlling the host from a node

Let's get to work!

Tap the Record button and play a few notes into your project. Note that you can play the app and record the audio directly into GarageBand without switching back and forth. You can even swipe up on the menu to minimize the controls for optimum playing room. When you're done, hit Stop (GarageBand also stops recording after you hit the limit of the loop size).

Finally, you can tap the GarageBand icon to go back to that app, as seen in Figure 16-7.

Figure 16-7:
Inter-App
Audio in
Garage-
Band,
post-
recording.

Everything sounds OK at this point, but we'd like to add another effect to our recording. The "Chipmunk" effect provided by GarageBand in Figure 16-7 doesn't really fulfill our needs right now, so tap the guitar cable icon again. From the menu shown in Figure 16-6, tap the arrow next to the Nanologue icon to see the menu shown in Figure 16-8.

Tap the arrow next to Effect, then tap the effect you wish to insert. Tap anywhere else on the screen (besides the menu) to go back to the screen shown in Figure 16-9.

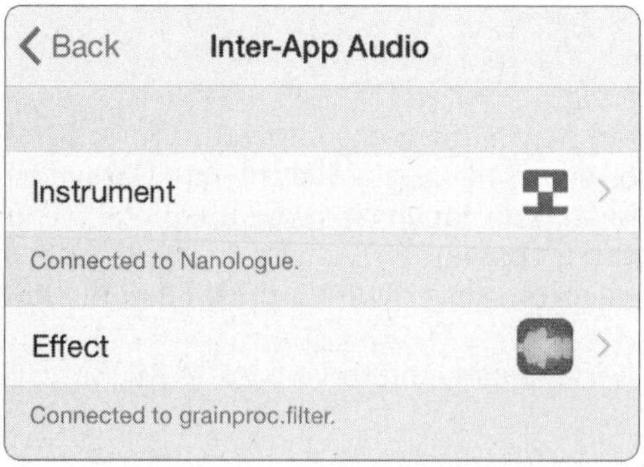

Figure 16-8:
Inserting an
Inter-App
Audio effect
in Garage-
Band.

‹ Back   Inter-App Audio

Instrument ⧉ ›

Connected to Nanologue.

Effect ▣ ›

Connected to grainproc.filter.

Figure 16-9:
Your
inserted
effect, ready
to go!

Set your effect to the settings you wish to use. Depending on how the effects handle IAA, you may see controls to return you to GarageBand. You may just have to tap the button on your iPad and tap GarageBand to get back to your virtual instrument. Either way, get back to GarageBand and listen back to your recording. Switch back to your node apps as many times as necessary to get the sound you want (nobody said everything would sound amazing on the first try — you'll probably need to tweak something every time). Keep going until you're done.

How different apps implement Inter-App Audio (differently)

IAA represents a standard and not an actual app. Therefore, the IAA controls in every node and host won't necessarily appear the same in every instance. For example, as shown in the earlier screenshots, Nanologue provides a set of controls in a pull-down menu for use with GarageBand when recording. AmpliTube provides a similar set of controls, but those controls appear in a different location than on Nanologue. And Tabletop (which we discuss in

Chapter 18) provides a couple of devices (Mastermind and Zignal) which permit MIDI and audio communication between IAA and your chosen apps. However, other apps (like Animoog at the time of this writing) don't provide additional controls when you wire them up using IAA.

Again, IAA represents a standard for developers to use when putting their apps together. This standard provides the framework for developers, but it doesn't put limits or specific recommendations on how they present IAA using their apps. So the burden rests on your shoulders to test each app to see how it functions as part of an IAA and decide if that functionality meets your needs.

That behind-the-scenes IAA functionality does permit low-latency audio transmission between apps, so the functionality is very valuable. And you can implement several different chains of IAA within hosts (depending on the host, of course), so you can use the host to include all kinds of sounds and effects in your projects.

If you've used plug-ins in desktop DAWs before (such as VSTs or Apple's AUs), you're familiar with the concepts of IAA already. Same type of functionality, just a different name and protocol.

Test your host apps by chaining in a large number of different apps via IAA. When you notice any issues like static, stuttering, or errors, back off of that number and make a note of the maximum number of IAA connections you can make. The number varies on the type of apps and the version of your iOS device, but you should be able to fit in a few apps before things start bogging down. You can also try lowering the frame rate in the host app or lowering the audio resolution from 24-bit to 16-bit.

Chapter 17

Using Audiobus

*T*he real world doesn't prevent audio devices from working together. You can take an instrument, run it through multiple effects devices, then output that audio to the recording console, amplifier, or PA of your choice. You can even run multiple instruments through that same effects chain by taking a mixer or some other signal splitter at the beginning of your chain. So why not reproduce that ability on your iPhone or iPad?

This chapter details the Audiobus app (on version 2 at the time) and everything you can do with it. Think of Audiobus as the virtual cabling you need to route your audio signal wherever you want it to go. You can even save your configurations for easy recall later. Try doing that with all of your physical cables and devices.

Audiobus 2 relies on iOS 7 and iOS 8 to function correctly. iOS 6 can use an earlier version of Audiobus, but most of the functionality outlined in this chapter won't be available on your iOS device.

Audiobus compatibility doesn't automatically equal Audiobus 2 compatibility. Check with the app developer and download new app versions as available.

Understanding the Basic Audiobus Structure

First, you must put the Audiobus app on your iOS device ($4.99 at the time of this writing, along with an in-app purchase of multiple audio streams for an additional $4.99 — we talk about that functionality more in the "Setting Up an Audiobus Session" section of this chapter). Tap the app after you download it to view the screen shown in Figure 17-1.

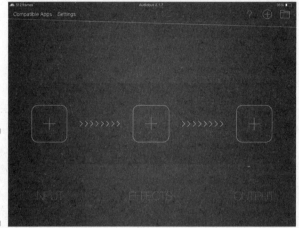

Figure 17-1:
The opening Audiobus screen in all of its glory.

On its own, the Audiobus app can't produce any sound whatsoever. What it *can* do is provide a framework for you to route audio from inside or outside your iOS device through multiple apps. Like Inter-App Audio (discussed in Chapter 16), Audiobus sees all compatible apps as a certain type of app. However, Audiobus recognizes three types of apps because it can't act as a host app itself.

Inputs

Input apps create the original sound to be routed through Audiobus. This category includes all of the usual suspects:

- ✔ Synthesizers
- ✔ Virtual instruments

✔ Drum machines

✔ Virtually everything else that makes a noise

All of the available input apps show up when you tap the plus sign above Inputs. Audiobus won't accidentally allow you to put the wrong app in the wrong location.

Effects

Effects apps take the audio from the input app (or apps) and process it, just like rackmounted effects or guitar pedals in the real world.

✔ Reverb

✔ Delay

✔ Compressor/limiter

✔ Pitch correction

✔ Granular processing

✔ Any other sort of sound processing and/or mangling

Note that, depending on the functionality of the input app, you might see the same app show up as both an input and an effects app. Don't worry about putting the same app in both locations, though. You can use all of the effects within an app in the input section and then use an additional effects app in the effects section.

Outputs

Output apps take the audio from the input and effect apps and act as the final stage of processing.

✔ Audio recorders

✔ DAWs

✔ Loopers

✔ Any other app that acts as the final repository for your audio signal

Again, you may notice apps showing up in both the output slot and another location. The setup just depends on what functionality you want to use where.

Place the app in the slot where the functionality you want to use would be best utilized. For example, the AmpliTube app can appear as an input, effects, or output app. If you're routing a guitar through your iPad for recording, place the AmpliTupe app as the input, put any additional effects in the effects slot, then put your recorder in the output slot. If you want to use the AmpliTube effects on a synth, place it in the effects slot with the synth in the input slot. Finally, if you want to use the recorder functionality in the AmpliTube app, place it in the output slot.

How Audiobus Differs from Inter-App Audio

Audiobus and Inter-App Audio both route audio from one app to the next, but they perform that function in two very different manners. As explained in Chapter 16, the IAA standard uses the standard provided by Apple in iOS to send audio from a node to a host. No app stands between that node and the host, but the manner of implementation depends on the app developers.

The Audiobus app also requires some implementation from app developers, but the app itself actually manages the audio transfer (as opposed to the iOS operating system). The visual representation of these apps lets you decide how you route that audio, and you can set up multiple connections in the same setting (as opposed to just creating a node-to-host connection).

Because the audio on your iOS device must go through at least one additional app (the Audiobus app) plus any other effects apps you place in your signal chain, you should expect a little latency in your performance and playback activities (although Audiobus recently integrated IAA functionality and reduced that latency). However, Audiobus allows you a little control over that latency within the settings (we discuss those settings in the "Setting Up an Audiobus Session" section, later in this chapter), so you can minimize the effects of the Audiobus app as much as possible. And, given the fact that you can set up more complex audio routing schemes and save those settings for instant recall, the latency may seem like a small price to pay for you.

Ultimately, there's a reason GarageBand remains compatible with both Audiobus and IAA — more versatility remains key to proper implementation of audio apps. Both Audiobus and IAA present attractive options for musicians, and you should be able to rely on the audio capabilities of both. Most apps offer both types of functionality, anyway, and more apps will fall in line as time goes on.

Finding Audiobus-Compatible Apps

Of course, you can always comb through the App Store or search over the Internet for apps that bill themselves as Audiobus-compatible. Or you can just use the app itself. When you open the Audiobus app (as seen in Figure 17-1), just tap the Compatible Apps link to view everything that you can use within Audiobus. Figure 17-2 displays the many, many options you can download for your own use.

Audiobus provides a full list of apps, but it also breaks those apps out by inputs, effects, and outputs. You can tap the App Store link next to each app to go to the App Store (network connection permitting, of course), and any app with a YouTube link features a video showing how the app operates. However, you also need to pay attention to two labels below the description of the app:

- ✔ **iOS 8 Ready:** You can use the app with iOS 8. Of course, most apps should be ready for iOS 8 by the time you read this, but this label remains important for those who just bought a new device or made the upgrade.

- ✔ **Supports State Saving:** This label indicates that you can save the connections and app settings within Audiobus for instant recall whenever you need. Because state saving requires additional developer effort, not all apps support this feature. But be sure that you check for this label for optimum Audiobus usage.

Figure 17-2: Just a sampling of the Audiobus-compatible apps you need to catch up with.

If you're looking for a specific name or type of app, type your search information in the provided field. You can also tap Subscribe to put yourself on the mailing list Audiobus developers provide to notify users about new app availability.

Check on the Audiobus Twitter feed for new developments as well. Just remember to use the `@AudiobusApp` handle.

Setting Up an Audiobus Session

The Audiobus interface lays out the signal path pretty well, but you need to make sure your settings are correct before you get started. Start your setup by tapping Settings to see the screen in Figure 17-3.

Start with your Audiobus app at 256 *frames* (number of samples you record per channel of audio). This measurement can seem a little complicated, but just know that the higher frame rate gives you more latency, and lower frame rate gives you less latency with the potential of causing your device to slow down or stutter. This potential increases as you add more devices to your Audiobus chain. So start at the recommended setting and alter as necessary.

You can also close unnecessary apps and lower the frame rate during recording, then raise the frame rate during mixing and mastering. Real-time functionality isn't as important when you're not recording, so you can give yourself a little more room then.

Figure 17-3:
Changing
settings in
Audiobus.

You can leave the Feedback Warnings switch alone if you wish — this setting just alerts you to conditions where you could experience feedback during operation. Trust me, you'll know when it occurs anyway.

And you only need to enable Measurement Mode if you want to better the audio quality you record through audio interfaces connected to the headphone jack. If you connect to your iOS device through the data jack (as you probably should), this setting makes no difference to you. Check the Input Gain slider as well. This slider indicates the level of audio you start with when recording audio through Audiobus. Start with the slider at about 75% and see if you experience any large amount of distortion. If your signal sounds okay and not puny or distorted, you're good to go. Slide it up to cure low signal with noise, and slide it down to reduce distortion. And, if you're not recording audio through the input, just leave it alone. Tap Done when you're finished.

Your first Audiobus session

Now that you have a firm grasp on your Audiobus settings, you can make some serious noise! Start by tapping the Inputs plus icon to see the list of available apps, as shown in Figure 17-4.

If you want to select the mic input for your iOS device, tap the System Audio Input icon. But hey, look — it's our old friend Bebot! Let's get started there by tapping the Bebot icon. You see the screen in Figure 17-5.

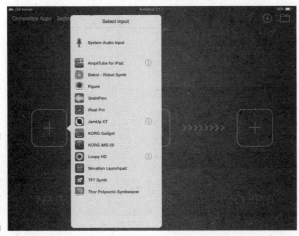

Figure 17-4:
Available
input
apps for
Audiobus.

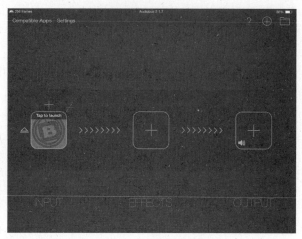

Figure 17-5:
Bebot taking
a nap before
starting in
Audiobus.

Tap the Bebot icon to wake the app up and get started. Audiobus automatically starts the app, shows you the screen, then goes back to Audiobus. Tap the Bebot icon again to return to the Bebot app. Everything looks the same, but a small menu appears at the left of the screen, as shown in Figure 17-6.

Play around with the Bebot app, and you'll notice that everything sounds the same. But you can tap the Audiobus controls to see the screen shown in Figure 17-7 and make some changes.

Figure 17-6:
Audiobus
controls in
the Bebot
app.

Figure 17-7:
Expanding
the
Audiobus
controls in
the Bebot
app.

The arrow control returns you to the Audiobus app, and the plus sign on the folder saves any preset changes you made to the Bebot app as part of the Audiobus state (we talk about state saving in the "Saving Audiobus presets" section later in this chapter). For now, return to the Audiobus app.

Tap the Effects plus sign to view the available effects apps, as shown in Figure 17-8.

These apps process the signal coming from Bebot, and you can add as many effects as you wish. Let's start with the JamUp XT app. Tap it, then tap the sleeping icon to wake up the JamUp XT app. We have sound to make — no sleeping allowed!

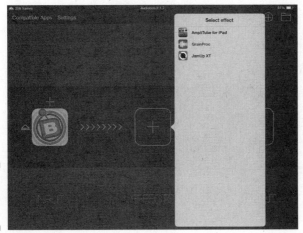

Figure 17-8:
Effects apps
in Audiobus.

Note that if you navigate to one of the apps now, you'll see an expanded Audiobus toolbar, as shown in Figure 17-9.

Tap any of the app icons to open the options for that app. Move around, change settings, whatever you need to do.

JamUp XT provides a separate Audiobus icon for quick movement — this implementation depends on developers who create the apps, but you'll always see the regular toolbar. Experiment with your apps to see which controls are available and which ones work best for you.

Navigate back to the Audiobus app and put in another effect. We already used a guitar amp simulator, so let's try the granular processing app now. Tap the plus sign above the JamUp XT app and select GrainProc. That app now appears after the guitar amp simulator, meaning the signal first goes to JamUp XT and then GrainProc. Take a look at Figure 17-10 to see how that shows up in Audiobus.

The order of your effects apps does make a difference — guitarists spend hours and hours putting pedals in different order to see how it affects their sound (putting a wah after distortion, placing delay or reverb towards the end of the chain). The audio signal changes with every effect, so feel free to experiment with the order to get the best possible signal for your use. But the usual signal chain follows the following order:

1. EQ and frequency effects

2. Gain or volume effects (like distortion or overdrive)

3. Modulation effects (like flangers, phasers, delay, reverb, and similar devices)

Figure 17-9:
Multiple apps in the Audiobus app.

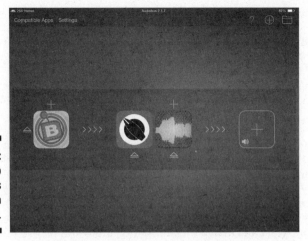

Figure 17-10:
Lining up
the effects
apps in
Audiobus.

You can add as many effects apps as your processor can tolerate. Newer devices, like the iPad Air 2, can handle more than the original iPad, for example.

After you have your effects in place, you can select the output app. Tap the Output plus sign to view the available options shown in Figure 17-11.

If you want to route the audio directly to the iOS device speaker, tap the System Audio Output icon. But we want to route the audio to something that will record the audio output, so tap the Loopy HD app.

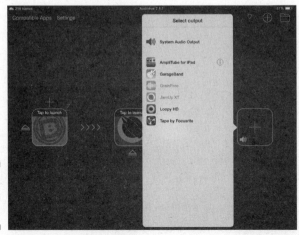

Figure 17-11:
Output apps
in Audiobus.

Any already-used app appears as grayed out in the menu, because you can't reuse an app multiple times in the same Audiobus session. Unless, of course, that apps offers multiple outs, like a DAW or Loopy HD. Check your app availability before you get down to business.

Now, if you navigate back to Bebot and view the Loopy HD controls in the Audiobus toolbar, you'll see that you have a few more options, as shown in Figure 17-12.

The Play button starts the Loopy HD playback, then changes to the Pause button that allows you to pause and return to the beginning of the loop cycle. Tap the Record button to record new audio from Bebot through the effects apps to a new loop in Loopy HD. Finally, tap the icon below the Record button to determine the number of bars included in the new loop you record. The loop plays at the same tempo as the other loops in the current Loopy HD session, but you can change the amount of audio you record per loop.

Obviously, this functionality changes greatly depending on the apps you use in Audiobus, but this session gives you the general idea of how to set up an Audiobus session.

Saving Audiobus presets

After you get your session set up correctly, save it for future use. Tap the folder icon in the top-right corner, then tap the plus sign/folder icon to see the screen shown in Figure 17-13.

Figure 17-12:
Controlling
Loopy HD
from the
Bebot
app with
Audiobus.

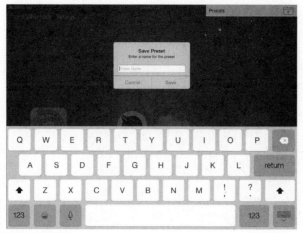

Figure 17-13:
Saving
Presets in
Audiobus.

Enter the name you wish to use and tap Save. Now, whenever you want to recall that session, just open up Audiobus and tap the folder icon to view your saved presets. Tap the one you want, and you're ready to go.

If apps in the preset support state saving, Audiobus can recall the settings on the app itself as part of the preset. That functionality goes a long way to making sure you get the right sound right out of the box every time. Otherwise, you need to adjust the settings for each app every time that you open the preset.

Check the state saving option for apps when you make your purchase to ensure they'll work as you expect later on.

Using Multiple Input Apps

Our current audio set up routes a lead instrument (Bebot's theremin) through the effects apps and into Loopy HD for the end recording product. But suppose we want to give a little backbeat for Bebot's musical stylings. Luckily, Audiobus lets you route multiple inputs through the same effects chain.

Tap the plus sign above the Bebot app and you'll see the list of input apps again. Let's pick Novation Launchpad for the looped beats it can provide, as seen in Figure 17-14.

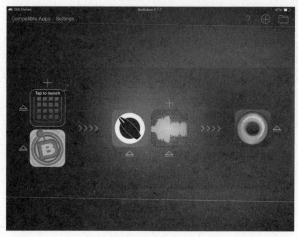

Figure 17-14:
Adding
Novation
Launchpad
to the
Audiobus
signal chain.

Tap the Novation Launchpad app and wake it up — you're ready to go. The addition of Launchpad helps out with the beat, but suppose you also want to add some additional keys to the mix. Tap the plus sign again and pick the Korg iMS-20 for some retro analog synth sounds. Wake it up and you'll see the screen shown in Figure 17-15.

Note that every input app you bring in goes through the same effects apps and records on the same track as the others. You can switch between all of the apps to play different parts, but they receive the same processing.

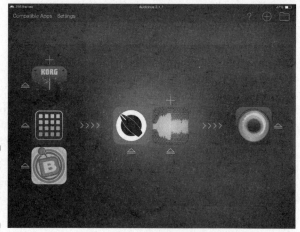

Figure 17-15:
Bringing in
the Korg
iMS-20 app.

Multiple audio streams

The situation in the preceding section could work for recording situations or certain live performances, but you probably want to separate input sources into different effects streams. Some effects like reverb help tie a recording together, but more extreme effects like distortion or phasing may overwhelm an entire recording. You may want to apply different amounts of distortion and compression to guitar than to drums, or you may only want to add delay to the vocals and not the rest of the song (an entire delayed song might make some listeners seasick, after all).

You have to pay the $4.99 in-app purchase, but that Multi-Routing in-app purchase gives you the ability to create multiple audio streams with different inputs, effects, and outputs. Tap the plus sign in the upper-right corner of the screen to fire up a different signal chain. In this case, you want to move the Launchpad app into its own chain to keep it out of the effects used on Bebot. Here's how to move everything over:

1. **Tap the eject icon next to Launchpad and the iMS-20 app.**

2. **Tap the plus sign in the upper-right corner of the screen to create a new signal chain.**

3. **Tap the plus sign for Inputs in the new signal chain and select Launchpad.**

4. **Tap the plus sign for Outputs in the new signal chain and select Loopy HD.**

5. **Wake up both apps by tapping them and coming back to Audiobus.**

After you complete those steps, you see the screen shown in Figure 17-16.

But wait — didn't we also have some keys? Sure did, so let's bring those back. Create another audio stream, add the iMS-20 app and another Loopy HD output, and you see the screen shown in Figure 17-17.

Theoretically, you could continue to create as many streams as you like, but your processor and memory will likely bog down if you add too many more streams. But you should still be able to see the possibilities here — you can create as many virtual signal chains as you and your iOS device can handle. This setup helps you solve several musical challenges, including the following:

✔ Separate signal chains for a guitar and rhythm tracks for live performances into a looper

✔ Different effects for instruments recorded into a DAW

- ✔ Adding effects to certain instruments that could not otherwise produce those effects on their own

- ✔ Using the same effects on different input devices to provide a more balanced sound (such as the aforementioned reverb example)

- ✔ Save and recall complex audio changes with a few taps

Because Audiobus allows you to customize your creations so much, you face only the limits of your imagination (and your credit card's ability to pay for the apps you want to use).

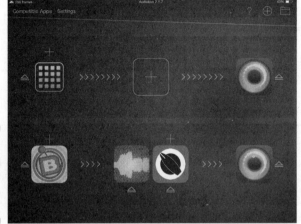

Figure 17-16:
Multiple
audio
streams in
Audiobus.

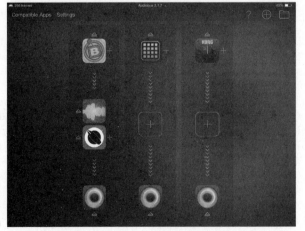

Figure 17-17:
Even
more mul-
tiple audio
streams in
Audiobus.

Staying in Sync

Audiobus not only allows you to route audio from input apps to output apps, but it also gives you some control over all of the devices from the side control bar. When you're recording parts to a DAW, you can switch over to the instrument you're recording and start the recording process from there. Depending on the MIDI functionality of the apps, you can even sync the input and the output apps for recording (to help start and stop loops at the correct times). Let's take a look at a couple of examples.

Recording audio into a DAW

For this example, we're going to put the Thor synthesizer app as the input app and GarageBand as the output app. Switch over to the Thor app and expand the control bar shown in Figure 17-18.

Tap the Record button and play your part on the Thor synth. When you're done, you can tap the Record button again to stop. Switch over to GarageBand, and you see the audio recorded from Thor (as shown in Figure 17-19).

Notice also that we put a track of Nanologue in there as well. You can use Audiobus to record multiple streams of audio into a single DAW with no issue.

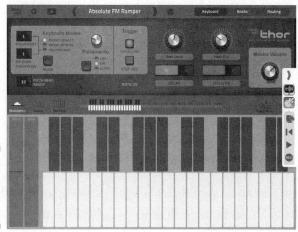

Figure 17-18: Recording Thor into GarageBand.

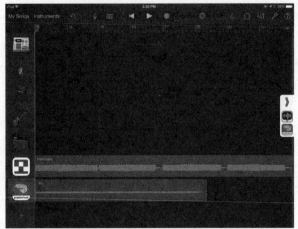

Figure 17-19:
Thor's
input in
GarageBand.

Recording loops into a DAW

The preceding process provides a straightforward solution for recording live parts, but what if you want to record parts from a drum machine or similar loop-based app? Again, Audiobus does a good job of routing audio, but you may need to do a little work to get loops to work correctly. This functionality depends on the apps you use to perform your recording — you're looking for the ability to handle MIDI clock and sync here. Check out sites provided by developers for blogs and videos that might help you out.

For this example, let's put the Korg Gadget into the input app and Loopy HD into the output. Follow the steps below to sync up your apps:

1. **Start up both apps, then go into Loopy HD.**

2. **Expand the sidebar in Loopy HD.**

3. **Scroll to the Tempo setting and set the tempo you want to loop at.**

4. **Tap Settings.**

5. **Tap MIDI.**

6. **Scroll down until you see the Clock Outputs section shown in Figure 17-20.**

7. **Tap Gadget and make sure the checkbox shows up next to the name.**

8. **Tap the Gadget icon in the Audiobus control bar and return to the Gadget app.**

9. **Tap the Loopy HD icon to show the controls.**

10. **Tap Record under the Loopy HD icon to start the recording. Gadget starts playing and Loopy HD records the audio to a loop.**

11. **When the loop stops recording, you can switch to another pattern and record that, or just close the Audiobus and Gadget apps and be done with it.**

Notice that if you leave Gadget and Loopy HD playing at the same time, you hear a slightly phased tone to the app? Because there's a slight delay in the original and the looped audio, you're hearing that delay expressed as that slight phasing. Turn off Audiobus and play the loop in Loopy HD by itself, and you'll be just fine. Remember that there's always a slight latency between the original audio source and anything recording in Audiobus because the audio had to go through another app.

Now, please remember that syncing varies wildly from app to app, so this process won't necessarily work for every audio app you encounter. The important thing to remember is that you need to set an app as the clock master to sync other apps to that single timing source. Without that sync functionality, you'll be at the mercy of tapping the control and hoping you hit it at the right time.

Figure 17-20:
Clock
outputs for
Loopy HD.

Chapter 18

Other Multi-App Possibilities

Audiobus and Inter-App Audio may provide the most powerful and versatile methods to get your musical apps working together, but you have a few other options as well. These methods may carry a few more limitations or work with fewer apps, but maybe you'll find them to be just the solution you were looking for.

This chapter focuses on solutions that involve third-party apps, multiple iOS devices, and a handy music app called Tabletop that ties together multiple musical sources in a single location. Keep reading and learn more ways you can play with musical apps on your iOS device.

Using Virtual MIDI

OK, so technically everything you do on your iPhone or iPad is "virtual" — because you aren't using any physical hardware beyond the iOS device, the software does everything in the virtual realm. And MIDI isn't really "real," because it's just the messages that devices exchange to control which events take place and when they occur. But Virtual MIDI uses CoreMIDI (the iOS service built into iOS) that basically allows synthesizers, drum machines, and sequencers to communicate with each other without needing another app to do all of the work. All you need are the apps that work together — and a little willingness to muck about in the settings for those apps.

How apps use Virtual MIDI depends on the imagination and resourcefulness of the developers who make the app. It all depends on what features they implement. This section demonstrates some common functionality using common apps, but your reality will depend on the apps you use.

Linking apps

Let's pair up a drum machine and a synth to handle the bass line for some backing tracks (or just to make some people dance, depending on what kind of party it is). Both Funkbox and Thor offers some solid Virtual MIDI integration, so this example shows you how to take those apps and make Virtual MIDI magic happen.

First, open up the Thor app and select a good bass preset. Tap the keyboard and see if you like the sound — tweak the controls until you've got something you're good with.

Now, open the Funkbox app and tap the Settings button. If the MIDI switch isn't already in the On position, make sure you switch it over to see the screen in Figure 18-1.

For now, leave all of the settings as they are, unless the Bass MIDI Sequence button is off. Make sure you tap that button and the red light next to that button comes on.

Next, tap the MIDI Routing tab to see the screen shown in Figure 18-2.

Notice how Thor shows up under the CoreMIDI Outputs section. In this case, Virtual MIDI uses CoreMIDI (the basic MIDI functionality integrated into iOS) to transmit the MIDI messages.

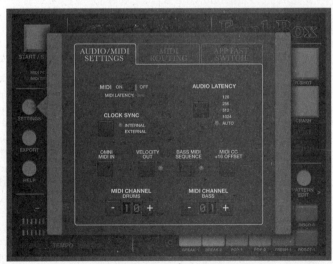

Figure 18-1:
Audio/MIDI settings in Funkbox.

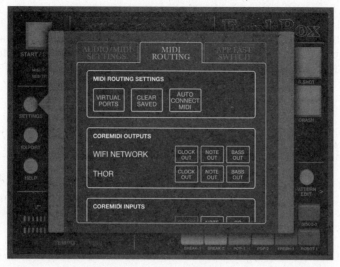

Figure 18-2:
The MIDI
Routing tab
in Funkbox.

Navigate back to the Thor app (trying not to exhaust yourself with all of this switching between apps) and tap the gear icon. Select the Source button under the MIDI heading and choose Funkbox from the listed options. When you tap Back, you should see the screen shown in Figure 18-3.

All of the steps basically put Thor at the command of Funkbox, with the synth accepting *note* (the pitch of the note) and *gate* (when the note actually plays) commands from the drum machine.

Figure 18-3:
The MIDI
menu in
Thor.

Go back to the Funkbox app and tap Start/Stop to hear the results. You should hear a funky drum loop backed by a bass line coming from the Thor app. The programmed beat from Funkbox determines the notes played by Thor, and Funkbox doesn't really provide a full-featured interface for actual notes. Instead, Thor receives the notes that match up with the notes used to trigger the Funkbox notes. It doesn't sound bad, but it doesn't give you the control you might want.

Adding a sequencer

A *MIDI sequencer* acts as the master control for all apps that accept incoming MIDI signals. Basically, the sequencer manages the song and passes along commands to all the apps listening for those commands. Bossy little app, isn't it?

The advantage of using a MIDI sequencer involves sending standard commands to all the apps and triggering them from a single source, rather than trying to decide which app controls the others and how. Every parameter about the song originates from the sequencer, and you can make any adjustment necessary from that location.

For this example, we use a fairly full-featured MIDI sequencer called Genome (available for around $13 from the App Store at the time of this writing). You can find other (both more expensive and less expensive) MIDI sequencers in the App Store, tailored both to live performance and to programmed sequences. Genome falls into the latter category, and we use it here for a couple of reasons:

✔ The aforementioned fairly full functionality of MIDI controls, including the ability to lay out loops and patterns

✔ A good linear, visual representation of the MIDI sequence

✔ A track-based representation of the 16 available MIDI channels

We should mention at this point that MIDI transmits information on 16 channels — no more, no less. The MIDI specification allows for 16 channels as a standard, so you can count on that no matter which MIDI sequencer or app you use. So with our Thor and Funkbox apps already open, open Genome to view the screen in Figure 18-4.

First, let's set up a pattern for Funkbox on MIDI channel 10. Why channel 10? The MIDI standard for drums and associated percussion uses channel 10. You could use other channels, but more than likely, any drum app or external drum machine you use will accept MIDI commands on channel 10. That's just the way it is.

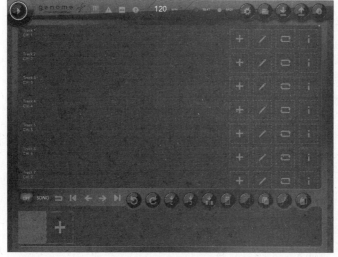

Figure 18-4:
Sequencing
Genome
(hey, I just
got that
joke . . .).

On track 10 in Genome, tap the plus sign to add a pattern for that channel. Then tap the pencil icon for channel 10 to see the screen shown in Figure 18-5.

You can tap on each square to play a drum or percussion hit. In this case, C3 triggers the bass drum, D3 triggers the snare drum, and F#3 triggers a closed hi-hat sound. Tap a quick pattern out for a standard rock beat, as in Figure 18-6, or just input whatever you want.

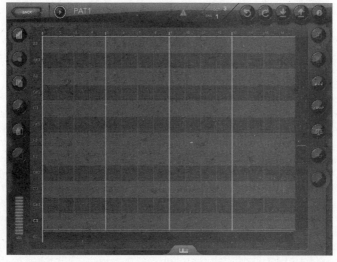

Figure 18-5:
The grid for
channel 10
in Genome.

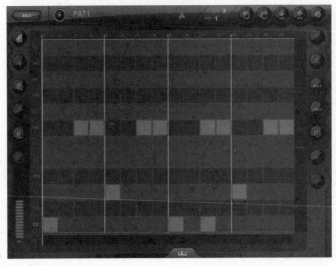

Figure 18-6:
A quick drum pattern in Genome.

The pattern entered commands any app listening for instructions on MIDI channel 10 to play those notes at the specified time. Tap Back to go to the main Genome sequence screen, then tap the pattern to activate it. Now, let's move on to a bass line.

Move over to the Thor app and tap the gear icon. In this case, tap Source and set it to Genome. Then tap the plus icon under Source until it says channel 1. If you haven't tired your fingers out yet, go back to Genome and tap the plus sign for channel 1. We created a simple bass line (shown in Figure 18-7) to go along with the extremely simple drum pattern.

Go back to the main sequence screen in Genome and tap the pattern in channel 1 to activate that pattern. Then hit the play button in the upper-left corner to hear the final product.

You may hear the pattern coming from Funkbox in addition to the drum hits you programmed in Genome. Turn down the master fader (labeled MST) to take the programmed pattern out of the sound produced by Funkbox.

Okay, so the example is pretty basic. The magic from here involves the additional patterns you can program. Just keep tapping the plus sign and adding new patterns. Each track plays one pattern at a time, and you can tap a new pattern to start it after the previous pattern finishes. From there, you can add different groups of patterns using the plus sign at the bottom of the Genome sequence screen. You can assign verse and chorus parts, or you can just put in different sequences that you wish to alternate in your performance. The sequencer handles all of the commands — you just tell it what to do.

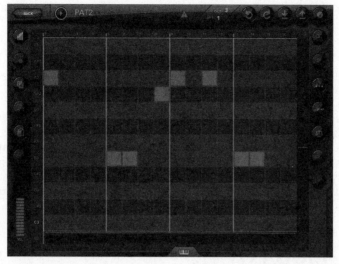

Figure 18-7:
Pairing a
bass line
with the
drum patter
in Genome.

The weird world of MIDI sequencers

Genome is a wonderful MIDI sequencer, but it's pretty standard for the way that it appears and handles MIDI. Because of the way you can interact with an iOS touchscreen, MIDI sequencers can manage MIDI data (and, therefore, MIDI-enabled apps in new and different ways). You can drag your fingers across virtual pads, knobs, sliders, and the like to make new and different sounds with your synth apps. From the higher-end Lemur app to the free Fifth Degree app, you can interact in many strange ways with your apps. And MIDI doesn't just control audio — you can use MIDI sequences to arrange light shows and trigger other effects. This type of control extends from modern devices to vintage synths, providing a level of control and interaction impossible with the original instruments.

Synth enthusiasts (and there are a ton of them online) create templates for apps like Lemur

and TouchOSC to help control synths. The possibilities are endless:

✔ Control virtual instruments on the iPhone or iPad.

✔ Control virtual instruments via MIDI on a computer via wireless or Bluetooth LE.

✔ Control a hardware synth via MIDI.

✔ Control just about anything that accepts MIDI over available connections.

The MIDI rabbit hole goes a long way — way too long to cover in this book. But keep investigating, as you never know what will help you out with your musical efforts. You'll certainly find a whole world of other people interested in the same subject, and you'll probably dig up more information than you could possibly use.

We left Genome at the default tempo of 120 beats per minute, but you can tap the tempo and change it to whatever you wish.

Using Korg WIST

What if you need to use multiple apps on multiple iOS devices? Getting everything started and stopped on time can be a matter of luck, or you can rely on a standard technology that keeps everything moving on track. A MIDI sequencer sending commands over a wireless network can work, but you cannot always rely on the presence or access to a wireless network (even if you establish one yourself). However, depending on the apps you use, you may have another alternative — WIST.

What is WIST?

The Korg company developed WIST as a way to keep multiple iOS devices using WIST-enabled apps in sync when you start and stop them. WIST keeps two devices (a parent and a child) in sync using information relayed over a Bluetooth pairing (much more reliable and secure than a wireless connection, in this case). The parent device transmits the start, stop, and tempo information. The child device . . . just follows along. WIST is simple and effective.

One issue with WIST is that, compared to the number of apps that support features like Audiobus or Virtual MIDI, the number of WIST-enabled apps seems pretty small. At the time of this writing, only about 42 apps let you sync with WIST. This list includes some familiar names from Korg, Yamaha, and Akai, as well as popular apps like Beatmaker and DM1. But given what's available on the App Store, you'll find a lot more apps that don't use WIST than do.

WIST only works with two iOS devices. No more, no less. Even if you use multiple WIST-enabled apps on the same iOS device, WIST only functions by pairing two devices together. If you're not using two iOS devices, just keep moving along.

Configuring multiple apps using WIST

Decide before beginning which device you want to use to control the WIST connection. In this case, use an iPhone to control your iPad. On your iPhone, start by opening Figure and tapping the WIST button on the System tab, shown in Figure 18-8.

Figure 18-8:
Starting a
WIST con-
nection in
Figure.

Turn Bluetooth on for both devices before you begin this process. WIST reminds you if you don't, but taking care of this step beforehand saves you some time.

Now that your iPhone is looking for a connection (aren't we all?), move over to your iPad and open up Korg Gadget. Tap the gear icon, then tap the WIST button to start the iPad's search, as shown in Figure 18-9.

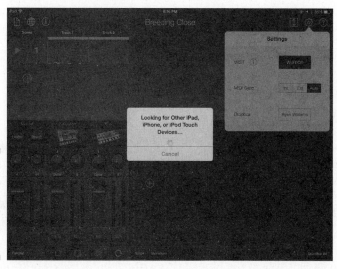

Figure 18-9:
Recipro-
cating a
WIST con-
nection with
Gadget.

If you still have problems making the connection after enabling Bluetooth, try rebooting both devices.

When both devices are looking, WIST makes the connection and shows available apps, as shown in Figure 18-10.

Figure 18-10:
Pairing up
your WIST
devices.

Tap the name of the other device in each WIST menu, and you're ready to go. The parent app can control the tempo, start signal, and stop signal for both devices. Each device plays whatever song is loaded at the time — WIST doesn't sync song information or anything like that. All it does is keep the enabled devices in sync. That may not seem like much, but it does it very well and solves an otherwise troublesome problem very gracefully.

Using Retronym's Tabletop

Retronym's Tabletop lets creative musicians put together several different devices together on the same playing field to achieve a greater whole. Some of those devices come with this free app, others come as part of in-app purchases, and some apps must be purchased entirely separately. You can even use Inter-App Audio to control devices that otherwise have nothing to do with Tabletop. This app doesn't make music as much as create a platform that you can customize for your own playing purposes.

The app itself is free at the time of this writing, but it only works on the iPad. So grab the newest iPad you can access, download the Tabletop app, and open it to see the screen shown in Figure 18-11.

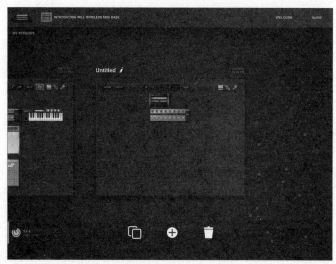

You can see the Untitled template in that screen, and you can also tap the plus icon at the bottom of the screen to see additional templates that come with the app. Tabletop primarily handles dance-oriented music, so the usual suspects show up in the template list (acid techno, dubstep, hip hop, and more). Be careful, though — most templates contain devices that require in-app purchase. The Tabletop platform may come for free, but you must spend a little extra to obtain full functionality. Such are the dangers of using apps in the "freemium era" of cheap entry and escalating costs of additional features.

However, you do get a decent sampling of apps to get you started:

✔ A touchpad sampler called Gridlok (familiar to fans of devices like the MPC)

✔ A polyphonic keyboard called RS3 (a simple two-octave keyboard with basic envelope controls, a note grid sequencer, and some useable patches)

✔ A pattern-based synth called M8RX (choose the patch, the pattern, and the scale you wish to use, then tap some notes on the grid to set up the pattern that plays when you tap Play in the Tabletop transport controls)

✔ An eight-channel mixer called Goblin MX8 (simple volume and pan controls for eight different inputs)

✔ A splitter unit called X2 (splits incoming signals into two different paths for use with different effects like *sidechaining* or running a dry signal in tandem with an effect signal)

The sidechaining compressor technique involves using an incoming signal to trigger the compression effect on another signal. For example, you could use the bass drum signal to trigger a compressor or gate to allow a bass guitar signal to come through (a very common use) or duck the volume of a backing track down to emphasize a vocal. The sidechaining effect depends on how you configure the noise gate or the compressor, but the entire effect relies on the incoming signal.

✔ A 3-band equalizer called 3Q (knobs for high, mid, and low frequencies with a bypass switch)

✔ A low-pass X-Y filter effect called FILTR (drag your finger across the X-Y pad to adjust the frequency and resonance of the filter in real time)

✔ An automated panning effect called Panhandler (automatically moves the audio signal from left to right in the stereo field depending on how you set the range of the autopan, the waveform, the rate, and whether it syncs with the overall tempo of your session)

✔ A virtual turntable called Spinback (load up an audio sample and manipulate it as if it were a vinyl record)

✔ A sequencer called the T101 Triggerator (set up different sequences and how many bars those sequences contain, then tap them in real time to start the patterns)

✔ An audio recorder called Magic Mic (not the movie, but an audio recorder with basic editing capabilities that uses the built-in iPad mic)

✔ Another audio recorder called (surprisingly enough) Recorder (another audio recorder that works with attached audio interfaces)

✔ An Inter-App Audio controller called Mastermind (a virtual controller that connects with IAA-enabled apps to bring those devices into the Tabletop - realm)

You can use multiple instances of these apps in a Tabletop session, and you get enough functionality to put together some decent tracks. However, remember that Tabletop is a platform, not a closed-off ecosystem. You can always add other devices if you're willing to spend a little more coin to do so. You must decide whether the expanded functionality and additional sound textures are worth the additional expense.

Take a look at the IAA apps you already have before you start purchasing additional Tabletop apps. Some may duplicate functionality and sounds, and you don't have to buy everything in the storefront to make music.

Adding Tabletop-ready apps to a Tabletop session

All of the apps in Tabletop live under the keyboard icon in the top-right corner of the main Tabletop screen. Tap that icon to see the screen shown in Figure 18-12.

Note that the control at the top of the menu displays both My Devices and Device Store. The highlighted My Devices section shows all the apps you currently own and that are present on the device. Tap the Device Store button to see what else is available in the store.

The store contains a wealth of additional synthesizers, drum machines, filters, and other effects. The vast majority of these devices come from Retronym, the company that created Tabletop. However, you can also bring in Akai's iMPC Pro and iMPC apps or Arturia's iMini and iProphet apps into Tabletop via the App Store as well. These Tabletop-ready apps function either on their own or integrate directly with Tabletop for use with the devices you already use within the Tabletop app. You will pay more for this functionality, but the versatility and sound quality of the apps may compensate for the additional expense. After you purchase the app, it will appear in your My Devices list, ready for use in your projects.

Figure 18-12:
A sample
list of
Tabletop
apps.

Using apps in Tabletop

After you assemble the devices you wish to use in Tabletop, you're ready to go. Tap the plus icon shown in Figure 18-11 and choose the Untitled template. You get the (relatively) blank slate shown in Figure 18-13.

The Mr. O device shown at the top of the screen takes output from the Goblin mixer and transmits it to whatever you use to listen to audio while you're recording — headphones, monitors, whatever you choose. Tap the keyboard icon to choose an app and drag it to the Tabletop screen. In Figure 18-14, we chose the Gridlock sampler.

Note how Tabletop automatically routes the audio out from Gridlock into the Goblin mixer. How helpful! Tap the Gridlok app to see the device up close, as shown in Figure 18-15.

Obviously, Gridlok's pad controls trigger the sounds loaded up, but let's take a look at the controls Gridlok shares with other devices in the Tabletop arsenal.

Well, before we move on, take a look at the pads in the bottom-right corner of Gridlok. Those joined pads offer an additional mute control — if you tap one side and then the other, the second sample mutes the audio of the first sample. This control can be helpful when playing closed and open hi-hat samples, for example. For the sake of realism, you wouldn't want the closed and open samples playing at the same time, so the mute function replicates the action of a drummer placing his foot on or taking it off of the hi-hat pedal.

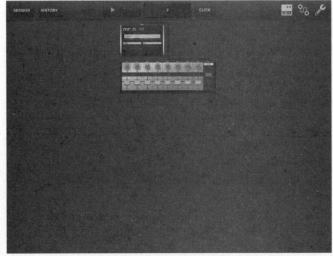

Figure 18-13:
The Untitled template in Tabletop.

Figure 18-14:
Dragging
Gridlok
to the
Tabletop.

Tap the Sequence button to see the grid displayed in Figure 18-16. We took the liberty of tapping in a quick drum sequence, and that's really all you need to do in this window. Just tap where and when you want the samples to play, and press Play to hear the results.

If you're unsure about which sample you want to use, tap the name of the sample in the list to the list. You hear the sound of the sample.

Figure 18-15:
Interacting
with Gridlok
to the
Tabletop.

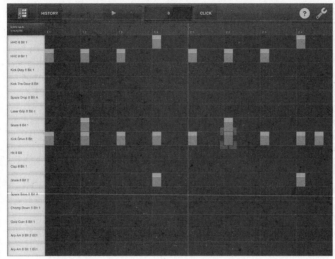

Figure 18-16:
A sample drum pattern in Gridlok.

Tap the Gridlok icon to go back to the main screen, then tap the wrench icon next to the Sequence button (as opposed to the larger wrench icon in the top-right of the screen, which we cover in the "Configuring a session" section, later in this chapter). You see quantize controls allowing you to customize where hits fall as you record in real time (which we go over next) and whether you want to erase recorded hits for the loop you selected on the pad (indicated by the lighted icon in the top-left corner of the pad) or for the entire Gridlok sequence.

Be sure you want to erase these hits before you hit those Quick Edit buttons. You can't undo this process.

If you want to record Gridlok (or another instrument) live, tap the Record button at the top of the screen to enable recording, then tap the Play button and start playing your part. We'd also recommend tapping the Click button to get a metronome to play along with. Tabletop defaults to two bars with four beats each. After you reach that limit, the recording continues, but you hear the hits you already recorded. These hits record using the Quantize settings you set under the wrench icon we covered in this chapter. You can also tap the Sequence icon to see these hits and modify them as you wish. For example, you can go in, double-tap a hit, and see the menu shown in Figure 18-17.

Most of these commands will be familiar to even the most casual computer user, but a couple deserve special attention. Tap Velocity to adjust how soft or hard the sample sounds off, and tap Duplicate to put a hit directly next to the previously recorded hit. Otherwise, you should be as comfortable dealing with these sections as you are with basic word processing functionality. Isn't it nice when those basic office skills carry over?

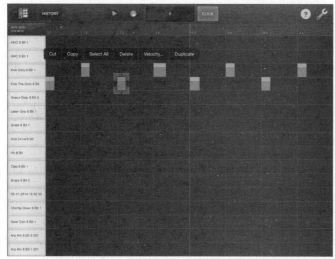

Figure 18-17:
Editing a
note in
Gridlok.

Don't tap iPhone and iPad screens too hard — you cannot create velocity information for an app by how hard you hit the screen! Some app developers may translate velocity by where you tap the pad or screen, but try it out first. And again, *never* hit the screen too hard!

Go back to the main Gridlok screen by tapping the Gridlok icon in the top-left of the screen so you can review the menus on the device. The top menu pulls up a bank of samples when you tap Load, and you can change any modifications you make to those banks by tapping Save. The bottom menu controls a specific sample for your selected pad, including recording a new sample for that pad. To record a sample, just follow these steps:

1. **Tap Record.**

2. **Record the sample using your mic or input.**

3. **Tap Tap to Stop to finish the recording.**

   That pad now contains the sample you recorded.

If you want to revert to the previously recorded sample, just tap Load and navigate back to the specific sample.

If you want to create an entire bank of new samples, tap Load on the top menu and select Empty. You can then load or record an entirely new custom bank of your own, because you're just that creative!

The sample and bank load controls are fairly common across all of the Tabletop apps, but each device contains its own controls. For example, Gridlok allows you to change the pitch, volume, and length of each sample pad, along with which channel the sample app goes out over. Of special note for Gridlok is the 1-Shot vs. Hold switch. The 1-Shot setting plays the entire sample once, whereas Hold plays the sample only as long as you hold the pad. Some samples continue to loop while you hold the pad, and others stop when the sample ends — that feature just depends on the sample you loaded, so be sure to experiment.

Let's take a quick look at some of the other instruments that come in the basic Tabletop configuration. Tap the magnifying glass icon in the top-left corner of the screen to go back to the main Tabletop screen, then tap the keyboard icon and drag an M8RX over to the screen. Figure 18-18 shows the interface for this particular instrument.

Just select the sound bank in the top menu and the pattern right below it. Then select your scale and set the note length (this control applies to all notes in the matrix). Finally, tap in the notes you wish to sound — the notes go from low to high vertically, and the horizontal controls determine when the notes play. Tap Play to hear how it sounds and edit from there. You can also change the pattern using familiar cut, copy, paste, and clear controls by tapping Edit Pattern.

Finally, let's take a look at the RS3 polyphonic keyboard. Go back to the My Devices list and drag an RS3 over to the main Tabletop screen. Tap the keyboard to see the screen shown in Figure 18-19.

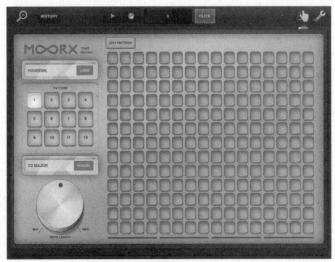

Figure 18-18:
The M8RX
grid.

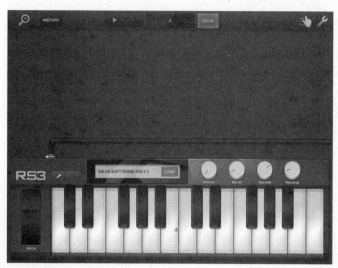

Figure 18-19:
The RS3
synth.

Nothing too surprising here — load a soundbank, adjust the envelope controls to tweak your sounds into exactly what you want, and use the keys and pitch wheel to play what you wish to hear. Otherwise, the wrench and sequencer controls work the same here as they do in Gridlok.

Tabletop offers so many devices and effects that we can't cover them all here — even the ones that come free. Tap the larger wrench icon in the upper-right corner of the screen and select Guide to review the detailed documentation for Tabletop. This guide contains specific documentation on every Tabletop device, including the ones you must pay extra for. This information can go a long way in helping you spend (and not spend) your money wisely! And head over to YouTube for demo videos if you want to hear the devices in action — search to your heart's content!

One more controller to check out before we move on — drag a T101 Triggerator over to the Tabletop screen and tap it to see the screen shown in Figure 18-20.

This controller lets you set up specific blocks that you can tap to begin playing while playing the main transport control (which include familiar Start, Stop, Record, Rewind, Fast Forward, and Loop buttons). Figure 18-20 shows two blocks that you can tap to begin instantly. You can also set the blocks to begin playing at the beginning of the next beat, bar, or block. The Trigger/ Switch toggle determines what happens if you touch the block.

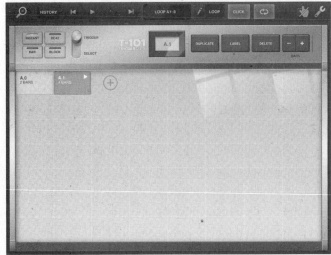

Figure 18-20:
The
Triggerator
in action.

✔ Trigger starts the selected block instantly or at the next indicated event.

✔ Select brings up the settings for that block so you can move them around while the other block plays.

The controls at the top-right of the device change individual block settings. Tap Duplicate to make another new block with the settings of the current block. Tap Label to give a better name to the block so you can recognize the contents more easily (such as "Verse" or "Chorus"). Tap Delete to remove that block. Finally, tap the plus or minus symbol to add or remove bars from the block, respectively.

To make a new block, just tap the plus sign on the Triggerator screen. When the Play symbol shows up on the block, you can go into the devices and change the sequences and notes as you wish. Go back to Triggerator and select a new block, then do the same. When you're finished, you can tap the blocks during playback to change how Tabletop plays the sequences.

Leaving the Trigger/Select switch on Trigger allows you to change the sequences. Select just lets you reorder the blocks without making edits.

You don't need to use Triggerator in Tabletop, but without this device, you can't easily move additional sequences around effectively. You'll just be stuck on the same two-bar loop.

From here, you can add effects to the instruments on the Tabletop main screen by dragging them onto the instrument you wish to . . . affect. Tabletop automatically routes the audio according to your wishes, and you can tap the effect to change setting as you wish.

To remove a device from the Tabletop, tap and drag the device to the top of the screen, where you see a trash icon. After you drop the device on the icon, it disappears from the screen.

Although the automatic routing is nice, what if you want to change the routing of some of the devices? For example, what if you want to put a splitter on the RS3 and put an effect on just one of those signal paths? No problem — drag the splitter and the effect onto the Tabletop screen, then tap the point-to-point icon at the top-right of the screen to show the virtual wiring of your session. All you have to do is tap and drag the wire from the green output to the blue input to change the wiring. Check out this scenario in Figure 18-21.

As long as the end of every chain ends up going to the Mr. O module somehow, you'll hear it. Put in as many mixers, instruments, effects, and other devices as you wish.

Configuring a session

To change the main settings for your session, just tap the larger wrench icon and pull up the screen shown in Figure 18-22.

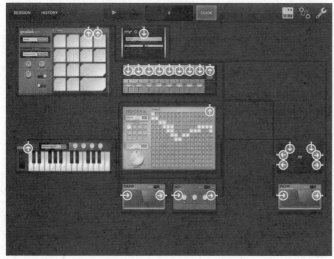

Figure 18-21:
Changing
signal flow
in Tabletop.

Figure 18-22:
Tabletop
session
settings.

The MIDI Learn button helps you configure an external MIDI controller for use with Tabletop (such as a keyboard or other controller). Tap the button to see the screen in Figure 18-23.

The highlighted blue controls can be mapped to a physical control. Tap the device, then tap the specific control. When you move the specific control, that key or control will play every time you use the physical controller.

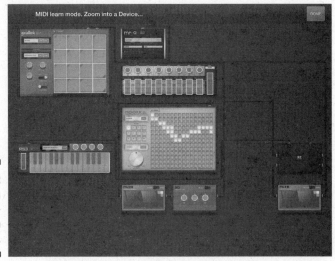

Figure 18-23:
Learning
MIDI con-
trols in
Tabletop.

MIDI implementation is pretty easy using this function. Tap Done when you're finished.

It may seem like common sense, but make sure that you correctly attach your controller to your iOS device and send the correct MIDI commands before you beginning learning MIDI controls. Otherwise, it just won't work.

Our old friend WIST shows up here as well — tap the WIST: Off button to start the linking process described in the "Using Korg WIST" section earlier in this chapter. And Tabletop uses common tempo and swing controls to set the overall tempo of the session. Finally, move the Record Count In switch to On if you wish to hear a four-count on the metronome before you start recording.

To round out the other Tabletop controls, tap the Session button to switch between sessions, and tap History to select commands you wish to undo. This feature thoughtfully provides the ability to select your undo actions, as opposed to just undoing your most recent actions. That way, you don't have to redo a whole lot of work just to change one error.

Controlling external MIDI apps via Inter-App Audio

Tabletop lets you use IAA to control virtual intruments, insert effects, and external audio recorders in line with the other provided devices, but it only makes the Mastermind Inter-App Controller available as part of the basic package. So let's take a look at that device, because it's the one we all get to use for free.

Drag the Mastermind controller onto the Tabletop main screen and tap it to bring up the main controller screen. Then tap the Select App icon to choose from your available apps. In this case, Figure 18-24 shows the controller linked up to Animoog.

Now you can use the wrench and sequence functions familiar to you already to trigger Animoog sounds. You can also record your lines using the onscreen keys and control dials.

The rotary controls send MIDI CC signals to the app controlled by Mastermind, so the effects change depending on the app. Consult your app to see what those controls do in your specific case.

Figure 18-24:
Controlling
Animoog
from
Tabletop
using
Mastermind.

Tabletop packs a lot of functionality into a single app, and you can bring your other apps along with you for the ride.

Part VI
Editing, Mixing, and Sharing Your Projects

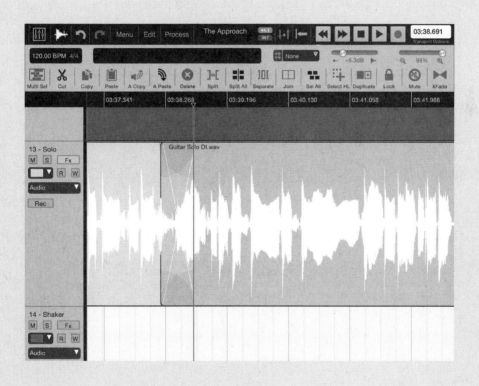

See how to export audio from your mobile device for online use at `www.dummies.com/extras/ipadandiphoneformusicians`.

In this part . . .

- Edit your recorded material together, cut out extraneous audio, and clean everything up.

- Use the mixing process to tweak levels, frequencies, and dynamics into the perfect mix.

- Move your finished tracks from your mobile device to the world, using a variety of file formats and Internet audio services.

Chapter 19

Editing Your Material

· ·

In This Chapter

▶ Tackling the basics of digital audio editing

▶ Creating and moving sections of audio within your larger track

▶ Smoothing your edits out with cross fades and other editor features

· ·

More than one audio recording app actually displays the image of an old reel-to-reel tape recording machine when you're recording audio. Even in this time of digital recording and inexpensive home-based recording rigs, the visual of a tape deck still calls to mind the common perception of a professional recording studio and signals to the exact action taking place. You are laying down tracks, no doubt about it.

Luckily, though, you don't have to worry about the inconvenience of actually maintaining this machines and having to actually edit the tape (involving using razor blades, tape, steady and precise hands, and a little bit of editing magic and luck). Part of what makes digital audio such an appealing and versatile tool is the ease of editing and the ability to undo catastrophic changes it provides. This chapter takes you through the steps of editing audio tracks on an editor hosted on your iOS device.

Getting to Know the Typical Editing Features

Believe it or not, using an audio editor doesn't differ too much from using a word processor program. After all, both programs take content within a file (either a text document or an audio file) and manipulate it in different ways to create a final piece of work. So although the actual functionality differs, the terminology will appear refreshingly similar.

Think of your audio file as one long document. The text document follows a linear structure (you read through the pages from top to bottom), as does the audio file (you listen through the file from beginning to end). However, your editing functions don't force you to work from the beginning to end. You can move to separate sections of the audio file and do whatever you need to do. Techie types call this style of audio manipulation *non-linear editing,* where you can move around and work on sections of the audio without having to address those sections in order. Jump around, do whatever you need to do.

Recording and importing

Most audio editors offer basic audio recording capabilities. You won't find multi-track recording on most of these types of apps (especially on the free ones), but you'll at least be able to get audio laid down into your iOS device. More than likely, though, you'll get most of your audio into your editing app of choice using some kind of import function. Just like opening an existing document in a word processor, importing allows you to take an existing audio file, open it up in your app, and make it do what you want to do.

Editing with cut, copy, paste, and delete

In a word processor, you use the mouse to drag the cursor over text, highlight that text, then right-click or use keyboard commands to affect that text. You could copy it to a different location, repeat that section again, or even delete it from the document entirely.

In an audio editor, you basically perform the same actions. But instead of highlighting and changing text, you select a section of an — audio file. For example, you could cut out a mistake in a vocal anfd just leave silence in its place — that hacking coughing fit never happened! This process takes just a little bit of work, and it's certainly better than trying to re-record that section of the vocal. You could also take a background vocal take and make copies of it to place at different places in a track. The point here is that you can take parts of the audio file, move them around, and make your changes without having to move back and forth through the entire file. Just modify the parts you want. The magic of non-linear editing!

iMovie users may also recognize this workflow from creating movies on the iPhone or iPad. Video or audio, the concept is the same.

Working with audio effects

This point may stretch our comparison of audio editors and word processors, but stick with us on this — the idea actually works. Think of changing the font and size of the text in a word processor. Maybe you also highlight sections of text, change the color, or add different types of art to the document. Make text bold, underline it, italicize it, do whatever you need to do. The audio editor lets you perform all kinds of changes on your audio as well. Turning up the volume on an audio track is similar to making the font larger, right? So even if you don't have a direct comparison to adding delay to a paragraph (smaller copies of the paragraph as the document goes on, maybe?), you get the point that these audio effects let you change your file a bit and give it a little extra personality.

Although we demonstrate audio editing in Auria, you should definitely feel free to download some of the free audio editors and review these kinds of effects before you buy anything. Everything that we talk about in this section either comes standard or via in-app purchase.

Adjusting volume level

Suppose you've got a quiet section of audio, and you need to make it louder. Just load it into the editor and crank up the volume! You could do this to the entire file, or you could just select a section of the file and boost the volume to that section (a quiet part of a conversation or a solo guitar part in an otherwise louder track). Audio editors can accomplish this task with ease.

Adjusting volume level at this level involves lowering or raising the volume on a specific section of audio, not the overall track or the recording in general. This ability lets you compensate for lower recordings or take the edge off of a particularly "hot" or loud recording. For example, take a look at the vocals in Figure 19-1.

In Auria, you can see different handles on an audio clip at the top of the clip and in the corners. The volume handle appears in the middle of the clip. Tap that handle and drag up and down to get the volume you're looking for, as shown in Figure 19-2.

Some audio editors also provide a volume or gain knob for a clip, but the iPhone and iPad allow you to drag the controls on the clip in a very precise and interactive way. Use whatever control you wish for your own best process.

Normalizing audio

When you *normalize* an audio file, you take the highest peak of that audio to a specified level. The rest of that audio file also increases by that level as well. Although it's not that different from manually adjusting a volume level, normalization performs a common function automatically. Most every audio editor handles this capability — even the free ones.

Although most normalization functions allow you to bring the peak of the audio file up to 0 dB, this use of normalization isn't usually a good idea, especially if you aren't dealing with your final track. Remember that you want to leave a little headroom to make sure you have some room to work with your files while you're mixing and mastering. A little headroom goes a long way.

Figure 19-1:
The original
vocal track.

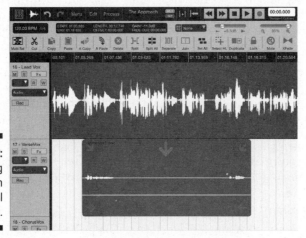

Figure 19-2:
Adjusting
volume on
the original
vocal track.

If you have a large peak in the audio, it might be better to reduce the amplitude on that particular peak and *then* normalize the audio, to make sure you normalize the entire file correctly.

Let's take a look at normalizing another clip. Normalizing isn't a control you set by dragging controls over a clip. The process analyzes the overall audio clip and adjusts the volume accordingly. Select the clip and tap Process to see the list of available processing effects, as seen in Figure 19-3.

Select Normalize to see the function in Figure 19-4. We tapped Scan already to perform the analysis of the audio to see the audio levels in question.

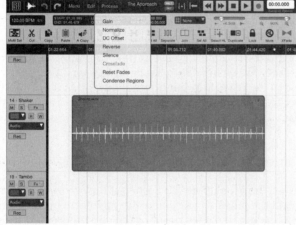

Figure 19-3:
Selecting the Normalize process.

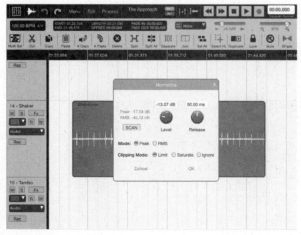

Figure 19-4:
Analyzing audio in the Normalize process.

The Normalize process in Auria allows you to adjust the volume level based on the previously mentioned peak value (the loudest peak of the entire audio file) or the *RMS* value (an involved mathematical formula that basically determines the average volume level of the audio clip). Suppose that you want to normalize this clip to –13 dB based on the peak value. Adjust the Level knob to as close to –13 dB as you can get and leave the Mode switch on Peak. The Release knob affects the Limit button on the Clipping Mode switch, where it determines how the *limiter* effect kicks in. The limiter prevents audio from going over a certain dB level, and the knob determines when the effects let go. You can leave it at a short period of time to affect only the peaks of the audio, or you can set it longer to smooth out more of the clip. The Saturate option offers a distortion-type effect to take place when the audio clips, and the Ignore option lets it all run wild. Leave the settings as is here and tap OK. You see the waveform increase in size, as shown in Figure 19-5, indicating a louder volume.

Fading in and out

If you've ever heard the volume increase at the beginning of a track or decrease at the end of a track, you've heard a *fade in* or a *fade out.* A fade refers to the gradual increase or decrease in volume, either quickly or slowly. But instead of trusting your steady hand to move the faders (hey, that makes sense now!) on a mixer, you can automatically move the volume up or down in just the right way.

Check out the keyboard track in Figure 19-6. We're going to fade this part in.

In this example, we drag the upper-left corner of the screen toward the middle of the clip to begin the fade in. Notice how the waveform became smaller at the beginning of the clip and becomes larger as the clip progresses in Figure 19-7.

Figure 19-5:
The normalized audio clip.

Figure 19-6:
The original keyboard track.

Figure 19-7:
Fading in the keyboard track.

Depending on the audio editor, you may encounter linear fades, exponential fades, logarithmic fades, equal power fades, and more (as seen in the squares in the upper-right corner of Figure 19-7). These terms describe exactly how the audio fade occurs, and you can see exactly how the fades look in the audio file. Each type of fade has its own use, but ultimately you should trust your ears to the right one for your case. You can always undo it if you don't like it.

Next, fade out the clip by dragging the top-right corner down. We picked a different type of fade out that acts a little more gradually than the type used to fade in the audio. Take a look at Figure 19-8 to see the final results.

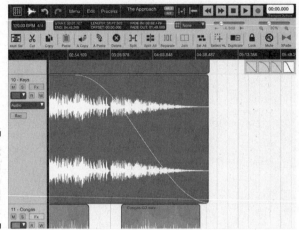

Figure 19-8:
Fading
out the
keyboard
track.

Reversing audio

Typing words backwards just gets you a jumbled mess, but reversing audio
gives you a cool effect (even if it's just simulating spinning a record backwards). Again, you can apply this effect to the entire track or just a section of
your audio.

In this case, we reversed the hi-hat track in the recording, as shown
in Figure 19-9.

After selecting the clip, tap Process and select Reverse. Notice the change in
the waveform shown in Figure 19-10.

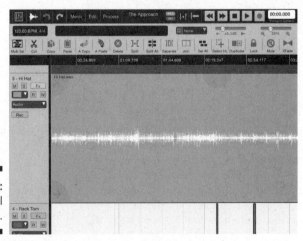

Figure 19-9:
The original
hi-hat track.

Figure 19-10:
The
reversed
hi-hat track.

Trimming audio

Suppose you have a track that includes a bunch of noise or silence at the beginning or end of the track. Most audio editors let you move the beginning or end of the track to start at a different point in the clip instead of the very beginning. This process alters the clip quickly and doesn't erase any audio in the process.

Take a look at the hi-hat clip in Figure 19-9 again. We want to move the beginning of that clip, so we select the bottom-left corner of the clip and move it to the point where we want the audio clip to begin, as shown in Figure 19-11.

Figure 19-11:
Trimming the
beginning
of the
audio clip.

You can do the same to the end of the clip as well, if you wish.

Adding silence

If you want to insert a bit of silence into a clip, you can select that portion of the clip and make it quiet. Audio editors can easily remove any waveform and insert the silence you require.

We want to remove one of the hi-hat hits from Figure 19-9, so we double-tap the clip and move the selection until we get the part of the clip we want, as shown in Figure 19-12.

After we tap Process and select Silence, the clip looks like the screen shown in Figure 19-13.

Note that this process doesn't just remove the primary part of the audio — it also takes out the background noise. All you get is pure silence.

Try copying a clip of ambient background noise and placing it on a track in place of the silence to make the quiet seem a little more natural (if not as silent).

Cleaning up

You can put quite a few effects under this section, including click and pop removal, noise and hiss removal, and other effects that take your original file and make it sound better or restore the sound to its former glory. These effects normally come with more expensive audio editors, but they can be worth the investment if you need them (like cleaning up files recorded from old vinyl records).

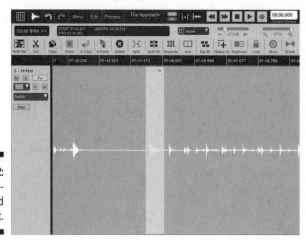

Figure 19-12: The soon-to-be-silenced hi-hat hit.

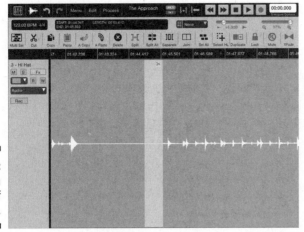

Figure 19-13:
Inserting a
little bit of
silence.

Auria offers a DC Offset function that lets you move the center of the audio waveform back to zero (if the waveform isn't based around zero, you could run into issues with amplification or normalization). This process isn't common, but it points out the kind of cleaning-up function audio editors can offer.

Adding the kitchen sink

Depending on the audio editor you use, you could perform all kinds of effects on your file, such as adding reverb, delay, distortion, or any number of wacky audio processing effects. You probably see these kind of effects in DAWs or amp simulators, but they also show up in audio editors as well.

Some audio editors can also let you use Audiobus or IAA to place your favorite effects in the audio editor for expanded use.

Exporting audio

When you finish off your audio editing, you can create a final file containing all of the work you performed up to this point. Just remember that when you save your edits while working, you're more than likely saving to a project file readable only by the audio editor itself (and maybe by other audio editors as well). When you complete your work and want to create the final audio product, choose the export function to create a new audio file with all of the changes intact. At this point, you can set the file type and resolution of the final file, from a tiny MP3 file to a mastered AIFF file ready for high-fidelity audio playback.

Because Auria involves multiple tracks, the menu command for exporting actually refers to *mixdown,* which accounts for all of the volume and pan settings, effects, and other settings within the project. Other audio editors use an *export* command to make a final file. Take a look at Figure 19-14 to see the export settings in Auria.

Figure 19-14:
Exporting the audio files.

We're going to leave this file as a WAV (uncompressed audio file), but you can select the most appropriate setting as you need. Notice the bottom of the menu, which determines exactly where the final exported file resides. Most audio editors offer similar choices, but we recommend saving a separate file in a cloud-based service first before uploading files to a audio playback service like SoundCloud. That way, you have a final copy you can edit or modify as you need instead of just a streaming track you have no final control over. Tap OK after you're done, and you've just exported a final track!

Always edit in lossless or uncompressed files, then export to lossy compression file types. If you edit and export from lossy compression, you will likely lose audio information in your file and maybe even introduce harsh and unpleasant audio artifacts into your file. Saving a little space at the beginning of the editing process could end up costing you in audio fidelity down the road.

Exporting audio may leave out metadata, like the artist name or album title. Check the final files and reenter the metadata if necessary.

Understanding non-destructive editing

The magic of non-linear editing involves knowing that, no matter what you do, you can always (well, MOST always, depending on the app) undo the change you just made. In the days referenced by the virtual tape machines found in some audio apps, a piece of tape that you cut stays cut — you can tape the pieces back together, but it probably won't sound the same. In this case, though, the Undo button takes it all away. That's why we call this type of editing *non-destructive* — you destroy nothing when you make edits.

Not only does non-destructive audio editing let you preserve the integrity of the audio file (by working on a project file and not the actual audio file), but you can be fearless in the effects you try on your audio files. Go ahead and do something wacky — you can always undo the effect and go back to what you had before.

Non-destructive editing also means that, if the app allows it, you can go make and selectively undo changes you made. For example, if you make a cut, compress the audio file, then run normalization, you may discover that you prefer the audio file better without the cut. You could backtrack through the entire file, or you can just undo the edit if the app allows it. This functionality depends on the app you use, but it is possible in some audio apps.

DAWs and audio editors usually use non-destructive editing methods, but it's always best to check before editing to make sure you don't accidentally delete anything permanently.

Cutting, Pasting, and Rearranging Sections

Audio editing doesn't just let you modify individual clips — you can create more and more clips if you wish. Take these sections, edit, and move them around as you need. They represent the paragraphs in your audio document, and you can do whatever you need to do with them.

Making the cuts

Audio editors offer a couple of options regarding cutting audio clips. The first option allows you to select a section of the audio clip and cut it out. In Figure 19-15, we selected a part of the audio clip that we want to cut.

The scissors icon appears in the upper-right corner of the selected region, so we tap that icon to create the cut shown in Figure 19-16.

Figure 19-15:
Cutting part
of the audio
clip.

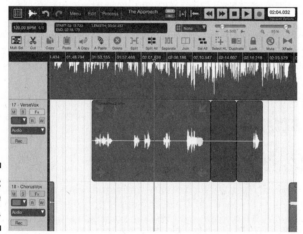

Figure 19-16:
Making the
final cut.

You can also split the audio clip at the point where the playhead rests. Note the position of the playhead in Figure 19-16. When we tap the Split icon, we create another clip (as shown in Figure 19-17).

This technique is helpful for creating a cut during playback.

You can always tap the Undo button to undo the cuts (unless you try operations that require a large amount of data, but you'll usually see a warning before edits of those kinds). Isn't technology a miracle?

Figure 19-17:
Splitting the audio clip at the position of the playhead.

Copying audio

Copying an existing audio clip couldn't be easier — just like copying a word or sentence in a word processor. In this example, we selected the clip and tapped Copy. We then moved the playhead to the location where we want to paste the clip and tapped Paste. The screen looks like Figure 19-18 when we're done.

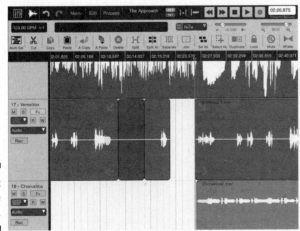

Figure 19-18:
Copying the audio clip.

Why would we want to do this? Simple — copying audio saves a lot of time. If you want to repeat a drum part, just take the clip and copy it over and over until you flesh out the song. And what is sampling besides making a copy? The true artistry comes in how you use these copies. Don't be afraid to chop up your clips, rearrange them (as shown in the "Moving audio around" section in this chapter), and make it your own.

Moving audio around

Next, take a look at how to move audio clips around the audio editor. Seriously, this process couldn't be easier. In the case of Auria, just tap and hold the audio clip, then drag it to its new location. Compare Figure 19-18 and Figure 19-19, after we moved one of the audio clips to a new location.

This functionality helps a great deal if you just want to nudge a part into the right place (so it will be in time with the correct tempo or just off enough to be funky) or move parts around dramatically for a remix effect. Move the clips wherever you need to and get your sounds in the right place.

Avoiding clicks

So after you perform a few cuts and splits here and there, maybe you notice that you hear some unpleasant clicks at the beginning or end of the clips. These clicks take place because the cuts occurred where the waveform doesn't rest at the zero line.

Figure 19-19:
Finding a
new home
for an audio
clip.

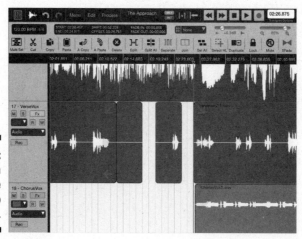

So what exactly does that mean? Think about every time you've seen an audio waveform in an app — there's a line running through the middle that represents a point where the waveform has no positive or negative movement. If you zoom in close enough on an audio waveform, you'll see it represented as a line moving through the audio clip. When you cut the audio clip where that line intersects the zero line, you remove the possibility of a clicking sound at the point of that code.

In Auria, find the closest possible view of the waveform and the zero line, and then place the playhead at that point, as shown in Figure 19-20.

You may need some additional practice to get this technique down, but keep at it. You'll get it, and you can always undo if necessary.

Adding crossfades

We already talked about fade ins and fade outs earlier in this section, and *crossfades* use those fades as part of its operation. Basically, a crossfade involves overlapping two audio clips, then adding a fade out on the first clip and a fade in on the second clip. If you've used DJing apps like djay or Traktor before, you're familiar with this concept. The cross part just means that you're adjusting the volume in different directions in the same track.

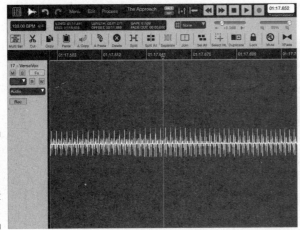

Figure 19-20: (Trying to) cut an audio clip without clicks.

So why would you want to perform a crossfade? Any time you want to join two audio clips, a crossfade helps make the blend smoother and more listenable. Several situations call for this kind of blend:

- ✔ Combining lead vocals or parts of a solo taken from different recordings into a single track (also known as *comping*)
- ✔ Mixing together two different songs as part of a mix
- ✔ Smoothing over loops
- ✔ Any time you need to combine two clips and you want to prevent unwanted clicks and pops

You could manually perform the crossfade, but most audio editors perform this operation automatically. Take a look at Figure 19-21, where we have two guitar solo clips that we want to blend together.

We drag the two clips over each other to the point where we're happy with the blend, and then we tap the XFade button (short for crossfade — feel technical by learning the shorthand!) to automatically create the crossfade (as shown in Figure 19-22).

After you create the crossfade, you can grab the handles to move the crossfade around for a little tweaking, and you can also choose the type of crossfade you wish to use, as shown in Figure 19-23.

You can tweak and modify the crossfade as much as you wish until you get it just the right way. It's a powerful tool — practice it and get it right!

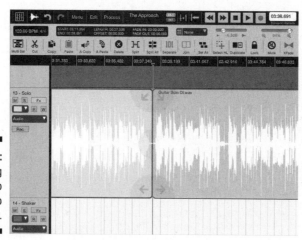

Figure 19-21:
Blending together two guitar solo tracks.

Figure 19-22:
The initial crossfade.

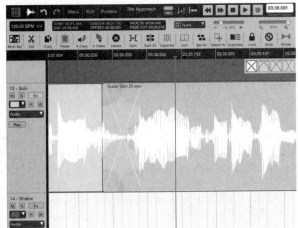

Figure 19-23:
Tweaking your cross-fade.

Cleaning up your tracks

You'll probably never get your audio tracks just right the first time through. If you could, nobody would need to build apps for editing audio after the fact. But more than likely, you'll need to do some additional work on your tracks. This section contains some common tasks you'll need to do and how to perform them.

Removing silence or unwanted noise at the beginning

You can either cut the sound out by splitting a clip and deleting it or using the trim functions in your audio editor to move the beginning or end points on the clip.

Some audio editors offer noise reduction functions that analyze a part of the audio, then use that analysis to remove the noise from the clip. The background noise at the beginning of your audio clip could be a great place to analyze that background noise without the main signal causing issues.

Removing breath sounds

Suppose you're working with a vocal or narration track that sounds great, but you want to remove breath sounds from the track. You can highlight those sections and insert silence to take that noise out. We find this technique preferable to cutting the sections out because you retain the natural timing of the vocal track, without risking moving the audio clips.

Adjusting volume and equalization

Most of the time, you want to handle volume and equalization concerns in the mixing process (which we discuss more in Chapter 20). However, especially if you're not doing any mixing (on a solo track, perhaps) or something is particularly egregious and you want to fix it now, go ahead and fix it in the audio editor. No time like the present to solve bad problems.

Adjusting large-volume issues

Suppose you recorded a live event that alternated between speaking on a mic and really loud songs. The audio editor is a perfect tool to make the volume a little more equal. Why do we mention this situation? Well, the volume changes are much larger, of course, and merit a little more attention rather than an overall volume adjustment.

Chapter 20

Mixing Your Music

● ●

In This Chapter

▶ Planning your mixes before you get started

▶ Tweaking your tracks with different effects

▶ Placing the tracks in the proper sonic space

▶ Automating mixing processes for the best possible results

● ●

A single chapter about mixing music can only hope to hit the highlights of what you should do with your tracks. Great minds wrote volumes on this topic, schools teach multiple classes on techniques, and years of learning and experience go into creating the best mixers on the planet. So, let us manage your expectations a little — the advice in this chapter isn't enough to make you into a stellar mixing engineer — overnight.

What this chapter CAN do is start you to the right road to mixing your tracks using the tools available to you on your iOS device. We take a look at available tools and how you can use them as part of the mixing process. And you can start letting your ears do the work as you create your masterpieces. Let's get started!

Adopting a Mixing Strategy

Before you jump into your mixing process, take a look at the overall product you wish to create. If you're creating an electronic dance track, you want the beat to carry and influence the entire track — how it comes in, when the breaks occur, and how you move into different sections of the track. For solo acoustic performances, maybe you want to focus on the vocals and build the song around that part. Even if the song doesn't have vocals, your music will have a part you want to emphasize and make the focal point of the track, even if that role changes from section to section (such as a jazz group where soloists take over for each other after initially playing the melody together.

The first step to mixing involves getting comfortable with the music. That doesn't necessarily mean that you need to find the comfiest chair and settle in, although you should be prepared to spend more than a little time with the process. Mixing isn't an immediate process — you're going to spend a lot of time tweaking and adjusting a lot of factors as part of your efforts, so prepare yourself. But really getting comfortable with the music involves knowing all the parts of the song, whether you performed them or not. You need to take the music and listen back to the tracks a few times (maybe after taking a little time away from the recording process to gain a clear mind and ear) to gain an understanding of the song as a whole.

When you play your tracks back, push up all the faders and get a rough balance to hear all of the parts together. Give each part close to the same amount of volume, and use the master fader to move down the overall level of the song to keep from introducing too much distortion and to spare your ears. Your goal is to hear all the parts at the same level so you can begin to tweak parts individually and create a bigger whole.

At least at this stage, you should always think about moving volume on other tracks down rather than boosting the volume to emphasize a single track. By doing so, you keep enough headroom in your mix to make sure peaks don't introduce distortion into your mix, and you leave yourself the space necessary to add effects and mastering processing later.

Nobody says the faders have to stay in the same position for the entire song! Don't get too attached to a single spot for your tracks — you can use automation to move volume levels as necessary, as we discuss in the "Controlling the Mix with Level Setting and Automation" section later in this chapter.

When you gain your understanding of the song as a whole and decide on the parts you want to emphasize, you can figure out how the other parts of the song support the tracks you want to emphasize (either by their presence or their absence) and make your tweaks from there. The rest of the sections in this chapter tackle how you can modify tracks to make them fit well together. Remember, you're trying to bring all the parts together to create a larger whole. Bricks, building blocks, however you want to think about them — the tracks build the foundation, the walls, and the accents of the building that is your finished track.

Let's take a look at a track in Auria, with all the faders pushed up, during playback. (See Figure 20-1.)

The first thing to notice is that the levels are pretty loud. At unity gain (0 dB), the tracks are already near (or even above) the levels we want for mixing. Time to drag the faders down to a more reasonable level!

Figure 20-1:
Initial
playback of
a recording
session.

Applying EQ

Equalization lets you adjust the frequencies present in a track to either
reduce problems or make the part stand out in an area that no other instruments occupy. Every instrument or port occupies a sonic space in your mix,
and your goal should be to find a place for each part in the mix to let that
part stand out.

So where do conflicts arise? You're more likely to see clashes where the
instruments try to occupy both the same role and the same sonic space.
Think about the low end, where the kick drum, the bass guitar, and the low
end of the keyboard hang out. Those frequencies can get muddy and mixed
up easily just by virtue of being in that sonic range, but the amount of instruments playing down there can cause issues as well. You can use equalization
to reduce frequencies on these instruments to make sure they all stand out.
You can also use a *high-pass filter* on the instruments that automatically cuts
all frequencies below a certain level to keep the track's rumble from getting
out of control.

On the other side of the spectrum, you can add a little high end to parts to
give them a little sparkle and shine, or take the high end down a bit to eliminate any harshness. Higher frequencies tend to stand out more on earbuds
and systems with smaller speakers, so making sure these parts stand out
without overpowering the song should be a high priority.

And then, of course, you must make sure everything else falls into place.
Keyboards and guitars take up a lot of sonic space, and you must find a place
for each part in the mix. That may mean taking something out of the rhythm

guitar to make space for the lead. Don't forget about vocals, either — you need to find the right frequencies for any singers to show off the unique nature of their voices. Every instrument and voice has a unique sound and emphasizes certain frequencies more than others.

This section gives you a little better idea of the frequencies common instruments use and where you can tweak those instruments to bring out the sound you want.

All values on this list are approximate. These instruments general find themselves in this range, but actual results may vary depending on construction and where you record the instrument. The ranges are also very large, covering the fundamentals of the note through all possible overtones.

- ✔ **Drums:**
  - *Bass Drum:* 50 Hz to 5 kHz.
  - *Toms:* 80 Hz to 7 kHz.
  - *Snare Drum:* 100 Hz to 10 kHz.
  - *Cymbals:* 200 Hz to 12 kHz.
- ✔ **Bass Guitar:** 30 Hz to 5 kHz.
- ✔ **Guitar:** 70 Hz to 5 kHz.
- ✔ **Keyboard:** 27 Hz to 4.3 kHz.
- ✔ **Brass:** Anywhere from 30 Hz to 2 kHz for a tuba to 170 Hz to 9 kHz for a trumpet.
- ✔ **Woodwinds:** Saxes and clarinets can range from around 120 Hz up to 13 kHz.
- ✔ **Male Voice:** Anywhere from 100 Hz to 16 kHz, depending on the vocal range of the singer.
- ✔ **Female Voice:** Anywhere from 250 Hz to 16 kHz, depending on the vocal range of the singer.

So what's with the big range of frequencies? Every note has a *fundamental* pitch (the main note you hear) and a series of *overtones* (different frequencies that you also hear that give the instrument its characteristic sound, also known as *timbre*). As you boost or cut frequencies along the range of the instrument, you change the characteristics of the sound.

- ✔ Frequencies from 20 Hz to around 250 Hz add the low bass and rumble to sounds, but can quickly overwhelm a mix.
- ✔ Electrical hum occurs at 60 Hz in the United States. If you hear that kind of hum or have grounding issues, this frequency is where the sound occurs.

✔ Frequencies from 250 Hz to 800 Hz can sound a little more bass presence, but watch that you don't make the sounds too muddy.

✔ Frequencies from 1 to 6 kHz can emphasize the fundamentals of most notes, but watch that the sounds don't overwhelm other instruments in the same range or become too tinny or honking.

✔ Anything above 6 kHz adds high-end frequencies (think treble, not really expensive frequencies) to the instrument, from the sizzle of cymbals to air and shimmer on other instruments. These frequencies can add to your mix, but they can quickly become annoying if you add too much.

✔ Vocal sibilance can occur between 4 kHz and 10 kHz, depending on the range of the voice. If you hear too much emphasis on the "ess" sound of your vocals, you may want to look at reducing those frequencies.

If you have to add more than three or four dB to an instrument, you might want to think about cutting other frequencies on the track to compensate. Boosting the EQ adds gain to the overall tracks, and you could be adding peaks that affect your headroom and possibly cause distortion down the road. You might also think about reducing the EQ of other frequencies in the signal (subtractive EQ) as opposed to raising the EQ of the frequency you want (additive EQ) to make sure your signal doesn't get too out of hand.

In the sample track, we want to bump up the boom on the kick drum — it's a little thin as it is. To alter the EQ in Auria, we tap the FX button, pull up the EQ section, and use the lower frequency EQ to select 60 Hz and bump that frequency up around 3 dB. (See Figure 20-2.)

Figure 20-2:
Boosting the bass on a kick drum.

Boosting bass frequencies without the aid of a professional monitoring system can get a little hairy, because a number of systems can't accurately reproduce those frequencies. (We're looking at you, earbuds.) Make sure you use a monitoring system that can handle bass frequencies (good monitors or subwoofers) before playing around with these sonic ranges.

The EQ used in this example is a *parametric EQ,* which allows you to select both the frequency and the amount of gain you can add or cut. Move the frequency around until you find the right frequency and then start cutting or boosting the gain.

Using Compression

Singers and instrumentalists alike can make glorious noise at all volume and dynamic levels. Why wouldn't we, when it's so much *fun?!* But all those variations can make the mixing process quite a daunting prospect. All of those changes in volume and dynamics make it hard for a track to "sit" properly in the mix, meaning that you have to tweak the track a little bit to help it blend with the other tracks and maintain a presence in the mix.

And that's where compression comes in. A little compression helps tame extreme peaks and valleys in an audio signal, adding more volume to the softer parts and easing the volume off in the louder parts. A lot of compression pumps up the track and puts it in the listener's face (or at least the listener's ears). Depending on the compressor you use, you can work on mono or stereo signals or handle the peaks in an audio signal versus the average level of the audio signal. Right now, let's take a look at the basic compression controls:

- **Threshold:** The audio level at which compression kicks in, usually expressed in dB

- **Ratio:** The amount by which the compressor reduces the audio level, also usually expressed in dB

- **Attack:** The amount of time a compressor takes to react to an audio signal, usually expressed in milliseconds

- **Release:** The amount of time a compressor takes to release the audio signal, also usually expressed in milliseconds

- **Soft or Hard Knee:** Whether the compressor uses a smooth, subtle response when compressing the audio (soft knee) or a more extreme response (hard knee)

- **Gain:** The amount of gain added to the compressed audio to make up for the gain reduction from the compressor

If you set your compressor for –8 dB and a 3:1 ratio and run a –5 dB signal through that compressor, that –3 dB reduces to –1 dB of output. The attack setting of 10 ms indicates the compressor engages after encountering 10 ms of that volume level, and the release setting of 50 ms indicates the compression lets go of the audio signal after than amount of time elapses. You can set it to a soft knee setting to smooth things out, and set the gain to compensate for the gain reduction of the compressor (most compressors offer meters to help you figure out how much gain you need to add back).

Yep, that's a lot of controls. And compressors offer a wide variety of functionality, from slight compression on a bass guitar or vocal track to extreme limiting on volume peaks. The following sections provide some common compression uses when mixing.

These values represent a good starting point, but you should adjust to taste. Seriously, every mixer starts in different places for different reason. Think of these numbers as the beginning of your sonic recipe, trust your ears, and listen and experiment as much as possible to know how your equipment works and what you want to get out of it.

All of these settings rely on a good, strong signal with proper gain staging. Otherwise, you may introduce noise or distortion into the track.

Vocals

Start with the threshold around –3 dB, a ratio of between 2:1 and 4:1, an attack of 1 to 5 ms, and a release of around 40 ms. This setting creates a slight effect that helps tame peaks in the vocals. Depending on the levels of the signal, you may need to lower the threshold so more of the audio signal triggers the compressor.

Guitar

Electric guitars may benefit from a little compression beginning at a –2 dB threshold, a ratio beginning at 2:1, an attack beginning at 25 ms, and a release around 200 ms. This setting can help clean electric guitar settings stand out a little more, but don't put too much compression on — your signal may lose definition and details. Running an electric guitar through an overdrive or fuzz setting adds a little compression, so you probably won't need to add much compression in that case.

Bass guitar

Slapped bass guitar can cause tremendous variations in dynamic levels —
after all, the bassist is literally hitting and pulling on strings harder as if it
were a percussion instrument. Start with a –8 dB threshold, a ratio of around
6:1, an attack around 10 ms, and a release of around 200 ms. This setting
helps takes the edge off of extreme peaks from overactive thumbs or plucking
fingers. If the bassist goes with normal finger plucking, you can ease off of the
threshold and ratio a bit.

Drums

Drum sounds include quick transients (the hit on the drum) and a quick
decay (the sound of the drum ringing after the hit). You can use compression
on single drums as well as the overhead mics usually placed on a kit.

For kick drums, start with a -5 dB threshold, a 3:1 ratio, a 5 ms attack, and a
200 ms release. You can also start with similar settings for the snare drum,
maybe nudging the threshold to –10 or –15 dB to compress the snare signal
more. Lighten up the compression settings for toms to let them ring a little,
and avoid compression on cymbals or hi-hats.

Piano and keyboards

Especially in the case of sampled sounds, you shouldn't need to add much
compression. These samples already saw some tweaking and finishing during
the initial recording process. You might experiment with some compression settings on wild synth sounds, but that's a matter left to your taste and
expression.

Additional types of compression

Up to this point, we've looked at compression as an effect applied to the
entire audio signal on a track. But you can use compressors for more subtle
and varied functions as well.

Sidechain

The sidechain compressor triggers compression settings based on an incoming
signal. You might also hear this effect known as *ducking*, where an incoming

vocal track reduces the volume of the backing tracks. A bass drum could also trigger compression settings to allow a bass guitar audio track through when the drum hits (and keep it quiet when it doesn't).

Parallel

Parallel compression sends a copy of the audio signal through a compressor, then blends the compressed signal in with the uncompressed signal. This effect tames some of the dynamic variation while still letting the signal sound "live."

Multiband

This compressor runs the audio signal through filters that split the audio signal into different frequency bands, then applies different compression settings to those bands. This effect is useful if you want to compress the low end of a track and let the rest of the track go unaffected (as seen in Figure 20-3).

Tracks versus overall mix

Compressing single tracks helps those tracks blend together better. Putting a stereo compressor on the final mix helps control the overall levels of a track. You usually see this type of compression (along with multiband compression) in the final mixing and mastering process. In Auria, you can see this kind of master compression on the master fader shown in Figure 20-4.

In the example track, we placed some compression on the bass guitar track to even out the dynamics, as shown in Figure 20-5.

Figure 20-3:
Multiband compression in the Final Touch app.

Figure 20-4:
Master
compression
in Auria.

Figure 20-5:
Compressing
the bass
guitar track.

Adding Reverb and Delay

Depending on how you record your tracks, you may already include reverb
or delay in your recording. After all, reverb is just the natural result of sound
bouncing off of the surrounding surfaces, whether those surfaces exist in a
small room, a grand concert hall, or some otherworldly place. And delay indicates an echo that comes back after a certain time (either in time with the
tempo or on its own). These time-based effects add a certain depth and presence to the tracks, as if you're determining the distance between the original
sound source and the listener. Be careful not to add too much and lose your

tracks in the wash (unless you're recording some shoegaze tracks, in which case, wash away!).

Reverb settings usually let you pick a room size (from closet to a concert hall, for example), then dial in the amount of reverb to use in relation to the original signal (also known as *wet* versus *dry* signal). Reverb plug-ins can also offer ways to adjust the wet signal, including how long the reverb rings out, how quickly the signal dampens, and other aspects of the effect. But the overall functionality simulates an acoustic environment and how your track would sound in that environment.

Delay settings include the amount of time between the dry signal and the delayed signal (which can be set to sync with the tempo of the song or as a set effect separate from that rhythm), the number of echoes you hear as part of the delay, and the volume level of the delayed signal. Most delays also include a wet/dry control to balance out the amount of original audio and the delayed audio. You can use these controls to set up anything from a *slap-back* echo (think the sound you hear on early rockabilly recordings) to the incredibly spacious (and spacy) echoes you hear in reggae and dub tracks. Depending on the intricacy of the delay, you may even cause the delayed signal to bounce around stereo channels (known as a *ping-pong* delay, partly because the audio signal acts like a ball bouncing around and partly because it's always fun to say "ping-pong") or *multi-tap* delay where the delay effects takes place in different rhythms, such as quarter notes or triplets from the same effect.

The mixing process usually adds reverb and delay to bring together all the tracks and make them seem part of a unified whole. After all, a band or other group of performers in the same space would encounter the same reverb or delay effect. Even if the tracks were recorded in totally different places at totally different times, you can put the same reverb effect on it and join them together in the same sonic space.

Because you might want to apply the same effect to multiple tracks, reverb and delay work well as *send* effects in the mix. In this case, you place the reverb effect on a separate track, then send a portion of the audio from the tracks to which you want to add reverb to that separate truck (often called a *bus*). You can determine the amount of signal you send and the volume level of the effect, which lets you precisely tailor the amount of reverb or delay you use.

In the sample track, we put the reverb effect in the Aux 1 slot. Tap the Aux FX button on the master track and select ClassicVerb in the first effects slot to see the controls in Figure 20-6.

Figure 20-6:
Placing reverb in the mix.

After we set the reverb settings to where we want them, we can turn the Aux 1 knob on each track to add the amount of reverb that sounds the best.

Too much reverb can cause things to get muddy and indistinct — make sure you add just enough effect (and no more).

Understanding the Soundscape and Panning

With reverb and delay, you help set the virtual distance between the listener and the instruments within a track. But that distance represents just a single factor in the overall soundscape of a track. Think of the soundscape as a stage on which your instruments perform. The reverb and delay help determine how close the instruments are to the audience (closer to the edge of the stage or buried towards the back). But you can also think of the volume level as determining the size of the instrument on the stage, with louder instruments taking up more room on stage than the quieter parts. And *panning* controls help place the instruments to the left or right of the stage.

When you first start recording tracks, you probably don't think much about where the instruments actually reside in the stereo mix. But just imagine how crowded the stage would be if all of the actors and actresses crowded together in the middle of the stage, competing for the same space as they try to recite their lines and move around. Any audience would watch this performance and think it was a total train wreck.

By panning the instruments left or right, you give the tracks their own sonic space without needing to boost or decrease volume levels. You also create a more immersive environment, where the tracks take up the whole stereo field and simulate a realistic performance.

It might help to draw a picture (mental or on paper, your choice) of how you view the tracks in your mind (whether you use a traditional rock band setup or something more expressive or abstract) to help you determine how you want to place your tracks in the soundscape. We use the rock band for the sake of familiarity, but let your imagination run wild:

- The lead vocalist usually goes at the center of the stage with a strong volume level (because he or she insists on it and might leave the group otherwise).

- The drums usually go center stage as well, but they appear a little farther back on the stage (indicating a little more reverb on the instrument).

- If you have two guitarists, you'll usually see them on opposite sides of the stage (unless one has to show the chords to the other or something).

- Sadly, the bassist usually sticks closer to the drums in the back.

- Keyboards can go anywhere on stage, as can the horn section or any auxiliary percussion.

- Background vocals can also appear anywhere in the mix, depending on who is singing and where.

Given this stage setup, you can pan the guitarists to opposite sides of the stereo field, place the vocals in the center, and put the kick drum in the center with slight pan tweaks to the drums and cymbals around that. Then put the other instruments in their own place, wherever you see them on the stage. This approach gives you a rough setting, and you'll need to make adjustments from there to get everything dialed in properly. But at least you get your initial placement.

Just because an instrument starts out at a certain point on stage doesn't mean it needs to *stay* in that place. Imagine the lead guitarist moving to the center of the stage for the solo, then going back after completing that epic rock moment. You can move the pan control (or automate it, using the controls detailed in the next section) to place emphasis on a part during a certain section of a song, then put it back where it needs to be to support the track.

In the example track, we set the pan controls to place all the instruments in the stereo track where we want them, as shown in Figure 20-7.

Figure 20-7:
Panning
tracks in
the mix.

Controlling the Mix with Level Setting and Automation

If you've ever seen a documentary set in a professional recording studio, you've probably seen a mixing board where the faders zoom up and down automatically, without any human contact. This kind of programming offers a lot of value, because otherwise you have to gather around a bunch of humans on larger mixers (or, optionally, an extremely intelligent octopus) to move the faders during the mixing process to make sure every part has the proper volume, effect, and pan settings at the right time. But those automated mixing boards cost a lot of money and probably won't fit into your home recording space (and is surely much bigger than your iPhone or iPad, anyway).

Luckily, with modern DAW apps, you can draw in these changes or record the automation on a per-track basis so that these settings occur automatically during mixdown. The process may not look as cool as all those faders moving up and down automatically, but it gives you the same results and saves a lot of space, time, and money.

In the example track, we set some volume and pan automation. In the edit screen, we selected Volume from the drop-down menu shown in Figure 20-8.

Figure 20-8:
Choosing
the
parameter
to automate.

We tapped the points in the track to begin and end the automation, then moved them to the correct positions (as shown in Figure 20-9).

We then chose the pan control in the drop-down menu and moved it from one side to the other. We also chose a little more graceful curve for the pan, as shown in Figure 20-10.

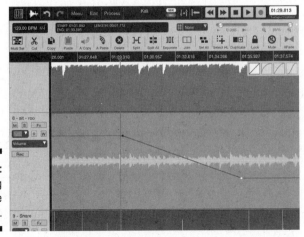

Figure 20-9:
Lowering
the volume
a little bit.

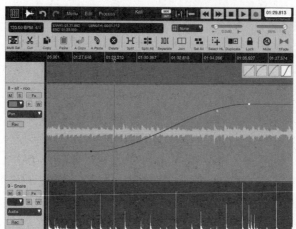

Figure 20-10:
Moving the track from side to side.

Mixing Better with These Tips and Tricks

Every track is different, so you can't always apply the same settings to every song you record. But this section gives you some sound (sorry for the pun) advice about making your mix the best you can.

- **Use your monitors and headphones:** Monitors give you a good impression of the overall balance of your mix, and headphones help you zero in on precise details (and avoid waking up the kids). Use both tools to help you find the right mix.

- **Listen on a variety of sources:** From your high-end stereo system to those crappy, crappy earbuds, every audio source can help you tweak your mix a little. After you finish a mix, listen to it on every device you can to see what you might need to fix. Just don't put too much faith in the earbuds.

- **Make the instrument sound right in the mix, not on its own:** Remember, you're not crafting a series of solo performances — you're making a final mix of your song. The parts only work well when they work well together. You can get a huge, booming drum sound that completely overwhelms everything else in the track and therefore bogs down the song. Tweak EQ, compression, effects, and more to get everything playing well together, and you'll be well on your way to getting a good mix.

- **Give yourself time and take breaks:** Ears and brains get tired, and you can't create good tracks with tired tools. Every time you finish a mix, take a little break before moving on and evaluating. Getting a little time and distance from the work gives you a fresh perspective and more rest to make better decisions.

✔ **You can start with presets, but they're not your final destination:**
Again, because every mix is different, presets won't fix everything. But
they will give you a good start from which to make changes. If your DAW
allows it, you can even create your own presets for use later. But don't
just choose the preset and let it lie there. Keep listening, keep tweaking,
and you'll get there.

Mastering

After you finish your mix, your tracks are ready for the mastering process.
Professional mastering engineers spend many years learning this craft, using
precisely honed and tuned skills in conjunction with expensive equipment
to adjust, modify, and sequence tracks (in the case of an album) to put the
finishing touches on your recording. So although this book can't contain all
of the knowledge about mastering (although several other books have tried),
let's review the steps that go into the mastering process, using the Final
Touch app shown in Figure 20-3.

1. **Pre EQ**

   After you finish the mix and get the best possible track, you may still need
   to perform a last little EQ tweak here and there. This steps allows you to
   start that process with some fine EQ adjustment. Remember — most of
   the work should be done by now. This step (shown in Figure 20-11) lets
   you add a little salt to taste, rather than pouring a whole cup on the dish.

2. **Reverb**

   If the track could use a little more depth, or maybe get a little more
   simulated realism from existing in a sonic space, you can place a little
   reverb on the entire track to give it some life, as shown in Figure 20-12.

3. **Dynamics**

   As we saw earlier in the "Compressor" section, the multiband compressor comes in useful here for taming the dynamics of certain aspects of
   the track while leaving the rest alone. You may need to knock the bass
   down a little even as you retain an uncompressed, lively top end in the
   cymbals. Used correctly, this step makes that possible.

4. **Stereo Imaging**

   Stereo imaging (shown in Figure 20-13) lets you stretch the track further
   into the stereo field and test the mono/stereo compatibility of your
   track. Switching to mono helps you find out if any frequencies cancel
   each other out and make the tracks sound thinner. You may have to go
   back to the mixing process to fix that issue, but better to find out now
   than after you release your music.

5. Post EQ

After all of those tweaks, a little more EQ may be in order (shown in Figure 20-14). Again, small tweaks, but this step helps you shape everything up.

6. Maximizer

This final step takes the track, bumps up the volume to the specified level (from pleasant to CLUB BANGING, although we advise caution with the CLUB BANGING level), and, in the case of Final Touch, establishes *dithering* settings. You might not need to dither your track, which involves introducing a little digital noise into the track to retain good audio quality as you move it from a higher audio resolution (such as 24-bit/96 kHz) to a lower audio resolution (such as the CD-quality 16-bit/44.1 kHz). But if you do make such a change, dithering can help you make that transition smoother.

Ultimately, the goal of the maximizer is to take the final product and boost it to the correct level for your listeners. This step is why you correctly set your headroom earlier in the recording and mixing steps — to allow the track to exist at the correct volume setting with all parts equally represented. Take a look at Figure 20-15 to see what a sampler maximizer looks like.

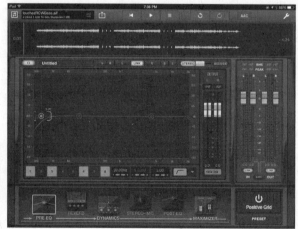

Figure 20-11:
The Pre EQ step in Final Touch.

Figure 20-12:
The Reverb
step in Final
Touch.

Figure 20-13:
The Stereo
Imaging
step in Final
Touch.

When you master your tracks, the song is done! Let it fly into the world!

Mastering your own tracks may save you some time and money, but never discount the potential that a real mastering engineer can provide. If you plan to seriously release your tracks as a potential money-making enterprise, consider the investment.

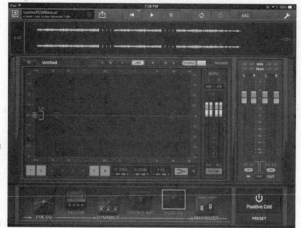

Figure 20-14:
The Post EQ step in Final Touch.

Figure 20-15:
The Maximizer step in Final Touch.

If you want to dig deeper into home recording, you can pick up even more knowledge in *Home Recording For Musicians For Dummies* from Wiley, authored by the always-knowledgeable Jeff Strong. Recording exists in its own world, and there's always more to learn.

Chapter 21

Exporting Your Finished Masterpiece

- -

In This Chapter

▶ Understanding the file formats available to you

▶ Choosing the right export option for your project or file

▶ Putting your music online

- -

*T*he end product of any successful mixing and mastering session is a final track worthy of sharing with the world. Or at least the people you wish to share your music with. In any case, once your tracks are ready, you must figure out how you'll deliver your music to the masses. After all, you can't just hand over your iPhone or iPad to everybody and play the track out of the apps you used to create it!

This chapter covers the file formats you can use to create your final tracks and the benefits and drawbacks of each. Most apps offers a multitude of export options, so you should become familiar with all potential file formats. You may not even need to create multiple file formats — think about placing your files on websites and services designed specifically to distribute your music and let them create the different versions from a single hi-res file.

Understanding File Formats

The alphabet soup of available file formats may seem a little confusing, but every format offers something useful to musicians. Take a look at the formats in this section and select the best format for your needs.

Before we get started though, a word of advice: You should always export your file into either a WAV or AIFF for safekeeping. Why? Because AIFF and WAV offer uncompressed audio that doesn't lose any data and can be read by all major recording and DAW apps. You can always make compressed audio files from these uncompressed files at any time later.

Never try to export a new file format from a compressed file format such as AAC or MP3. Putting that audio data through two compression processes further degrades the audio quality. Always export compressed files from an uncompressed source.

WAV

WAV files can provide uncompressed audio file at a variety of bit depths and sampling rates. Because WAV offers high levels of quality, you can use this format to create final master recordings of audio files for use as a source for other formats, from physical media to streaming files. And you'll probably want to use these different formats, because WAV files can become quite large the longer you record.

If you plan on performing further editing on the file after export, you should also consider WAV or AIFF (discussed in the next session). Always edit in uncompressed files. Again, you should only put audio files through one round of data compression.

AIFF

Microsoft uses WAV files as the default for uncompressed audio, but Apple uses AIFF files as its chosen default. Don't worry — these file formats have been around long enough that audio editors can handle either one without issue. And although they may use different types of coding, both WAV and AIFF files produce the same basic end product: an uncompressed audio file suitable for archiving, compressed audio exports, or other editing uses.

Given that you're working with an iOS device, though, you may want to pay special attention to the AIFF format. Apple Loops uses the AIFF format and offers a little more flexibility within apps like GarageBand. If you know you're sticking with Apple products for your editing and processing needs, AIFF may provide better looping and metadata options for you down the road. If you're collaborating with Windows folks, though, you may want to consider WAV.

MP3

MP3 is the file format that changed the world, and its ability to compress audio down to easily transmitted and stored file sizes keeps it alive long after its introduction many years ago. If you plan on sharing your audio with the widest possible audience, go with MP3: Everybody can handle MP3 files.

That said, MP3 files (which use *lossy* compression schemes that subtract audio data from the original recording) don't provide the best possible audio quality, and your listeners may prefer a more high-fidelity experience than MP3s can provide. Then again, if you stream the audio over earbuds, that audio quality may not make that much of a difference. Just remember to use the highest possible audio quality you can when creating your MP3 files. In this day of high speed cellular networks and broadband Internet, you have no reason to skimp on audio quality at this point.

AAC

Songs you buy from the iTunes Store come in AAC format, also a lossy compressed format. That said, Apple tweaked the format to provide slightly better audio quality than MP3 at a similar file size. Again, if you're sure your listeners will listen on OS X- or iOS-powered devices, AAC may provide a better audio experience.

So much more goes into your audio signal chain than the file format: Good headphones or speakers, the device used, the background audio, and so much more combine to provide the optimum listening experience. All you can do is give your listeners the best possible song. The rest of the experience is out of your hands.

ALAC/FLAC

ALAC (which stands for Apple Lossless Audio Codec) and *FLAC* (which stands for Free Lossless Audio Codec) audio both provide a smaller file size while offering uncompressed audio quality. It sounds like the best of both worlds, and FLAC has caught on as a popular format for those who trade recordings of live shows (legally obtained, mind you) or those who want better quality audio out of their digital recordings.

Unfortunately, the native Music player on your iPhone or iPad (along with iTunes) will not handle FLAC files out of the box. You can purchase apps or plug-ins to work your FLAC files into your listening rotation. However, you may find that Apple's version of lossless compression (ALAC) fits better into your iOS lifestyle (as this format does work natively with iTunes and the Music app). If you plan on sharing your music with a wider audience, though, FLAC files may reach beyond Apple-based listeners more effectively. In any case, recording in 24-bit audio now allows you to make the transition more easily, no matter which format you use.

Other formats

Depending on where you procure your audio files, you may run across other audio formats like WMA (the Windows version of lossy audio compression), Ogg Vorbis (the open-source version of lossy audio compression), OggPCM (the open source version of uncompressed audio, like WAV or AIFF), and many more. These file formats usually belong to more specialized devices or older codecs, so you probably won't run across them very often. More than likely, you'll be looking for a way to convert these files to another format so you can use them on your iOS device. Just remember that moving from one lossy compression format to another will cause degradation in the audio quality.

Knowing Your Export Options

So when it comes time to export your files, what steps should you perform? If you know the possibilities, your choices become pretty clear. This section tackles the options in order to make sure you keep your files sounding as good as possible.

Go high fidelity early

When you export your music, you should initially export to an uncompressed audio file at the highest possible resolution. So if you recorded your audio at 24-bit, 96 kHZ sample rate, you need to export to a WAV or AIFF format at the very beginning. This file represents your first generation master recording, from which all of your future audio files will spring.

Thankfully, you can make as many copies as necessary from this file as you wish. Unlike analog recording, where each copy degrades the audio quality a bit, the zeroes and ones that make up your audio files don't get worse as you make more copies. The only change comes from any data compression the file format may perform.

If you go lossy, go high quality lossy

When iTunes first rolled out, it sold files at 128 Kbps. Today, that resolution sounds puny compared to the other options available to you. But not everybody needs uncompressed audio, either. You simply cannot fit enough WAVE or AIFF files on a mobile device to fill the random, short-attention-span listening habits of the average music listener. So you're probably going to have to make some lossy compromises, especially if you want to sell files on an online service.

That said, make sure you create any lossy audio files at 320 Kbps, if possible, or at 256 Kbps, if necessary. (256 Kbps is where iTunes sets its files.) It's likely that your listeners won't be able to tell the difference between the two files (especially if they're listening on earbuds in a noisy environment). But given that storage is relatively cheap and some might be able to tell the difference, the increased size isn't that big of a hit here.

You can export compressed files from either the app you used to record the audio or from your uncompressed audio file, whichever you prefer.

Check with your partners

If you're working with a service that distributes music or creates physical media like CDs or vinyl records, make sure you check with them to see what kind of files they need — *especially* if you're dealing with vinyl records, since files that are too loud or don't follow the RIAA standards for equalization may cause the creation process to fail (and waste time and money). You'll find that investing into a mastering service that specifically handles vinyl is worth the money.

Yet another good reason to keep an uncompressed audio copy around? So you can go back and make changes that don't cause you to waste time and money.

Export your projects, too!

Exporting doesn't just revolve around your final listening file. You also want to export a copy of the finished project file, if possible. You can't listen to your project file in a music app, but you can go back and create additional files (or changes) from the project.

Depending on the app, you could also work on your initial project in a computer-based DAW. For example, Auria exports projects in AAF format, which DAWs like Logic Pro X and Pro Tools can handle with ease. This kind of export helps assure that, even if you lose your iOS device, you can still work with your music down the road.

Finally, you might also want to export different versions of your tracks (with and without vocals, with and without effects, and so on) for use in different tasks down the road.

How to Use SoundCloud

SoundCloud doesn't just provide a central site hosting millions of hours of music (although it does that well). The site doesn't offer social links, allowing you to follow your favorite artists and share posted tracks with those users that follow you (although it handles that task with ease). SoundCloud takes this functionality and wraps it with the ability to use *widgets* (bits of code that embed music on other sites) to share posted tracks all over the Internet, using social networks, websites, and mobile apps alike. SoundCloud basically allows you to share your music with the world and let the world take over from there.

Reviewing the types of accounts

You can sign up for a SoundCloud account easily enough — just go over to SoundCloud's website at `http://soundcloud.com` and open an account like any other social network. The basic free account lets you interact with SoundCloud users and upload up to three hours of audio at no charge.

You can upgrade to Pro or Unlimited status, which gets you extra hours of uploads. But you also get more access to information about the folks who listen to your music, how you can present your music to your listeners, and more control over how your listeners can interact with your account. This structure represents a similar take on the "freemium" structure adopted by mobile apps. So why would you want to upgrade? Here are two good reasons:

- ✔ You're incredibly prolific and want to post more than three hours of music.

- ✔ You want to know how and when your listeners listen so you can better target them. This means knowing if a geographic location contains a lot of fans for a tour stop or if a social network like Twitter hosts a lot of chatter about your music so you can join in on the conversation.

Otherwise, you can probably stick with the free account for the time being. This account lets you perform the basic sharing and conversation tasks you need to start getting your music out.

Uploading your tracks

After you create your account, you can upload tracks to SoundCloud in two different ways:

✔ Export the final track to your computer and upload that track to SoundCloud via your web browser.

✔ Upload the track directly to SoundCloud from the music app you used to create it.

The best method to use depends on your situation. If you have the time to run your track through several different apps, then export a high quality final track and move it to your computer, that might present the best option for you. However, if you're in the field and want to upload your file for immediate release, go ahead and make your move. You can even record audio directly from your mobile SoundCloud app.

The audio quality of your SoundCloud files depends on how you intend to distribute them. SoundCloud permits both streaming and downloads, and the downloadable files don't change their file format or resolution. You can use huge uncompressed files like AIFF or WAV, lossless compressed files like FLAC or ALAC, or lossy compressed files like MP3, AAC, or WMA (among others).

The only thing SoundCloud doesn't do is charge for tracks. You can do just about anything from this site but sell your music.

If you stream your audio, though, every track becomes a 128 Kbps MP3 file. No matter what file format you initially used, SoundCloud *transcodes* that file to the new format.

To avoid compressing the same track twice, make sure you upload uncompressed files for songs you wish to allow downloads for. SoundCloud will transcode the file anyway, so make sure you give it the best possible starting point.

If the app you used to record your track allows direct posting to SoundCloud, the process becomes pretty simple for you. The SoundCloud export option usually appears after you finish your recording. For example, after you make a recording in Loopy HD, you can tap the SoundCloud button to see the screen shown in Figure 21-1.

Figure 21-1:
Starting
your jour-
ney to
SoundCloud.

Sign into your SoundCloud account to see the options shown in Figure 21-2.

The name, location, and image fields of the track are easy enough to understand. So take a look at the switches under those fields.

The Public/Private switch lets you determine who can listen to your track. Public makes your music available to the world, whereas Private posts it for your use only. You can also add email addresses that let you offer access to other listeners.

Figure 21-2:
Setting
SoundCloud
upload
options in
Loopy HD.

The Add/Don't Add switch lets you link your tracks to the Loopy group in SoundCloud, so other users of the app can listen and comment on your work. SoundCloud hosts many, many groups — some associated with genres, some with apps (Korg Gadget also offers a user group with rankings and other features), some with no connection to reality (just like the rest of the Internet, really). Finally, you can link other social networks to your app to automatically create tweets or posts when you post a new track.

Sharing the music

Even if you don't automatically alert your social networks when you first post a track to SoundCloud, you can sound the alarms once you're ready. For example, maybe you finally want to share a private track with the world. When you're ready, open your mobile SoundCloud app and navigate to the track you wish to share. Notice the social network icons displayed in Figure 21-3.

Tap the icon, enter your social network credentials as needed, and post the track. All of your fans and followers can now access and share your tracks with their friends as well.

This point is where SoundCloud hopes you'll pay for the Pro or Unlimited accounts — they know who is playing your track and where, but they want you to pay for that knowledge. You'll have to decide for yourself if this price is worth it. If you're doing it for fun, it might not be worth the expense. If you're trying to make money off of your efforts, though, this information could be lucrative.

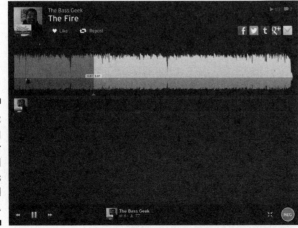

Figure 21-3:
Sharing
your
SoundCloud
tracks
on social
media.

SoundCloud can (and will) pull down any tracks that use material from copy-written material. Do it too much, and you could be faced with a suspended account. Use only material you have permission to use.

Sharing Your Music on Social Media

Even if you don't opt to upload your tracks to SoundCloud, you can still post your tracks to social media to share with all (or just a few). Again, the mobile app developers who create the apps you use determine whether you can post your tracks directly from the app to your social media accounts, but most apps can connect with Facebook, Twitter, YouTube, or other accounts to put your music online. For example, in GarageBand, you can select a song and tap the Export icon to move your song to a social media account (as shown in Figure 21-4).

Tap the account you want to use and link the app to your social media account. You're off! Most apps will offer basic Facebook and Twitter func-tionality, as shown in Figure 21-5. Figure also offers additional export options (such as email, SoundCloud, and more), but it puts Twitter and Facebook front and center because they offer the most reach at this time.

Facebook offers several layers of sharing permissions, from your own private use to sharing with friends to sharing with everybody. But if you post a track to Facebook and set permissions, it can also restrict who your friends can share it with. If you want the fullest possible audience, consider posting the track on a central repository such as SoundCloud and sharing the track from there. That way, even people who aren't on Facebook can get access to your track.

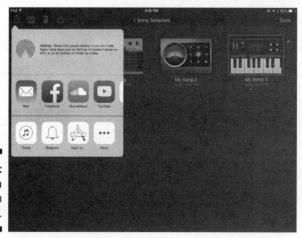

Figure 21-4:
Exporting a song from GarageBand.

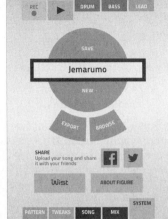

Figure 21-5:
Posting
Figure
tracks to
Facebook
and Twitter.

Heading to Bandcamp

Even with iTunes, Amazon, and other online music stores, you still encountered some hurdles when trying to sell your music online. You had to go through services like CD Baby or Tunecore to place your tracks in those services, or you had to work out your own system online. But with the advent of Bandcamp, you can easily put your music online for sale at a variety of price points (from name-your-own-price to a specified minimum amount to a set price). You can even offer subscriptions to your work for a yearly membership fee. Bandcamp also lets others share word of your music through a variety of methods, including:

- Links to embeddable tracks
- Sharing to social media
- Public collections hosted on Bandcamp fan sites

Bandcamp offers several different options and account types, and you can customize those options to fill your needs. Payments go directly to a PayPal account.

Link your PayPal account to a separate online bank account and not to your main checking or savings account for the sake of security. You can move funds from the specific account to your main accounts once the funds go through PayPal.

Export all of the tracks you plan to use on Bandcamp as uncompressed audio. Bandcamp offers different options for download, including MP3, FLAC, and ALAC. But the service handles all transcoding from those files. From there, you can follow a basic social media plan for your music:

1. Upload your tracks to Bandcamp.

2. Embed the streaming widgets on your website (you *do* have a website, right?).

3. Share the streaming tracks on social media with a link.

4. Thank everybody who buys your music with a personal note. Hopefully this will lead you into the problem of writing too much email or social media notes. And Bandcamp will also allow you to exchange downloads in exchange for email addresses, so you can increase the size of your mailing list.

If you're planning on making a push to sell your music, create separate Twitter, Facebook, and other social media accounts for your music. That way, you can stay on message with your music and not your personal photos or thoughts on reality television.

Part VII
The Part of Tens

 See ten other musician's tools for your iPhone or iPad at www.dummies.com/extras/ipadandiphoneformusicians.

In this part . . .

- ✔ Track down some can't-miss audio apps you need for your mobile device.

- ✔ Put some free audio app tools in the palm of your hand.

- ✔ See what other musical tasks you can perform with your iPhone or iPad.

Chapter 22

Ten Music Apps You Can't Live Without

● ●

*W*e looked at quite a number of apps in this book already (enough to put a significant dent in your wallet, perhaps), and it's safe to assume that those apps wouldn't appear in these pages if they didn't provide a great deal of value for what you pay for them. After all, if these apps were duds, why talk about them? That said, the previously mentioned apps don't represent the totality of what's available. In this chapter, we take a look at ten of the most intriguing and useful apps you can put on your iPhone or iPad.

Korg Gadget

The cost of this app goes beyond the common one-to-five-dollar range — but look at all you get for that price: Korg Gadget combines over 15 different music-making devices (including drums, synthesizers, and other . . . well, gadgets) in a remarkably full-featured music creation program. Excellent MIDI control and export options (including interfacing with popular computer-based DAW Ableton) round out this excellent app.

Notion

The iPad offers many options for reading charts and sheet music. Notion, however, gives you the ability to actually write and edit sheet music directly from your iPad. And after you write out your music, you can play it back using samples recorded by the London Symphony Orchestra in the Abbey Road studio facility. Not a bad way to hear your works come to life.

Thor

Originally a component of the popular Propellerhead computer-based DAW Reason, Thor lives the solo life on the iPad. This modular synthesizer combines several different oscillators and filters with spectacular audio routing capabilities and even a built-in sequencer. Thor packs an entire synthesizer workstation into your iPad.

iMaschine

This groove-based music production app combines well with the Maschine hardware controller, but you can use it on your own to create amazing sample-based groove music. Tap out your creation on real or virtual pads, and you're ready to go.

DM1

This drum machine makes creating beats or drum tracks amazingly simple. This apps gives you a fully functional drum machine at a can't-miss price.

iMPC Pro

Fans of hip-hop know what the MPC sampler means to producers. This app puts that history-making controller right on your iPad. Create up to 64 tracks, and use a host of included samples or create your own.

iStroboSoft

Every so often, you have to tune your guitar or bass. This app uses your iPhone mic (or another audio connection) to put the respected Peterson strobe tuner at your fingers.

Musyc Pro

This app gives you an entirely new touch-based music-making app with built-in effects. And although it contains 88 instruments, the unique interface makes it fun to play and record on.

SampleWiz

This standalone sampler lets you record, manipulate, and arrange your sounds in such precise details that you probably won't believe you can do such things with a handheld device. But you can, we promise. Tweak to your heart's content!

FL Studio Mobile HD

Fruity Loops took their notable computer-based DAW and put a portable version on the iPad. You get much of the same functionality, and whatever you make on the go can upload to your Fruity Loops DAW, if you're inclined. But it works just as well as a standalone app.

Chapter 23

Ten Great Free Music Apps

. . . .

*N*ot everything you put on your iPhone or iPad must cost you a ton of money. The App Store offers plenty of noisemakers for free. A good deal of them are introductions to other, more full-featured apps that are available at a higher cost, but some come to you out of the goodness of the developers' hearts. Let's take a look at what's out there for the taking.

Novation Launchpad

This app gives you 16 virtual pads and some interesting effects that let you produce dance-based music almost immediately. Sure, Novation wants to sell you some additional sounds for a small fee, but the free samples that come with the app still handle themselves well.

Take

Propellerheads gives you a scratchpad that lets you loop up to four tracks of audio from your mic over some prerecorded beats. Just sing or hum along to capture your inspiration wherever you wish.

AmpliTube Free

AmpliTube Free starts you off with some basic guitar and bass sounds for you to play around. You can add some additional gear and recording capabilities if you wish. Still, nobody should turn up his or her nose at the free gear IK Multimedia offers with this app.

Keezy

You can think of Keezy as a lightweight sampler, or you can just play around with its included soundboards. Keezy makes music creation for all ages.

Modular Synthesizer

This free app gives you the feel of an old analog synthesizer (complete with cables and jacks!) paired with Audiobus compatibility and some amazing sounds.

Tape

This app gives you exactly what it looks like — a virtual two-track tape recorder. If it's possible to do retro recording on an iPhone or iPad, this app accomplishes the task.

LP-5

LP-5 puts five sampler-based tracks on your device and tailors the interface for use in a live performance. This free version restricts you to the samples included in the app, but you can upgrade to the full version and import your own.

Hokusai

If you need to tweak some audio tracks, or even mix some recordings together, Hokusai gives you a simple, easy-to-use editor with Dropbox capabilities.

TF7

TF7 puts a pad-based interface and FM synthesis right on your iPad. Again, the app will prompt you to buy additional functionality, but you can fully enjoy the free version as well.

GrainProc

This granular synthesis effect takes the audio you send it (such as vocals or instruments) and lets you manipulate it with a variety of effects. This app is definitely for the more experimental users.

Chapter 24

Ten Other Musical Uses for Your iOS Device

● ●

This book primarily focuses on creating music using virtual instruments and performing live or recording your own music. But musicians know that you need much more support to handle everything you need to do musically. This chapter takes a quick look at what else your iOS device can do to help you improve as a musician.

Tuners

Yes, most guitar amp simulators include tuners, but you can also buy more full-featured tuners that offer different tuning options (like the iStroboSoft app) or that help you tune all of your strings at the same time (like the Polytune app).

Metronomes

Yes, you need a metronome. This tool helps you get your rhythm down pat. Sure, drum machines can also keep time, but you run the risk of getting caught up in the feel of a drum pattern as opposed to the rhythm itself. Plenty of metronome apps exist, including those that handle odd-meter tempos and subdivisions.

SPL Meters

Need to know how loud you are? Put an SPL meter on your phone and use the built-in mic (or an attached mic) to measure your dB level and tame yourself if you get too loud.

Real-Time Analyzers

Sound pros use analyzers to view frequency bands as the sound is produced so they can adjust the EQ accordingly. Use these apps to find out exactly where the feedback comes from and how you can reduce it.

Notation Apps

If you need to put together a score on your iPad, apps like Notion can help you create the sheet music you require on the fly. Store your music on the iPad or print it out for others to use (because you don't want others touching your iPad, right?).

Sheet Music and Tablature Apps

If you read music but don't need to create it, plenty of apps exist that let you download and read sheet music straight from your iPad (or iPhone, but that screen is awfully small). Guitarists can also use tablature, if they wish.

Computer DAW Controllers

If you're recording on Logic Pro X, but your computer is all the way across the room, you can use your iPad to remotely control your recording session from wherever you are. Some DAWs offer dedicated controls, but you can also customize others to work with your DAW of choice.

Live Sound Mixer Controllers

Companies like Yamaha, PreSonus, and Mackie offer apps that let you control your digital mixer from your iPad. Wander around the venue and make sure the band sounds great from all angles.

Instrument Remote Controls

Just like DAWs and mixers, you can remotely control instruments and amps from your iPhone or iPad. Stroll around the stage or adjust your amp settings from your mic stand.

Education and Learning Apps

Apps like Capo and iReal Book help you learn all styles and genres of songs by either playing tracks for you or even analyzing songs and showing you the proper chords. Almost makes it too easy, doesn't it?

Index

About the Author

Ryan Williams is a technical writer and musician living in New Orleans, LA. He received his master's degree from the Indiana University School of Music at Indianapolis in 2003. His previously published works with Wiley include *Teach Yourself VISUALLY Bass Guitar, Windows XP Digital Music For Dummies,* and many, many others. He has shared the stage with everybody from Grammy-award-winning hip-hop artists to full bagpipe-and-drums corps, but not at the same time.

Mike Levine has a wealth of experience as a writer and editor of magazines, books, and websites in the music and music-technology fields. He's currently the U.S. editor for the French website *Audiofanzine*, and is the former editor of *Electronic Musician* and *Onstage* magazines. Levine's four books include *How to Be a Working Musician*, and *The Warren Haynes Guide to Slide Guitar* (with Warren Haynes). Levine is also a multi-instrumentalist who writes and produces music for television in his home studio, and plays in three bands. Visit his website: www.mikelevine.com.

Author's Acknowledgments

Ryan Williams: First, I owe many, many thanks to Mike Levine for getting the project rolling, helping to organize the basic building blocks of the final book, and for the insanely great writing he contributed. I also could not put this book together without the invaluable work of Steve Hayes, Linda Morris, Chris Morris, and everybody at Wiley Publishing. Technical editor Matt Fecher deserves much credit and praise for adding his insights and app programming background to the mix. And finally, thanks to all of the musicians and supporters of music, both here in New Orleans and all around the world, for continuing to inspire and amaze me with the art they create. Today's technology works best when it supports the larger artistic effort and connects musicians and audience directly.

This book is dedicated to my loving and patient wife Jennifer, who tolerated the long hours of writing and research that went into creating this book (as well as the noise that went along with it). On to the next adventure!

Publisher's Acknowledgments

Acquisitions Editor: Aaron Black

Senior Project Editor: Christopher Morris

Copy Editor: Christopher Morris

Technical Editor: Matthew Fecher

Editorial Assistant: Claire Johnson

Sr. Editorial Assistant: Cherie Case

Project Coordinator:

Cover Image: ©iStock.com/SimmiSimons